202
THINGS YOU CAN
BUY AND SELL
FOR BIG PROFITS

JIM STEPHENSON

EP
Entrepreneur.
Press

Managing editor: Jere L. Calmes
Cover design: Beth Hansen-Winter
Composition and production: Eliot House Productions

This publication is designed to provide accurate and authoritative information in regard to the
subject matter covered. It is sold with the understanding that the publisher is not engaged in ren-
dering legal, accounting, or other professional services. If legal advice or other expert assistance is
required, the services of a competent professional person should be sought.

Library of Congress Cataloging-in-Publication Data is available.

ISBN 1-932531-22-X

Printed in Canada

10 09 08 07 06 05   10 9 8 7 6 5 4 3 2 1

CONTENTS

CHAPTER 3

Everything Else You Need to Know to Operate a Buy-and-Sell Enterprise _____ 31

CHAPTER 5

Where You Can Sell Things for Big Profits _ _ _ _ _ _ _ 95

CHAPTER 6

The Best 202 Things You Can Buy and Sell for Big Profits _ _ _ _ _ _ _ _ _ _ _ _ 129

INTRODUCTION

Last year, I read an article about a 15-year-old high school student who was making over $5,000 per month part-time selling vintage T-shirts online. I was fascinated and wanted to know more. What I learned is that she was doing nothing more than purchasing vintage and secondhand T-shirts at garage sales, flea markets, and used clothing stores, paying as little as $1 each, and reselling them to collectors and everyday consumers through various online marketplaces for prices ranging from $10 to as much as $200 for rare and highly collectible T-shirts.

This got me thinking, "Wow, could it really be that simple? I wonder how many other people are also making big profits buying and selling?" As it turns out, a lot of people are. There is a janitor who purchases sunglasses in bulk for $2 each and resells them at weekend swap meets for $20; a retired police officer who earns $100,000 a year buying collector cars in North America and reselling them overseas; a single mother who supports her family buying used restaurant equipment at auction sales and reselling that equipment directly to restaurant owners in her area for as much as five times her cost.

In fact, my research led me to the conclusion that thousands of people worldwide have discovered they can earn as much, or more, than their current income by buying new and used products cheaply and reselling for a profit. Online auction and retail marketplace giant eBay has more than 100 million registered users around the globe. Over 450,000 registered users claim that selling products through eBay is their sole source of income. Not part-time, but their full-time sole source of income. Guess what? EBay is only the tip of the iceberg. People are also using flea markets, trade shows, classified ads, and additional online marketplaces to sell new and used goods and earn big profits in the process. With the help of this book, so can you.

What do you want to achieve? Do you want to

- earn a full-time living?
- work from the comfort of home?
- pay your way through college?
- supplement your retirement income?
- pay down your mortgage faster?

All of this is easily within your reach and can be achieved by starting and operating your own buy-and-sell enterprise. People just like you are doing that right now, and many more are joining their ranks daily. As manufacturing, technology, and middle-management jobs continue to disappear overseas into cheaper labor markets, buying and selling in North America and in other industrialized areas of the world has become the new economy. The old adage "Work smarter, not harder" has never been more true than it is right now.

The Internet, or more precisely eBay, certainly has propelled buying and selling as a career choice into the mainstream and into pop culture. People from every walk of life, level of education, and age group are choosing to buy and sell rather than fight it out to get a traditional job and then fight even harder to keep it. Many people are discovering they can work less, earn more, and be a lot happier in the process. Helping to fan the buy-and-sell phenomenon flames are television shows such as "Antiques Roadshow," "The Collectors," "Trash to Treasure," and "Flea Market Finds."

My objective in creating this book was clear: include the best products to buy and sell, the best places to buy, and the best places to sell. There are numerous books about buying and selling, but they are all aimed at one specific topic, such as flipping real estate, or one specific selling venue, such as starting a flea market vendor business. *202 Things You Can Buy and Sell for Big Profits* is the only book that will take you through every step required to start and run a buy-and-sell enterprise for success and profit. The book explains the best products to sell, the best places to buy them cheaply, and the best places to sell them for maximum profits. You will learn why buying and selling is the new economy. The book also explores the advantages of buying and selling, what special skills are needed, how much money you can earn, and what you should buy and sell. Overall, after completing this book, you will have acquired valuable information and knowledge on all the critical topics.

Legal Issues

You will discover answers for all of those tough legal questions, including:

- *Licenses and permits.* What business licenses, permits, and sales -tax ID numbers are required to start and run a buy-and-sell enterprise, and where do you get them?
- *Business structure.* What legal business structure is right for your needs and your new buy-and-sell enterprise: sole proprietorship, partnership, limited liability corporation, or corporation? The advantages and disadvantages of each option are explained.
- *Insurance.* Do you need insurance to buy and sell? In some cases, yes. So you will learn what property, inventory, and liability insurance is, why it may be needed, and where you can secure the insurance coverage you need to protect your family and assets.

Financial Issues

You will find out how to deal with all of the financial issues pertaining to starting and operating a buy-and-sell venture, including:

- *Cash requirements.* How much money will be required to start your buy-and-sell enterprise, and what are the sources available to you in terms of obtaining the required capital? You will learn how to start your buy-and-sell venture for peanuts and in some cases to get suppliers to fund your venture almost entirely.
- *Money management.* Learn how to set up your books, work with accountants and bookkeepers, and open commercial bank accounts. You will discover how to establish merchant accounts so you can provide your customers with convenient purchase payment options, including credit cards, debit cards, electronic money transfers, and retail financing and leasing options.

- *Pricing.* You will learn how to calculate fixed costs, direct costs, income, and profit so that you can establish a selling price that will leave you in the black, not seeing red.
- *Taxation.* What taxes are you required to pay on the money you earn buying and selling, and what are the tax advantages of a buy-and-sell operation? Both issues are fully explained.

Getting Started

You will learn how to get a buy-and-sell enterprise rolling, including:

- *Setting up.* Learn how to set up and organize your workspace, including equipment requirements, time management tips, storage needs, and an inventory recording and tracking system.
- *Technology.* Discover the technologies that can be used to help increase sales and profits, while saving you time and money.
- *Trade accounts.* Establish trade accounts with suppliers. Learn how to buy on terms, negotiate the lowest price, and learn about drop-shipping, delivery, and order-fulfillment services.
- *Build a Web site.* What you need to know to get on the Internet and start doing business there, such as building your site, selecting the right domain name, and registering with search engines.

Sales and Marketing

You will discover what is required to market your products like a seasoned pro, including:

- *Developing a marketing strategy.* Learn how to develop a marketing strategy that is right for your needs, enabling you to meet and exceed your objectives and goals. You will learn how to identify potential customers, provide great customer service, overcome challenges, and grow your buy-and-sell enterprise into a profitable business concern.
- *Personal selling.* The information featured takes you through the entire sales cycle, from prospecting to presenting to closing the sale and negotiating the highest possible price for your goods. Once complete, you will have the ability to master personal selling.
- *Advertising.* Create great ads that sell, learn the sources for free and very inexpensive advertising, secure free valuable publicity, and discover how to use promotional fliers and signs to triple your sales and profits.
- *Online marketing.* Consumers spend billions every month purchasing products online, and you will learn about online permission-based marketing

and advertising to reach them so you can claim your portion of the very lucrative Internet pie.

The Best Buying Sources

You will discover what the best buying sources are, including:

- *Wholesalers.* You will find the contact information for hundreds of national and international wholesalers of brand-name, highly saleable merchandise that can be bought low and sold for as much as ten times your cost.
- *Liquidators.* Every year retailers and manufacturers unload billions of dollars' worth of brand-name, top-quality merchandise directly to liquidators at insane rock-bottom prices. You will find out who these liquidators are, how to contact them, and how to get the best deals on the best products for resale.
- *Manufacturers.* Find hundreds of manufacturing sources nationally and internationally so you can skip the middleman markup and buy direct. Included is the contact information and what they manufacture.
- *Craftspeople.* Often you can look no further than right in your local community to find great, highly saleable crafts that you can buy low and sell high. Working with local craftspeople to market their goods can make you rich, and this book will show you how.
- *Sales agents.* Thousands of manufacturers nationally and internationally are represented by sales agents. You will learn where they are, how to contact them, and how to negotiate great deals.
- *Classified advertisements.* One of the best sources for finding great second-hand products to resell for big profits is right in your local classified advertisements. Learn how to buy products from classified ads and resell the same products at huge profits.
- *Garage sales.* There is an endless supply of fantastic garage sale bargains in every community. You will learn how to be first in line, what types of used products to look for, and how to negotiate rock-bottom prices.
- *Flea markets.* The majority of flea market vendors do not know the true value of their merchandise, and because of this, treasures can be found at every flea market, every time you go. You will learn how to separate the treasures from the junk, buy low, and resell directly to collectors for big profits.
- *Auctions.* Without question, auctions and government surplus sales represent some of the best opportunities to find products, equipment, and merchandise at pennies on the dollar and resell these goods at huge profits. You will learn who organizes these auctions and how to find out what is being sold long before the sale.

- *Online marketplaces.* Go online and buy cheap merchandise, art, antiques, and more, all at the click of a mouse and at incredible prices. You will learn where the best sites are and how to find the best deals.

The Best Selling Venues

You will discover what the best selling venues are, including:

- *EBay.* People just like you have struck it rich and continue to do so selling products through eBay. You will learn how to set up your own eBay seller's account, list products, market your goods, and start making money like thousands of people are already doing, all from the comfort of home.
- *Classified advertisements.* Find out how to place advertisements in your local paper that will make the telephone ring off the hook with customers eager to buy your goods at top dollar. You will learn what sells best, the best days to run your ads, the best categories to place an ad under, and what to tell people that will make them take action and buy.
- *Auctions.* Buying and selling is knowing where to buy and where to sell. It is possible to buy an item at one auction and sell the same item at another auction for huge profits, and this book will explain how to do it.
- *Garage sales.* Get the great tips you need to plan, organize, and host super profitable year-round garage sales. Find out what sells best and how to advertise the event so hundreds of people show up, ready to buy.
- *Flea markets.* Find out where the best flea markets are, how to select the most visible vendor space, what products sell best, how to merchandise your goods, and how to sell hard, get your price, and take no prisoners.
- *Direct-to-collectors.* You can sell your goods at incredible profits direct to collectors or direct to businesses. You will learn what equipment and products are best suited to accomplish this and how to get started.
- *Kiosks.* Find out how renting mall and portable kiosks where you can sell your goods can make you rich. You will learn what products sell best, how to merchandise them, and what time of year is best to rent kiosk retail space.
- *Homebased showrooms.* You can even set up a showroom right in your own home to showcase and sell your products. You will learn how to do it, what zoning requirements must be met, how to keep your neighbors happy, and, most importantly, how to explode sales and profits right from home.
- *Your Web sites.* Discover how you can market your products to a world-wide audience of buying consumers via your Web site and other online

marketplaces such as Web malls, cyber storefronts, online classifieds, and e-auctions.

- *Trade and consumer shows.* The trade-show sales environment can be a fast-paced, exciting, and profitable one, and the information and tips in this book will show you how to find the best shows, display your merchandise, and command top dollar on each sale.

The Best 202 Products to Buy and Sell

You will discover the best 202 new and used products, equipment, and merchandise to buy and resell, such as antiques, sunglasses, tools, fitness equipment, jewelry, toys, and vintage clothing. Each product feature also includes:

- *Product description.* A complete product description explaining what it is used for, who buys it, and what makes it such a great product to buy and resell.
- *Best buying sources.* Multiple buying sources are featured for each product, including a price range, when applicable, and contact information.
- *Best selling venues.* You will learn where to sell your products and for how much. Each product features the best places to sell your goods.
- *Resources.* Of course, one of the keys to success will be your ability to buy low and sell high. You have to know where you can purchase highly saleable merchandise at the lowest-possible price, and where the same merchandise can be sold at the highest-possible price to maximize your return-on-investment and profits. After all, the entire premise of a buy-and-sell enterprise is to buy low and sell high. That is why you will find hundreds of valuable resources throughout this book. The resources featured include American, Canadian, and international private corporations, business associations, government agencies, individuals, Web sites, publications, products, services, and lots more.

Icons used represent the following:

   🖱 A mouse icon represents an online resource Web site address.

   ☎ A telephone icon represents a resource's contact telephone number.

   📖 A book icon represents a book or other publication that offers further information.

All of the resources featured were active links, telephone numbers, and mailing addresses at the time of writing. However, over time some information changes or is no longer available. In an effort to ensure that resource information remains active for the long term, I have endeavored to find reputable businesses, organizations, publications, and individuals to feature as resources. But featuring a resource in this book is by no means an endorsement of the company, product, or service.

▇   ▇   ▇

202 Things You Can Buy and Sell for Big Profits is the most authoritative and comprehensive buy-and-sell book available. It gives you the ability to identify the best products, where to buy them cheaply, and how to sell them for the most profit. Harness the power of this book by putting it to work for you today.

WHAT IS A BUY-AND-SELL ENTERPRISE?

A buy-and-sell enterprise is nothing more than purchasing cheaply new or previously owned products that we all need, use, or want, and reselling these same items for more than cost. The difference between what you paid and what you sold it for, of course, is your profit. The mantra of every buy-and-sell enterprise is simple, and easily memorized: *Buy low, sell high*. That is precisely the purpose of this book—to show you how you can start and operate your own independent buy-and-sell enterprise so you can buy low and sell high, and make a bundle of profit in the process. Buying and selling for profit is nothing new. It has been around for thousands of years; the only difference is that the currency has switched from goats and bread to paper and plastic. With that said, however, there are two primary reasons why buying and selling has recently *exploded* from being the closely guarded secret of a few, to the popular occupation of hundreds of thousands of people worldwide, who are now buying and selling as their sole source of income. The first reason is the advent, wide acceptance, and use of the Internet, and the second reason is what I refer to as the new economy.

The Internet Makes It Easy to Buy and Sell

The proliferation of the Internet gives entrepreneurs from every walk of life and from every geographic location access to a global audience of buying consumers, eager sellers, information, and resources as in no other time in history. The Internet has not only made it easier to sell products into the global marketplace utilizing online sales venues such as eBay, e-commerce Web sites, e-classifieds, and e-storefronts, but to also source a nearly limitless number of in-demand products, which can be bought cheaply from domestic and overseas suppliers and resold for a handsome profit. Once this task was out of the reach of most small businesspeople because of the amount of time and money required to research and often travel to foreign and domestic product suppliers to inspect, negotiate, and ink an agreement. Much of that has changed. Now with the simple click of a mouse you can buy products cheaply from thousands of suppliers spanning the globe, and resell these same products worldwide through numerous online marketplaces, or locally through community retailing opportunities like your weekend flea market—all for incredible profits.

The New Economy Is Buying and Selling

The new global marketplace has also created a second reason why buying and selling is not only the wave of the future, but also likely to become a large part of what makes up the new economy in industrialized nations such as the United States and Canada. It is no secret that manufacturing, technology, and middle-management jobs continue to disappear daily, swallowed up by overseas economies with cheaper labor, raw product, and production costs. In fact, some studies suggest the job drain in these areas is occurring at an alarming rate, faster than most people, including politicians and policy makers, are aware of or care to admit. Call centers in India, furniture manufacturing in Indonesia, and chemical processing in China. The resulting fallout in North America is a dramatic increase in the numbers of new small-business start-ups. Many people who have been or who will soon be affected by the new global economy have chosen self-employment as a way to keep in tune with changing times, make money, and secure their long-term future. History has taught us evolve or end up like the dinosaurs—extinct!

The Advantages of a Buy-and-Sell Enterprise

When you consider the advantages of a buy-and-sell enterprise over traditional retail or service-provider businesses, it quickly becomes apparent why many people have wisely elected to buy and sell, and why buying and selling will make up a large percentage of new business start-ups and the new economy. Consider some of these reasons.

- *Low investment.* The vast majority of buy-and-sell enterprises require only a minimal investment to start. Most require under $2,000, including inventory.
- *Minimal financial risk.* Because almost all of the money you spend to get started goes into buying inventory, there is limited financial risk involved. If you decide to quit, you can simply sell off stock, recoup all or most of your investment, and live to fight another day.
- *Incredible profit potential.* As mentioned in the introduction, a 15-year-old high school student is earning $5,000 a month part-time selling vintage T-shirts! Needless to say, the profit potential is excellent.
- *Work from home.* For people wanting to work from home, a buy-and-sell venture is a great choice, because most can largely be operated and managed from home.
- *Flexibility.* No other business opportunity or career choice offers as much flexibility as buying and selling, especially if you concentrate on online sales. Part-time, full-time, seasonally, or occasionally, you set your own schedule and level of commitment as determined by your goals and objectives, not your boss's.
- *Minimal skill requirements.* With the exception of a few specialized products such as real estate and antiques, there are few skill requirements needed to start, operate, and prosper in a buy-and-sell enterprise, and those skills that are needed can be mastered by novice entrepreneurs over time. This is a rare opportunity where ambition and motivation are more important than special skills.
- *Tax advantages.* Operating a legal buy-and-sell business has numerous tax advantages and business write-offs, which will leave more money in your pocket and less in Uncle Sam's.

Who Can Buy and Sell?

The answer is simple—anyone. One of the best aspects about starting and operating a buy-and-sell venture is that everyone is qualified. Buying and selling knows no boundaries—anyone with a need or desire to earn extra money, work from home, or to start and own a business can buy and sell, regardless of age, experience, education, and financial resources. This is perhaps what makes buying and selling the ultimate self-employment option for the vast majority of people; it's cheap, easy, quick, and proven to work and generate huge profits. Imagine the flexibility that buying and selling offers. You can buy and sell part-time to pay off debts. You can buy and sell full-time to replace your current income and in all likelihood earn more. You can buy and sell seasonally, enabling you to pursue other interests like travel. Or you can buy and sell to help supplement your retirement income and stay active in your golden years. Much of what is discussed in this book is aimed at helping you capitalize on your existing knowledge, experiences, skills, and interests, and channeling these into selecting the right things for you to buy and sell.

Buying and Selling Part-Time

The first, and most logical, option for most people is to start buying and selling on a small and part-time basis; perhaps selling merchandise on eBay, renting a booth at a busy weekend flea market, or placing classified ads in your local newspaper. Starting small and part-time enables you to eliminate risk by limiting your financial investment, and allows you to test the waters to make sure buying and selling is something you enjoy and want to pursue. If all goes well, you may decide to transition from your current job, devoting more time to your new buy-and-sell enterprise each week, and decreasing the time at your current job until you are buying and selling on a full-time basis.

There are many advantages to starting off part-time, including keeping income rolling in, taking advantage of health and employee benefits, and building your business over a longer period of time, which generally gives it a more stable foundation. If it turns out you are not the type of person who is comfortable with buying and selling, you have risked little and still have the security of your job. I strongly recommend that everyone with an existing job start off buying and selling part-time before taking the leap of faith into full-time.

Buying and Selling Full-Time

As the commitment would suggest, you can also throw caution to the wind and buy and sell full-time. This option would appeal to people without a current job or business, or to people who want to start a full-time business, but not necessarily a traditional business, like fixed-location retailing or providing a service. There is nothing wrong with starting off full-time, especially if you take the time required to conduct research, develop a business and marketing plan, and have the necessary financial resources to start the business and pay yourself until the business is profitable.

The main downside to starting off full-time is risk. If you jump ship and leave your job, you risk loss of current employee benefits and have no guarantee of steady income, contributing spouses or partners excluded. The upside to starting off full-time is potential rewards, including the opportunity to make more money than you can at your current job. You also gain control of your future and, therefore, your true potential to succeed.

Your decision to operate your new buy-and-sell business on a full-time basis will largely be determined by your current financial situation, your own risk-reward assessment, and your goals and objectives for the future. Jumping in full-time will appeal to the true entrepreneurial mind-set, people who prefer to steer the ship, rather than stoke the boiler.

Buying and Selling Seasonally

Seasonal buy-and-sell enterprises run during one specific season, although some, such as a roadside vegetable stand that starts in the summer and ends in the fall, combine more than one. A seasonal buy-and-sell venture can still be operated with a full- or part-time effort, but the majority are run full-time to maximize revenues and profits over the normally short timespan. Just about any product can be bought and sold seasonally or occasionally, but some are better suited to seasonal sales than others. Examples of products you might buy and sell seasonally, depending on your geographic location, include vegetables, snowmobiles, boats, landscape supplies, Christmas trees, patio furniture, sunglasses, and fishing bait.

A seasonal venture will appeal to people with a special interest in a seasonal product or activity and to people who want the ability to earn enough money during part of the year in order to do as they please with the remainder of the year—travel, pursue education, or work a job in another season. The potential to earn a very good living buying and selling only part of the year is real, as proven by the thousands of people who are currently doing it. This option should not be overlooked, especially by people who want the flexibility to pursue interests other than working year round.

Buying and Selling to Supplement Your Retirement Income

The fourth option is to buy and sell when and as needed or wanted to supplement your retirement income or just to have fun and stay active in your golden years.

Retirement businesses have become extremely popular in the past decade for a number of reasons. First, the cost of living has dramatically increased, often outpacing wages and retirement savings. The result is lots of people heading into retirement needing a little extra income to cover expenses and provide an adequate lifestyle, or to maintain their preretirement lifestyle. Second, people are living longer and healthier now than in decades past and are seeking new challenges daily because they have the spirit, drive, and health to do so. Perhaps the biggest change is attitude. The days of sitting on a porch in a rocking chair growing old are long gone. People want to be vibrant and active, and operating their own buy-and-sell business is a way to stay active physically and mentally. In fact, many innovative retired entrepreneurs have learned how to combine their buy-and-sell business with travel, and work their way across the country, buying, selling, traveling, and enjoying their retirement the entire time. Stay awhile in any RV park, and you will soon discover many people who buy and sell at flea markets, online, and through community events to fund their retirement and travel. They sell watches, crafts, books, and sunglasses, and they trade in antiques, at their own pace and on their own schedule—while stopping to take in the sights and make new friends along the way.

Capitalize on Your Knowledge

Do not fret if you lack skills such as person-to-person selling, negotiating, bookkeeping, time management, and creating effective advertisements. No question these are important skills to have, but at the same time they are secondary because with practice all can be learned and mastered. These skills are covered in detail in Chapters 4 and 5. More important is the question of what knowledge do you have that can be leveraged and used to your advantage in a buy-and-sell enterprise?

Knowledge is one of your biggest and most marketable assets. The more you know about a product, its value, the industry, and the people who are most likely to buy, the better off you will be and the shorter the road to profitability. For instance, if you know how to repair small engines, that knowledge can be used to acquire (cheaply, or even for free) outdoor power equipment in need of repairs, that you can fix and resell for big profits. If you have knowledge of antiques, this can be applied to buy antiques at below-market prices and resell for more. Or, if you have been an avid boater for 20 years, this knowledge can be leveraged to your benefit to buy and sell boats.

Knowledge enables you to:

- know how to fix something that is broken, and thereby greatly increase its value and marketability.

- know how much a specific item(s) is worth and how much profit can be earned from buying and reselling it.
- know the best places to buy items and the best places to resell.
- know how many people buy this specific item, where they are located, and how this market can be accessed.

How Much Money Can You Earn Buying and Selling?

The $64,000 question is: How much money can you make buying and selling? As intriguing as the answer to that question could be, the question should really be: How much money do you need or want to earn from buying and selling? If you work at a job for $20 per hour, calculating your maximum pretax income is easy—multiply the number of hours your boss will let you work or you are capable of working each week by your hourly rate, and you'll know your maximum income potential. Buying and selling is much different. While there are certainly upper limits in terms of income and profit potential, at the same time the measure of one's success is generally determined by ambition and motivation and not by a clock.

In researching this book, I spoke with many people who are buying and selling on both a part- and full-time basis. Some people were legitimately earning $100,000 a year, some two times and three times that amount. But all people in this income range were truly motivated to work hard and smart and were very ambitious because they had goals they wanted to reach. Likewise, I spoke with people earning $10,000 a year who were quite happy with their accomplishments and the return on their investment and time.

Once again, the income and profit you earn will largely depend on your financial needs, your goals, and your personal motivation. Additional factors influencing profit potential include product costs, overhead costs, marketing costs, selling prices, competition, and sales volumes. With that said, if you follow the proven buy-and-sell concepts and ideas outlined in this book and if you are prepared to work both hard and smart, there is a better than average chance you will earn more buying and selling than you are, or can, working in your current field.

LEGAL AND FINANCIAL ISSUES OF A BUY-AND-SELL ENTERPRISE

Starting a buy-and-sell enterprise is like starting any other type of business; there are no shortcuts and you have to follow the letter of the law. A few of the legal and financial issues that you will need to deal with are registering a business name and selecting a legal business structure, obtaining a business license, obtaining a sales tax ID number, choosing insurance, opening a commercial bank account, and preparing and filing business and income tax returns. Expenditures on professional legal and financial advice here is money well spent. Lawyers with small business experience will be able to advise you on which legal business structure best meets your needs, insurance and liability issues, drafting of legal documents, supplier and vendor agreements, and many other legal issues. In short, they will decipher the legalese for you and help make sense of complicated matters pertaining to business. Likewise, certified accountants will decipher the tough financial information you need to know in order to comply with state and federal tax regulations.

Legal Business-Structure Options

The starting point of the buy-and-sell enterprise from a legal standpoint is the selection of a business structure—sole proprietorship, partnership, limited liability corporation, or corporation. Issues such as budget and personal liability will be determining factors when selecting a business structure for most entrepreneurs. Many people choose a sole proprietorship if they are on a tight budget and comfortable with liability issues. A partnership is the right choice if you will be running your new business with a spouse, family member, or friend. A limited liability corporation (LLC) or corporation will be the right choice if your plans include expansion and you want to minimize personal-liability concerns. The advantages and disadvantages of each are discussed below.

Regardless of the legal structure you choose, you will also need to select and register a business name. You can name the business after your legal name, such as Jim's Hot Tub Sales, or you can choose a fictitious business name, such as Northern Hot Tub Sales. Have two or three name options ready to go, in case another business is already using your first choice. Business registration costs vary by state and province, though generally they are less than $200 to register a sole proprietorship, including name-search fees. Normally, you have to show proof-of-business registration in order to establish commercial bank accounts, buy products wholesale, and secure credit-card merchant accounts. So there are no shortcuts; you have to register your business.

RESOURCES
- American Bar Association, ☎ (202) 662-1000, ♂ www.abanet.org
- Canadian Bar Association, ☎ (800) 267-8860, ♂ www.cba.org
- Canadian Business Service Centers, small-business registration services and information, ♂ www.cbsc.org
- Canadian Corp, online filing, ♂ www.canadiancorp.com
- Corp America, online filing, ♂ www.corpamerica.com
- Small Business Administration (SBA), small-business registration services and information, ♂ www.sba.org

- 📖 *Legal Guide for Starting and Running a Small Business*, Fred Steingold and Ilona M. Bray (Nolo Press, 2003)
- 📖 *The Ultimate Great Big Book on Forming Corporations, LLCs & Partnerships*, Michael Spadaccini (Entrepreneur Press, 2004)

The Sole Proprietorship

The sole proprietorship is the most common type of legal business structure, mainly because it is the simplest and least expensive to start and maintain. A sole proprietorship means your business entity and your personal affairs are merged together as one—a single tax return, personal liability for all accrued business debts and actions, and control of all revenues and profits. It is, however, still important to separate your business finances from your personal finances for record-keeping and income tax reasons. For instance, interest payments on credit cards used for business purchases are 100 percent tax-deductible, while interest payments on personal credit cards used for personal purchases are not tax-deductible.

The biggest advantage of sole proprietorships is that they are very simple and inexpensive to form and can be started, altered, bought, sold, or closed at any time, quickly and inexpensively. Also, other than routine business registrations, permits, and licenses, there are few government regulations. The biggest disadvantage of a sole proprietorship is that you are 100 percent liable for any number of business activities gone wrong, which can mean losing any and all personal assets, including investments and real estate, as a direct result of debts, or successful litigation against the business.

The Partnership

A partnership is another popular low-cost legal business structure because it allows two or more people to start, operate, and own a buy-and-sell enterprise. If you do choose to start a business with a family member or friend, make sure the partnership is based on a written partnership agreement, not just a verbal agreement. The agreement should address issues such as financial investment, profit distribution, duties of each partner, and an exit strategy should one partner want out of the agreement. The absence of a formal agreement can be extremely problematic should disagreements arise that cannot be resolved, or should one of the partners die or want out of the business. Like a sole proprietorship, business profits are split among partners proportionate to their ownership and are treated as taxable personal income.

Perhaps the biggest advantage of a partnership is that financial risks and work are shared by more than one person, which allows each partner to specialize within the business for the benefit of the collective team. Record-keeping requirements are basic and on a par with a sole proprietorship. Unfortunately, partnerships also have disadvantages. The most significant is that each partner is legally responsible and personally liable for the other partners' actions in the business because a nonincorporated partnership offers no legal protection from liability issues. All partners are equally responsible for the business's debts, liabilities, and actions.

The Limited Liability Corporation

A limited liability corporation combines many of the characteristics of a corporation with those of a partnership in that like a corporation, it provides protection from personal liabilities, but the tax advantages of a partnership. Limited liability corporations can be formed by one or more people, called LLC members, who alone or together organize a legal entity separate and distinct from the owners' personal affairs in most respects.

The advantages of a limited liability corporation over a corporation or partnership is that they are less expensive to form and maintain than a corporation, offer protection from personal liability that partnerships do not provide, and have simplified taxation and reporting rules in comparison to a corporation. Because of these advantages, limited liability corporations have become the fastest-growing form of business structure in the United States.

The Corporation

The final and most complicated business-structure option is the corporation. When you form a corporation, you create a legal entity that is separate and distnct from the shareholders of the corporation. Because the corporation becomes its own entity, it pays taxes, assumes debt, can legally sue, can be legally sued, and, as a tax-paying entity, must pay taxes on its taxable income (profit) prior to paying any dividends to the shareholders. But the company's finances and financial records are completely separate from the finances of its shareholders.

The biggest advantage to incorporating your buy-and-sell business is that you can greatly reduce your own personal liability. Because a corporation is its own entity, it can legally borrow money and be held accountable in a number of matters from a legal standpoint. In effect, this releases you from personal liability. The major disadvantage is double taxation. Corporation profits are taxed, and then the same profits are taxed again in the form of personal income tax when distributed to the shareholders as a dividend. Unfortunately, the same does not hold true if the corporation loses money. Financial losses cannot be used as a personal income-tax deduction for shareholders.

Licenses Needed to Operate a Buy-and-Sell Enterprise

All businesses must be licensed. In fact, chances are you will to need to obtain several licenses and permits, depending on the type of product(s) you sell and how the product(s) is sold. At minimum, you will need a business license, vendor's permits, and a resale certificate or sales-tax permit ID number. Additional permits and licenses that may be needed include a health permit if you sell food; police clearance certificate if you sell home-security products; import and export certificates if you bring products into the country or ship products out. A home-occupation permit is required to work from home in some states as is a building permit if you significantly alter your home to suit your new venture. A tobacco vendor's permit is required if you sell any tobacco products. If you are thinking about skipping any of the required licenses and permits, don't. You need them to buy wholesale, open commercial bank accounts, open merchant credit card accounts, sell products from home, and import and export goods. If you get caught operating a business without licenses, you can face hefty fines.

Business License

To legally operate a business in all municipalities of the United States and Canada, you will need to obtain a business license. Business license costs vary depending on your geographic location, expected sales, and the type of business or products you sell. Because they are issued at the municipal level, contact your city/county clerk's or permits office for the full requirements for a business license. The Small Business Administration (SBA) also provides a directory indexed by state, outlining where business licenses can be obtained. This directory is located at ✆ www.sba.gov/hotlist/license.html. Additionally, in the United States and Canada you can also contact the chamber of commerce to inquire about business license requirements and fees. Contact the chamber: United States, ✆ www.chamber.com, Canada, ✆ www.chamber.ca.

Permits

The name may vary depending on geographic location—resale certificate, sales-tax permit, ID number—but whatever you want to call it, you need a permit to collect and remit sales tax. Almost all states and provinces now impose a sales tax on products sold directly to consumers, or end users. It is the business owner's responsibility to collect and remit sales taxes. The same sales tax permits are needed when purchasing goods for resale from manufacturers and wholesalers so the goods can be bought tax-free. (Taxes will be paid by the retail customer when resold.) The SBA provides a directory indexed by state, outlining where and how sales-tax permits and ID numbers may be obtained, including information on completing and remitting sales tax forms. This directory is located at ♂ www.sba.gov/hotlist/license.html. In Canada there are two levels of sales tax. One is charged by most provinces on the sale of retail products to consumers, and the second is charged by the federal government. The latter is known as the goods and services tax and is charged on the retail sale of all goods and most services. You can obtain a federal Goods and Services Sales/Harmonized Sales Tax (GST/HST) number by contacting the Canada Customs and Revenue Agency at ♂ www.ccra-adrc.gc.ca.

Insurance

You will need insurance coverage depending on the products you buy and sell to protect inventory, customers, personal assets, and your family from theft, damage, and liability. In short, if you operate a business, you need the protection and peace of mind provided by business insurance.

Most people operate their buy-and-sell enterprises largely from home. They often wrongly assume their current insurance coverage extends to cover these business activities. This could not be farther from the truth, because from the insurance companies' perspective, they cannot take the risk of insuring what they do not know about. The vast majority of buy-and-sell businesses are registered as sole proprietorships, and if there is a successfully litigated claim made against such a business, the owner could be held personally liable. In all likelihood the plaintiff would attempt to seize personal as well as business financial assets. So regardless of size, it is important to be fully insured in business.

The first step is to choose an insurance agent or broker who is familiar with the specific insurance needs of the small-business owner. Not only will the agent be able to translate insurance legalese into easily understandable, plain English for you, but she will also be able to find the best coverage for your individual needs and at the lowest cost. There is a plethora of business insurance available for every imaginable contingency, but the coverage needed is property and liability insurance. Many sales venues such as farmers' markets, public markets, flea markets, and mall kiosks require vendors to show proof of liability insurance as a condition of renting booth or table space.

RESOURCES
- Independent Insurance Agents and Brokers of America, offers a free online find-an-agent search service indexed geographically, ♂ www.iiaa.org

– Insurance Brokers Association of Canada, offers a free directory, listing more than 25,000 insurance agents and brokers indexed geographically, ☞ www.ibac.ca

Property Insurance

Because most entrepreneurs operate or manage their buy-and-sell businesses from home, property insurance, which generally covers buildings and contents, is your first line of protection. Depending on how extensive your property insurance is, often it will provide protection in the form of a cash settlement or paid repairs in the event of fire, theft, vandalism, flood, earthquake, wind damage, acts of God, and malicious damage. Property insurance is the starting point from which you should branch out to include specialized tools and equipment, inventory, and other liability riders, depending on what you buy and sell. Contacting your insurance agent and asking questions specific to your business, equipment, and inventory will quickly reveal what is or is not covered by your existing policy. In most cases, you will want to increase the value of the contents' portion if you use expensive computer and office equipment. You also want to insure cash on hand, accounts receivable records, and inventory, which will require a special rider added to your basic insurance. Also, make sure your insurance covers inventory, tools, and equipment while in transit, as well as at selling venues you might utilize such as flea markets, auctions, and community events.

Liability Insurance

Most homeowners have some sort of liability protection built into their basic homeowner's insurance policy. This is also true of people who rent, because landlords are obligated by law in most places to carry property and liability insurance on rented buildings and land. No matter how diligent you are in terms of taking all necessary precautions to protect any person or customer by removing potential hazards from your home, property, business, and products, you could still be held legally responsible for events beyond your control. So it should go without saying that the best protection is liability insurance coverage. This type of extended liability insurance is often referred to as general business liability, or umbrella business liability. General business liability coverage insures a business against accidents and injury that might occur at the home, at a customer's location, retailing venues, or other perils related to the products you sell. It provides protection from the costs associated with successful litigation or claims against your business or you, depending on the legal entity of your business, and covers such things as medical expenses, recovery expenses, property damage, and other costs typically associated with liability situations. Also, even if your business is not directly involved in manufacturing the products you sell, you still must be proactive in terms of product-liability insurance concerns. In litigation situations, it is not uncommon for plaintiffs who have suffered damages as a result of product malfunction to name numerous defendants in their claim, including the product retailer.

How Much Money Do You Need to Start Buying and Selling?

Another important consideration is how much money you need to start a buy-and-sell enterprise. The amount needed depends on the type of product(s) you will be buying and selling, as well as other factors such as transportation, marketing, and equipment requirements. Some people will already have many of the things needed to operate their business, while others will have to purchase or rent these items. I have included a handy worksheet (see Figure 2.1) at the end of this section to help you calculate how much money will be needed to start your business.

If this is your first foray into the world of business ownership, you should know that in addition to start-up capital you will also need working capital. Start-up capital is needed to purchase equipment and office furniture, to meet legal requirements, to pay for training, and to purchase initial inventory. Working capital is needed to pay bills, and gives you an income until the business generates revenues and profits or is otherwise self-sufficient. You will also need working capital for other activities such as renting flea market booth space. The next logical question is where you will get the money to start. You have options—personal savings, family or friends, bank loans, credit cards, leasing and renting, and supplier terms. The advantages and disadvantages of each are discussed below.

Personal Savings

The fastest and simplest way to finance your buy-and-sell enterprise is right from your own bank account, especially if the investment is small and manageable. Self-financing means you do not have to worry about applying for a loan, accumulating unnecessary debt, or paying interest on borrowed money. You can use your personal savings, cash in an investment certificate, or use retirement funds, mutual funds, stocks, or insurance policies.

A word of caution: Money you remove from fixed certificates or retirement investments may be subject to additional personal income tax or specific penalties for early withdrawal or cancellation. Consult a financial planner before cashing, selling, or redeeming any investment or certificates. Also keep in mind that depending on the investment you want to liquidate, you might actually be earning a higher rate of return than the interest rate you can secure for a business start-up loan.

FIGURE 2.1: Buy-and-Sell Start-Up Costs Worksheet

Use this handy worksheet to calculate how much money you will need to start your buy-and-sell business. Ignore items not relevant to your business, and add items as required.

Section A. Business Set-Up

Business registration	$ _____
Business license	$ _____
Vendor's permits	$ _____
Other permits	$ _____
Insurance	$ _____
Professional fees	$ _____
Training/education	$ _____
Bank account	$ _____
Merchant accounts	$ _____
Payment processing equipment	$ _____
Association fees	$ _____
Deposits	$ _____
Other _____	$ _____
Subtotal A	$ _____

Section B. Business Identity

Business cards	$ _____
Logo design	$ _____
Letterhead	$ _____
Envelopes	$ _____
Other _____	$ _____
Subtotal B	$ _____

Section C. Office

Computer hardware	$ _____
Communication equipment/devices	$ _____
Software	$ _____
Furniture	$ _____
Other office equipment	$ _____
Office supplies	$ _____
Office renovations	$ _____
Other _____	$ _____
Subtotal C	$ _____

Section D. Transportation

Upfront cost to buy/lease transportation	$ _____

FIGURE 2.1: Buy-and-Sell Start-Up Costs Worksheet, continued

Section D. Transportation

Registration	$ _____
Insurance	$ _____
Moving equipment	$ _____
Shipping/delivery supplies	$ _____
Other _____	$ _____
Subtotal D	$ _____

Section E. Web Site

Domain registration	$ _____
Site development fees	$ _____
Search engine/directory fees	$ _____
Equipment	$ _____
Software	$ _____
Content/tools	$ _____
Hosting	$ _____
Other _____	$ _____
Subtotal E	$ _____

Section F. Marketing

Research and planning costs	$ _____
Signs	$ _____
Brochures/fliers	$ _____
Catalogs	$ _____
Initial advertising budget	$ _____
Initial online promotion budget	$ _____
Other _____	$ _____
Subtotal F	$ _____

Section G. Merchandising

Product samples	$ _____
Pricing/value guides	$ _____
Display racks/cases	$ _____
Kiosks/carts	$ _____
Portable booth	$ _____
Other _____	$ _____
Subtotal G	$ _____

Section H. Inventory

#1 _____	$ _____

FIGURE 2.1: Buy-and-Sell Start-Up Costs Worksheet, continued

Section H. Inventory

#2 _____	$ _____
# 3 _____	$ _____
# 4 _____	$ _____
# 5 _____	$ _____
Subtotal H	$ _____

Adding Up the Costs

Business set-up	$ _____
Business identity	$ _____
Office	$ _____
Transportation	$ _____
Web site	$ _____
Marketing	$ _____
Merchandising	$ _____
Inventory	$ _____
Total start-up costs	$ _____
Working capital	$ _____
Total investment needed	$ _____

Another innovative way to fund your venture is to create a list of all personal items you no longer want or need, and sell them by holding a garage sale, by using eBay, or by renting a flea market booth. Not only can this raise the money needed to get started, but you also gain valuable sales experience in the process.

Borrowing from Family and Friends

You could also borrow money from a family member or friend to get started, but there is a downside. If the buy-and-sell business fails, will you be able to pay back the money you borrow? If not, the relationship could be damaged beyond repair. Having said that, many extremely successful business ventures have been built on money borrowed from friends and family members, which is often referred to as a love loan. If you decide to borrow from friends or family to fund your buy-and-sell start-up, treat the transaction as you would if you were borrowing the money from a bank. Have a promissory note drawn up and signed, noting all the details—principal loan amount, interest, and repayment dates. And whatever you do, make sure you stick like glue to your repayment schedule to avoid disputes.

Bank Loans

If you have good credit, you can apply for a small business start-up loan from a bank or credit union. The loan can be secured, meaning it is guaranteed with some other type of investment, such as a guaranteed investment certificate, or it can be unsecured, with the funds advanced because of your credit worthiness. Secured loans have lower interest rates, by as much as 5 percent. Another option is to talk to your banker about setting up a line of credit. Secured lines of credit also enjoy lower interest rates than unsecured credit lines. One advantage of a line of credit over a standard business loan is that most only require you to repay interest based on the account balance, and not on the entire principal and interest. For example, a $10,000 line of credit fully extended with a per annum interest rate of 5 percent would require minimum monthly payments of $41.66 ($10,000 multiplied by 5 percent divided by 12 months = $41.66). Of course, this is interest repayment only, and you would not be paying down the principal amount. But this flexibility provides exactly the kind of breathing room new business ventures need to get rolling.

RESOURCES

– Bank of America, small business loan programs, ♂ www.bankofamerica.com
– Key Bank, small business loan programs, ♂ www.key.com
– Royal Bank, small business loan programs, ♂ www.royalbank.com/sme/
– Wells Fargo, small business loan programs, ♂ www.wellsfargo.com

Credit Cards

The biggest drawback to using your credit cards to fund your business start-up is that most have high annual interest rates, often in the 20 percent range. This makes them a less attractive financing option if you cannot pay off the balance for an extended period. They are, nonetheless, still a funding option, especially if they are your only one. If you are going to use your credit cards to fund your start-up, try to pay off your balance before starting. This will leave you carrying less debt, with lower monthly obligations, and with the opportunity to borrow more money against the cards to buy valuable products for resale. Shop for credit cards with the lowest interest rates and no annual fees. Also use cards that reward purchases with air miles or redeemable shopping points. Many banks and credit unions offer small business credit cards (such as the Visa Small Business Card) that offer many special services—travel insurance, and lower interest rates.

RESOURCES

– American Express Small Business, ♂ www.americanexpress.com

– MasterCard Business, ♂ www.mastercardbusiness.com

– Visa Small Business, ♂ www.usa.visa.com/business

Leasing and Renting

Leasing or renting equipment is another financing strategy that might not fund your entire buy-and-sell enterprise start-up, but can greatly reduce the amount of hard cash you need to get things rolling. Renting equipment or tools means you do not take ownership in any form. You simply pay the rental rate for the time you need the equipment and return it when it's no longer needed. Leasing also means you do not own the equipment, but you are legally bound to pay for a portion of the entire value of the equipment plus interest by way of scheduled monthly lease payments. The benefits of renting or leasing equipment such as computers is you need little if any money upfront, which leaves your cash free to buy merchandise that can be resold for a profit right away. Also, rental and lease payments are deductions, unlike the sliding scale of tax depreciation used on owned equipment.

RESOURCES

– Alpha Lease, ♂ www.alphalease-equipment-leasing.com

– GE Asset Funding, ♂ www.gesmallbusiness.com

– Lease Source, ♂ www.leasesource.net

Supplier Terms

Another way to bootstrap your way into your own buy-and-sell business is to ask your new suppliers for a revolving credit account, which gives you up to 90 days to pay for goods and services you need to operate your business or for resale to customers for a profit. People with strong credit will have few problems opening revolving credit accounts with suppliers. If your credit is not so strong, you will need to establish a payment history with most suppliers prior to their granting you credit privileges. The advantage of revolving credit is that you can often sell your goods long before you have to pay your supplier. In effect, your suppliers are bankrolling your business and you get to skim off the profits, all without having to use your own cash.

Banking and Bookkeeping

Money management can be tricky business because, in addition to customers, cash flow is what keeps your buy-and-sell business humming along. Consequently, understanding money management has to become a priority, even if you elect to hire an accountant or bookkeeper to manage the books. You will still need to familiarize yourself with basic bookkeeping and money management principles and activities such as understanding credit, reading bank statements and tax forms, and making sense of accounts receivable and payable.

Once your business is registered and ready to roll, you will also need to open a commercial bank account, separate from your personal savings or checking account. Setting up a business bank account is easy. Select the bank you want to work with (think small-business friendly), call, and arrange an appointment to open an account. When you go, make sure you take personal identity as well as your business-name registration papers and business license because these are usually required to open a commercial bank account. The next step will be to deposit funds into your new account (even $100 is okay). If your credit is sound, also ask the bank to attach a line of credit to your account, which can prove very useful when buying large quantities of products and during slow sales periods, and make inquiries about credit-card merchant accounts and other small-business services at that time.

Setting Up the Books

When it comes time to set up your financial books, you have two options—do it yourself or hire an accountant or bookkeeper to do it. You might want to do both by keeping your own books and hiring an accountant to prepare year-end financial statements and tax forms. If you opt to keep your own books, make sure you invest in accounting software such as QuickBooks, because it is easy to use and makes bookkeeping almost enjoyable. Most accounting software also allows you to create client accounts with invoicing and mail-merge options, and to track account bank balances, merchant account information, and accounts payable and receivable. Depending on features, good small-business accounting software may be purchased for $50 to $150.

Keep in mind that even with the proliferation of accounting software, hiring an accountant to take care of more complicated money matters is often wise. Like many professionals, accountants pride themselves on the fact that they do not cost you money, but rather make you money by discovering items overlooked on tax returns, by identifying business deductions you never knew existed, and by creating financial plans that will enable you to enjoy the fruits of your labor later in life without having to worry about where the money will come from. If you are unsure about your bookkeeping abilities even with the aid of accounting software, you may want to hire a bookkeeper to do your books on a monthly basis, and a chartered accountant to audit the books quarterly and prepare year-end business statements and tax returns.

If you are only holding the occasional garage sales to raise a few extra bucks, there is little sense or need for accounting software and accountant services.

Simply invest a few dollars in a basic ledger, and enter prices paid versus prices sold for all goods, along with expenses such as advertising. The ledger book will run you about $5, and keeping on top of it should take all of about five minutes a week.

You have to use a common-sense approach when calculating how much to invest in your business set against expected revenues and profits. Also remember to keep all business and tax records in a dry and secure place for up to seven years. This is the maximum amount of time the IRS and Revenue Canada can request past business revenue and expense information. Likewise, also be sure to track and record every cent coming in and going out of your business, regardless of the amount. And get a receipt for everything you buy or spend money on for business. Keep a logbook in your glove box for times when no receipts are issued, such as when feeding the parking meter. You can record these expenses in the logbook and enter them later into your accounting program or ledger.

RESOURCES
- American Institute of Professional Bookkeepers, ☎ (800) 622-0121, ♂ www.aipb.com
- Chartered Accountants of Canada, ☎ (416) 977-3222, ♂ www.cica.ca
- Canadian Bookkeepers Association, ☎ (250) 334-2427, ♂ www.c-b-a-c.ca
- QuickBooks, ♂ www.quickbooks.com
- Quicken, ♂ www.quicken.com
- United States Association of Chartered Accountants, ☎ (212) 334-2078, ♂ www.acaus.org

Purchase Payment Options

In today's super competitive business environment, consumers have come to expect many payment options for purchases. A steadfast, cash-only payment policy is no longer acceptable even for the small buy-and-sell enterprise, especially if you plan on doing business online. You must provide customers with many ways to pay, including cash, debit card, credit card, and electronic cash. There is a cost to provide these payment options—account fees, transaction fees, equipment rental, and merchant fees based on a percentage of the total sales value. But, these expenses must be viewed as a cost of doing business in the 21st century and not as a reason to avoid providing customers these options. There are two ways to reduce these fees. First, shop for the best service with the best prices. Not all banks, merchant accounts, and payment processing services are the same, and fees vary widely. Second, check with small-business associations such as the chamber of commerce to see if they offer member discounts, as it is not uncommon to save as much as 2 percent on credit card merchant fees, for example. Remember, consumers expect choices when it comes time to pay for their purchases, and if you elect not provide these choices, expect fewer sales.

Accepting Cash and Checks

The first way to get paid is good old hard cash, which is great because it is instant, with no processing time required. As fast as the cash comes in, you can use it to buy more goods to sell and increase revenues and profits. The major downside is that cash is risky because you could get robbed or lose it. In that instance, collecting from your insurance company could prove difficult if there is no paper transaction as proof. Even if you prefer not to receive cash, there are people who will pay in cash. For this reason, invest in a good-quality safe for your home and for use on the road. Also get in the habit of making daily bank deposits during daylight hours. I don't recommend that you accept paper checks, but if you do, ask to see picture ID and write the customer's driver's license number on the back. If the amount of the check exceeds a few hundred dollars, ask the buyer to get the check certified or pay with a bank draft instead. The last thing you want to be left holding is a rubber check.

Accepting Debit Cards

Buying or renting a wireless or wired debit card terminal allows you to accept debit card payments, which is much better than accepting checks, and in some cases better than cash, because you do not have the theft concerns. Most banks and credit unions offer business clients debit card equipment and services. The processing equipment will set you back about $40 per month for a terminal connected to a conventional telephone line and about $100 per month for a cellular terminal, plus the cost of the telephone line or cellular service. There is also a transaction fee charged by the bank and payable by you every time there is a debit card transaction, which ranges from 10 cents to 50 cents per transaction, based on variables such as dollar value and frequency of use. Having the ability to accept debit cards will often give you a competitive advantage and make it easier for people to buy and impulse shop. Offer debit card payment options if you will be selling at flea markets, from a homebased showroom, mall kiosks, community events, or at farmers' or public markets.

Merchant Accounts and Accepting Credit Cards

Many consumers have replaced paper money altogether in favor of plastic when buying goods and services. In fact, giving your customers the option to pay for purchases with a credit card is often crucial to success. This is especially true if you plan to do business on the Web, because credit cards and electronic cash are used to complete almost all Web sales and financial transactions. Therefore, most buy-and-sell entrepreneurs will want to offer customers credit-card payment options, and to do this you will need to open a credit-card merchant account. Get started by visiting your bank or credit union, or contact a merchant account provider such as Cardservice International or the others listed below. If your credit is sound, you will run into few obstacles. If your credit is poor, you may have difficulties opening a merchant account or have to provide a substantial security deposit. If you are still unsuccessful, the next best option is to open an account with an online payment service provider, which is discussed in the next section.

CREDIT-CARD MERCHANT ACCOUNT ADVANTAGES

- Accepting credit cards increases impulse buying. Studies have proven that merchants who accept credit cards can increase sales by up to 50 percent.
- If you have your own merchant account, you can accept credit card payments online, over the telephone, by mail, or in person.
- You can sell products on an installment basis by obtaining permission to charge your customers' credit card monthly, or as per agreement.
- Processing time is relatively quick, and money is often deposited in your bank account within 48 hours.
- You can ship products knowing you have been paid in full and do not have to worry about CODs, bum checks, or slow payers.

CREDIT-CARD MERCHANT ACCOUNT DISADVANTAGES

- It can be difficult to qualify for a merchant account, especially for small businesses with a limited operating history or small sales volumes.
- It can be costly to set up and maintain a credit-card merchant account, including:
  - Setup and application fees, $300 to $1,000
  - Equipment and software purchases, $200 to $1,000
  - Equipment and software leases, $25 to $100 per month
  - Administration and statement fees, $10 to $100 per month
  - Processing and transaction fees, 2 to 8 percent of total sales
- Credit card companies can hit you with stiff chargeback fees, ranging from $10 and up for goods returned and credits returned to customers' credit card accounts.

- 1st American Card Service, ♂ www.1stamericancardservice.com
- Cardservice International, ♂ www.cardservice.com
- MasterCard, ♂ www.mastercard.com
- Merchant Account Express, ♂ www.merchantexpress.com
- Monster Merchant Account, ♂ www.monstermerchantaccount.com
- Visa Financial Services, ♂ www.visa.com

Online Payment Services

The basic purpose of online payment services is to allow people and businesses to exchange currency over the Internet electronically. Online payment services are very popular with consumers and merchants alike. In fact, PayPal, one of the most popular online payment services, and coincidently owned by eBay, has more than 40 million members in 45 countries and offers personal and business account services. Both types of accounts allow funds to be transferred electronically amongst members, but only the business account enables merchants to accept credit card payments for goods and services. The advantages of online payment services are they are quick, easy, and cheap to open, regardless of your credit rating or anticipated sales volume, and you can receive payment from any customer with an e-mail account. You can also have the funds deposited directly into your account, have a check issued and mailed, or leave funds in your account to draw on using your debit card. The number-one disadvantage is that customers are redirected to the online payment service Web site to complete the transaction. This can confuse people who in some cases will abandon the purchase. Overall, the advantages of online payment services far outweigh any disadvantages. If you plan on doing business on the Web, you will need to offer your customers online payment service options.

RESOURCES
- PayPal, ♂ www.paypal.com
- Veri Sign Pay Flow, ♂ www.verisign.com
- Yahoo Pay Direct, ♂ www.paydirect.yahoo.com

Taxation and the Buy-and-Sell Enterprise

There is no escaping the taxman, regardless of how big or small your business may be. If you earn business profits, the government will want its share. In the United States and Canada, business income/profits are taxed at the federal, state/provincial, and municipal levels. The best and most up-to-date information and advice you can obtain about small business and income tax will come directly from the Internal Revenue Service in the United States and the Canada Customs and Revenue Agency in Canada. These government agencies oversee federal business and income taxation. Likewise, certified accountants can help you navigate the murky taxation waters, and there are also many books specifically developed to help the small-business owner understand and prepare tax forms. Small-business taxation is complicated and can be very frustrating for the novice entrepreneur to understand. Even seasoned entrepreneurs do not like dealing with tax issues and preparing forms because the rules and regulations change regularly.

RESOURCES

- Canada Customs and Revenue Agency, ☎ (800) 959-2221, ✆ www.ccra-adrc. gc.ca
- Internal Revenue Service (IRS), ☎ (800) 829-3676, ✆ www.irs.gov
- 📖 *Small Time Operator,* Bernard B. Kamoroff (Bell Springs Publishing, 2004)
- 📖 *Top Tax Ideas for Small Business: How to Survive in Today's Tough Tax Environment*, Thomas J. Stemmy (Entrepreneur Press, 2004)

Paying Taxes

In the United States and Canada if you earn income, regardless of the source, it is subject to taxes at the federal and state or federal and provincial levels. How your business is legally structured will determine the taxes you pay, both personal and business, as well as the forms required on which to file and remit payment. As a sole proprietor or unincorporated partnership, the income your business earns after expenses is your personal income, and you are taxed accordingly. If your business is incorporated, you are taxed on the income you receive from the corporation in the form of wages and bonuses, and the corporation is taxed on the profits it earns after all expenses are deducted. Additionally, post-tax corporate profits are taxed once again when distributed to shareholders in the form of dividends. Also keep in mind that if you have any employees, you will need to obtain employee identification numbers, prepare and submit employee income tax reporting forms, and withhold and remit the employee and employer portions of Medicare, employment insurance, and Social Security. Again, tax issues are very complicated for small-business owners.

INTERNAL REVENUE SERVICE SMALL BUSINESS TAX FORMS AND PUBLICATIONS

The IRS provides small-business owners with a number of free publications to explain small-business taxation issues. These publications can be used as a guide for completing small business and self-employment tax forms. You can pick up IRS small-business information, tax forms, and publications in person at your local IRS office, call to have the publications delivered by mail, ☎ (800) 829-3676, or download them online, ♂ www.irs.gov/business/small.

- Sole Proprietorship, *Publication 334: Tax Guide for Small Business*
- Partnerships, *Publication 541: Partnership Tax Guide*
- Limited Liability Corporations (LLC), *Publication 541: Partnership Tax Guide* and *Publication 542: Corporation Tax Guide*
- Corporation, *Publication 542: Corporation Tax Guide*

CANADA CUSTOMS AND REVENUE AGENCY SMALL-BUSINESS TAX FORMS AND PUBLICATIONS
Canada Customs and Revenue Agency also provides small-business owners with a number of free publications to explain small-business tax issues. These publications can be used as a guide for completing small business and self-employed tax forms. You can pick up CCRA small-business information, tax forms, and publications in person at your provincial business service centers, call to have the publication delivered by mail, ☎ (800) 959-2221, or download them online, ♂ www.ccra-adrc.gc.ca.

- Sole Proprietorship, *Publication T4002: Business and Professional Income*
- Partnership, *Publication T4068: Guide for the Partnership Information Return*
- Corporation, *Publication T4012 T2: Corporation Income Tax Guide*

Allowable Expenses

There are a number of tax advantages from operating even a simple and small buy-and-sell enterprise. Because of allowable business expenses, it is very possible to claim a portion of your current household expenses, such as rent or mortgage payments and utility bills, against your business and personal income, especially for the sole proprietor. Whenever you are unsure about which expenses are allowable and which are not, it is best to contact a certified accountant. The following are the 20 most common allowable business deductions, providing all or a portion of the expense used for business.

1. A portion of rent or mortgage payments, utilities, property tax, and maintenance.
2. Communications costs including telephone, toll-free lines, fax, Internet connection, cellular telephone, pagers, and answering services.
3. Rental payments on equipment, furniture, and computers.
4. A portion (depreciated scale) of equipment purchases including computers, software, office furniture, and display cases.

5. Transportation costs, including gas, maintenance, insurance, and a portion of lease payments, or a depreciated scale on owned vehicles used in business.

6. Wages and benefits, regardless if full-time, part-time, temporary, or seasonal.

7. Professional fees paid to lawyers, accountants, or consultants.

8. Marketing costs, including advertising, public relations, seminars, brochures, catalogs, fliers, trade shows, direct mail, and seminars.

9. Booth rent at flea markets, farmers' markets, and trade shows.

10. Commissions paid to auctioneers, eBay, and other salespeople and sales venues.

11. Business-related insurance premiums.

12. Office supplies such as paper, printer ink, pens, garbage bags, and paper clips.

13. Interest on business loans and credit card purchases for business.

14. Training and education, including classes, books, and seminars.

15. Business travel and a percentage of entertainment costs.

16. Postage, courier, and shipping costs.

17. Customer gifts, charity, and sponsorships.

18. Business and association membership dues.

19. Business licenses, permits, and registrations.

20. Business cards, stationery, and letterhead.

3

EVERYTHING ELSE YOU NEED TO KNOW TO OPERATE A BUY-AND-SELL ENTERPRISE

Perhaps this chapter does not include everything else you need to know to operate a buy-and-sell business in the literal sense, but it does give a brief, yet very informative rundown on the more important topics and issues. In this chapter you will learn about selling from home, building strong trade accounts, developing a minimarketing plan, mastering personal selling, creating advertising that works, taking your buy-and-sell enterprise online, and a host of additional helpful information and tips to put you well on the path to profitability. Buying and selling as a business is very broad because there are many options in terms of how you buy, how you sell, and the types of products you buy and sell. Therefore, the information in this chapter and other chapters in the book is meant to give you a general understanding of important business fundamentals and marketing basics so you do not run into trouble early on. This affords you the opportunity to fine-tune your business and marketing skills on the job once you are up and running.

Buying and Selling from Home

Can you legally operate a buy-and-sell business from your current residence? Chances are you can, although probably with some restrictions. Unfortunately, there is no standard, across-the-board set of rules on allowing businesses to operate from a residential location. Each and every community in the United States and Canada has its own home-business zoning regulations and specific usage guidelines. The majority of municipalities do allow small home businesses to operate from a residence, providing the business activities do not negatively impact neighbors and the neighborhood in general. From a zoning standpoint, the potential issues include exterior signage, parking, noise, fire, storage of hazardous substances, deliveries and shipping, and customers visiting your home. Long before you decide to buy and sell from home, you need to check out your local zoning rules, regulations, and restrictions. Visit your local city or municipal planning department or bylaws office for further information.

Setting Up Your Workspace

The products you sell and how they are sold will determine the type, size, and location of the home workspace that you need. Homebased workspace options range from any old corner of the home to a separate outside structure. I have used a converted garage, a den, a living room, a basement, and a spare bedroom for various home business ventures over the years, and each has advantages and disadvantages. Careful consideration must be given to the needs of your family and how space in the home is currently being utilized for day-to-day living as well as for special occasions, seasonal activities, and guests. Because setting up a home workspace requires balancing the needs of your business with the needs of your family, compromises will have to be made on both fronts.

No or Few Customer Visits

If you will have no or few customers coming to your home, workspace issues are not as important, but there are still areas to consider. First off, if money is tight, select a room that will require the fewest alterations and preferably one with a door that shuts to keep business in, and family, friends, and pets out when necessary. But make sure your workspace is large enough to operate your business. Working out of two or three separate areas of the home is far less productive than working from one area; you are constantly searching for things rather than working. Also, try to make your workspace a single-use area. Ideally, the room should not double as the dining room at night or the children's playroom.

Selling Full-Time from Home

If you will be selling full-time from home, the first considerations are: Do you have the interior/exterior space required to showcase products and accept customers? Do you have suitable parking, and can you provide customers with access to washroom facilities? In addition, you also want to be able to separate your living space from your selling space, to provide privacy for both customers and your family. A separate entrance for customers or an existing entrance close to the workspace is important. Another consideration is the appearance of your home. Peeling paint, threadbare carpets, and broken porch boards send customers the wrong signals about your business and products. If your home needs a sprucing up, then do it before you get started.

Storage Issues

Whether you have customers coming to your home or not, you will need storage space for equipment, inventory, and business records, as well as adequate space for receiving products and shipping orders. Provided you have enough storage space to meet your needs, the space you use will also need to be easily accessible, dry, and free of critters. It must also be secure so there is no risk that valuable business equipment, inventory, and records will be stolen. If you do not have suitable storage space, is there suitable storage for rent close by with good access, and how much does it cost?

Equipment and Technology

Every buy-and-sell business has different needs in terms of office furniture, equipment, and technology devices. If customers will be visiting your home showroom, your furniture, equipment, and displays will need to reflect this, both in appearance and function. If you do not have customers visiting your home office, you will have more leeway because it won't really matter if the colors are mismatched, if you purchased your desk secondhand at your neighbor's garage sale, or if you choose to build a few of the items yourself. All that really matters is that your furniture, equipment, and technology devices do what you need them to do, be reliable, be comfortable, and get the job done. The following are the basic needs.

- *Desk and comfortable chair*. You will need a desk large enough for a computer monitor with tower storage underneath, a printer, and a telephone/fax machine. Also, if you only splurge on one piece of office furniture, a comfortable and ergonomically correct chair should be that luxury item, especially if your business keeps you on your seat for long periods of time.
- *Paper file storage*. Even in this electronic age, businesses still generate lots of paper files. But you do not have to invest in a file cabinet immediately if money is tight. Instead, for about $5 you can purchase accordion-style file storage boxes that can hold up to 100 documents, which should be enough file storage space to get you going.
- *Worktable*. Purchase or build a worktable separate from your desk if space allows. Worktables are indispensable and can be used for opening and sorting mail, book- and record-keeping duties, packing and unpacking inventory, and much more.
- *Computer system and software*. You will need a complete computer system, including monitor, printer, modem, keyboard, and mouse. The main considerations will be processing speed and data storage capabilities. Desktop computer systems range in price from $600 for a basic model to $3,000 for a top-of-the-line home office computer. Expect to pay in the range of $1,500 to $4,000 for a portable notebook/laptop computer. You will also need software. Depending on the products you buy and sell and how they are sold, you might need software in one or more of the following areas: word processing, accounting, database management, Web site building and maintenance, shopping cart, payment processing, inventory tracking, and desktop publishing.
- *Digital camera*. Digital cameras are indispensable to buy-and-sell entrepreneurs. You can take pictures of products, and because the images (photographs) use digital technology, they are easily transferred to your Web site, e-mails, classified ads, or desktop publishing programs to create fliers, brochures, presentations, catalogs, posters, and signs. Good-quality digital cameras cost in the range of $400 at the time of this writing.
- *Telephone/fax machine*. You will need a good old desktop telephone with business functions such as on-hold, conferencing, redial, speakerphone, broadcast, and message storage capabilities. Contact your telephone service provider; many offer customers multifunction business telephones on installments, with payments added to your telephone bill. If your budget allows, you might consider purchasing an all-in-one office document center with a telephone, fax, printer, scanner, and copier; current costs are in the range of $400 to $1,500.

Things You Can Buy and Sell for Big Profits

- *Cellular telephone.* A cellular telephone is a must, enabling you to keep in constant contact with customers and prospects, no matter where you are. Cellular telephone service plans are cheap, in the range of $50 per month. Also, consider purchasing a cell phone with Internet features so you can receive, check, and send e-mails, not to mention track eBay auctions, if desired.
- *Internet connection.* You will also need an Internet connection so you can access the Net, eBay, and send and receive e-mails. Unlimited dial-up access generally costs in the range of $15 per month; high-speed access generally runs in the range of $20 to $50 per month, but you will also need to upgrade your modem at an additional cost if you choose high-speed.

Keeping Track of Inventory and Delivering the Goods

Newton was right: For every action there is an equal and opposite reaction. The fun action is selling your products and making a profit. The equal and opposite reaction is not so fun, because you will need to manage your inventory and find ways to deliver products on schedule and at the lowest cost. This is best classified as boring, hard work.

INVENTORY MANAGEMENT

The first hard-work issue is inventory management. If you are selling big items one at a time, you're off the hook. However, if you are selling small items through various venues and are a high-volume seller, you will need to put an inventory management system in place. Starting with the physical aspect, you will need a place to put your inventory, one that is easily accessed, dry, and secure. If you do not have space at home, you will need to rent space, and security, cost, size, and proximity to your home will all need to be considered. I find public mini-storage services are the best, because you are not tied to long-term warehouse leases, nor do you have to worry about utilities and maintenance, which are included in your month-by-month rent. At home or off-site, you will also need to build or purchase new or used shelving to house your inventory. Ideally, the shelving should be adjustable to accommodate various-sized products.

In terms of inventory management, once again you have options, and much of your decision will be based on volume of sales. If you are an occasional or small buyer and seller, simply invest in a spiral notebook, create a few columns for product description and units, and you are pretty much set. Likewise, you can also create your own inventory management system using your computer and a spreadsheet program such as Excel. Large-volume sellers should, however, invest in inventory or retail management software. Most inventory management software offers valuable, time-saving features such as customer database options, invoice creation, label-making, inventory tracking, bar code scanning, tax codes, and automatic inventory reordering. Prices vary depending on features and peripherals such as fixed and wireless scanners. Listed in the Resources are two directories for business software companies, or you can find inventory management software by conducting searches on Google and Yahoo.

PRODUCT DELIVERY

There are many options available for how to get products from your business to your customer's location. You can deliver the item yourself, have a courier service pick up and deliver, use the postal service, or hire a cartage company. Your decision will be based on factors such as cost, schedule, and what is being shipped. Whether you deliver or hire it out, product delivery is a major part of your business. It reflects to customers the kind of service you provide and can have a positive or negative effect on repeat business and word-of-mouth advertising depending on how customers perceive the overall experience. Shipping costs vary depending on product weight, overall dimensions, schedule, geography, and value.

You will also need to consider how you will pack items for transport and the costs of packing-and-shipping materials such as boxes, bubble warp, envelopes, tape, Styrofoam® pellets, and plastic bags. All of the big courier and freight companies offer packing materials for sale, but shop around because in small quantities or individually, these are very expensive. Office supply stores like Staples generally have the lowest costs on packing-and-shipping supplies. These delivery charges will all have to be calculated and built into retail pricing before you sell items. If you sell the same products regularly, then costing out packaging and shipping charges is a snap, because outside of how far the product is being shipped, costs remain the same. However, if you sell various products and you do not know from one week to the next how big or how many, you will need to calculate packing-and-shipping costs individually and add these to retail prices prior to selling. All the big courier companies, the U.S. Postal Service, and Canada Post have software available to frequent shippers that calculates shipping charges based on the information you enter. A few other benefits of this software are that it allows you to print customer labels, track packages, and arrange for pickups and deliveries online. Listed below are a few of the major courier companies and postal services. You can log on to their Web sites to find additional information about shipping and opening accounts.

RESOURCES

- Canada Post, ♂ www.canadapost.ca
- DHL, courier and freight services, ♂ www.dhl.com
- FedEx, courier and freight services, ♂ www.fedex.com
- Purolator, courier and freight services, ♂ www.purolator.com
- Soft Scout, business software directory, ♂ www.softscout.com
- The Software Network, business software directory, ♂ www.thesoftware network.com
- TNT, courier and freight services, ♂ www.tnt.com
- The United States Postal Service, ♂ www.usps.com
- UPS, courier and freight services, ♂ www.ups.com

Product Pricing

Pricing new, used, and collectible products for resale is more difficult than most people new to the buy-and-sell game think, yet pricing is a very important element of the marketing mix. If your prices are too high, you will meet with great resistance to buying. If your prices are too low, you may also meet with resistance because of perceived quality issues, and you probably won't make any money on the sales you have.

There are a number of factors influencing how you price products for resale—product costs, overhead, competition, method of distribution, wages, and your desired return on investment. If your pricing is correct, consumers won't think twice because they will feel the price is fair and commensurate with the perceived value and benefits. However, as soon as your price goes below or above the threshold of what consumers feel is in the fair range, you will meet sales resistance. Whether you are selling new, used, or collectible products and items, you still have to cover the basics, your fixed costs, direct costs, and income and profit. It is a combination of the aforementioned and common sense that will help you determine what prices you have to, and can, charge for your products. The first factor is overhead—that is, the fixed costs of doing business. Even though fixed costs cannot directly generate a profit, they nonetheless must be present in order to operate the business. The telephone bill must get paid regardless of how many sales you make or how much revenue is generated. Some overhead costs do increase as sales volume increases, necessitating good record-keeping and bookkeeping habits to keep on top of changes. Additional examples of fixed costs include business permits, transportation, bank charges, professional fees, and marketing expenditures.

The next factor affecting product pricing is direct costs associated with the sale and delivery of a product. An example of a direct cost is the wholesale cost of a pair of sunglasses. If the sunglasses cost you $5 each, the cost to have each pair shipped to your home is $1, and you spend a further $1 repackaging and labeling the sunglasses for resale, then your total direct cost for each pair is $7.

The third basic factor influencing product pricing is your wages and profit. People often confuse the two, but they are separate issues. Income is what you trade your time for—$25 per hour, for example. Profit is the return on your investment and the reward for the risks entrepreneurs take by starting and operating a business.

Pricing New Products for Resale

There are a number of ways to price new products for resale. The simplest is generally a cost-plus approach, which means that you multiply your product cost by a markup factor such as 100 percent. If you paid $25 wholesale for a cordless drill and applied a 100 percent markup, the retail selling price would be $50. But at the end of the day, competition will be seen as the greatest influence. If the majority of resellers charge $35 for a cordless drill on eBay, you would be hard pressed to sell for more unless your cordless drill had substantially more user benefits and features. Of course, if you were the only vendor selling cordless drills online or elsewhere, you might be able to sell one for $75 in the absence of competition.

Sales value also has to be factored in to pricing. If you pay $1 for a lighter and resell it for $3, you might be getting a whopping 300 percent markup, but at the same time you have to sell a whole bunch of lighters to cover fixed costs, and income, while also generating a profit. On the other side of the coin, you might only earn 5 percent on the resale of a piece of real estate, but on a $300,000 sale this adds up to $15,000. Once again, a commonsense approach must be taken when choosing products to resell and their prices.

For the small buy-and-sell operator, the best product pricing approach is to conduct research in the marketplace to find out what the same or similar products are selling for, how they are being sold, and who is buying. Research techniques include:

- Going online to eBay and other marketplaces to study prices
- Searching through newspaper, flier, and magazine advertisements for prices
- Mystery-shopping at retail stores and doing price comparisons
- Subscribing to product catalogs for pricing information
- Calling retailers and asking how much they charge for the type of product(s) you are going to sell
- Asking suppliers. They are one of the best sources of up-to-date product pricing. They can tell you about suggested retail selling prices, sales tips, and if you are lucky, the prices other resellers are charging.

Obviously, it is in your best interest to search for innovative ways to distinguish what you sell from the competition's products and methods of distribution so you can sell your products for more and in greater volume.

Pricing Used Products for Resale

Pricing previously owned merchandise for resale shares similarities with pricing new products, especially in terms of pricing research. Use many of the same price research techniques—online searches, classified advertising, and mystery-shopping comparison for small items at thrift shops to help determine market value of the used goods you are selling. There are also price guides available for more expensive products like cars, boats, and recreational vehicles. Where available, I have included these guides in Chapter 6: Resources.

Price guides typically describe the product, including model and features, and assign a value based on these criteria as well as the condition of the item. Used car dealers have used price guides for decades to help establish a buying and selling price for trade-ins.

You can also have professional appraisals performed on higher-priced items to help substantiate and support the asking price. This is especially true for items like real estate, cars, fine jewelry, and boats. Keep in mind that professional appraisals and surveys can be quite expensive, and you will need to factor in this cost when buying and pass the cost along when selling.

Many resellers create *a sliding-condition scale* for pricing items. In perfect condition, items are priced at 70 percent of new cost, while items that are still saleable, but past their glory days, are priced at 30 percent of new cost. Some products also retain value better than others. For instance, computer towers are notorious for having poor resale value due to rapidly changing technology, while computer monitors hold their value better because technological advances in monitors aren't as quick or common. Ultimately, pricing used products for resale is very much what the market will bear, but you can greatly increase the odds of securing top dollar by selling products that are in good condition, work, and are in demand, and by selling through the right venues and to the right audience.

Pricing Antiques and Collectibles for Resale

Pricing antiques and collectibles for resale is another game entirely, mainly because antiques, collectibles, and memorabilia items are seldom needed like a dependable used car to get the kids to school, a stove to cook on, or clothes for people's backs. Antiques and collectibles are things people want, not need, and the target audience can be very narrow, especially for uncommon collectibles and highly valued antiques. Let's face it, few consumers have an extra $25,000 lying around to buy an original Tiffany lamp. Therefore, pricing is largely reflective of what the marketplace will bear.

There are price, value, and condition guides available for every imaginable type of antique and collectible. Many are listed as resources in Chapter 6. Value guides are unquestionably a good starting point for pricing and in most instances invaluable, but only to a point. Antiques and collectibles values go up and down daily, influenced by many factors. For instance, the value of nautical collectibles, especially cruise line memorabilia, skyrocketed after the release of the movie *Titanic,* as does the value of first-edition Hemingway novels for a few weeks a year around the anniversary of his birthday.

Pricing antiques and collectibles is as much about choosing the right sales venues and target audience as it is about the actual item, probably more so. Therefore, success comes to antiques and collectibles traders who pay close attention to what's going on in the marketplace at all times. Professional appraisals and authentications also help to substantiate and support asking prices. Indeed, in many situations having antique, collectible, and memorabilia items appraised and authenticated will greatly increase their value. Authentication is especially valuable.

Building Strong Trade Accounts

A business can only be as strong as each supporting partner. If you sell new products purchased from manufacturers, wholesalers, distributors, importers, or craftspeople, you have to choose your suppliers wisely. In order to sustain long-term stability and profitability, relationships with your product suppliers must be mutually beneficial and equitable. Buying decisions cannot be based solely on low price; you also have to factor a good match, reliability, and support into the equation.

- *A good match.* The first rule of choosing suppliers is to only do business with people you like, trust, and respect. You might love your supplier's products, but if you do not like, or cannot get along with the people running the company, there is little hope for establishing a long-term, stable, equitable business relationship.
- *Reliability.* If your suppliers cannot deliver what you need when you need it, this will have a very negative impact on your business. Supplier reliability is perhaps the most important criteria you should consider when establishing trade accounts. Your supplier's promise to you is your promise to your customers. If your supplier lets you down, you in turn let your customers down, and lose sales and profits every time it happens.

- *Support.* You also have to consider the support that suppliers offer in terms of warranties, customer service, and selling aids such as product samples, brochures, fliers, catalogs, promotional signage, event displays, and Web site and e-commerce support. The higher the level of support and service supplied to you, the higher level of support and service you can provide your customers. Most buy-and-sell enterprises are one-person shows, so all support you receive from your suppliers is critical.

Buying on Terms

The payment terms you can negotiate with your suppliers are often more important than a lowest unit-product cost. With the right terms, you have the opportunity to sell products to your customers, get paid, and keep your profits before paying your suppliers. Ideally, you want to secure 90-day payment terms on a revolving-account basis, but you will generally find most suppliers prefer 30 days and offer discounts for cash orders or early settlement. People with strong credit will have few problems opening revolving-credit accounts with suppliers. If your credit is not so strong, you will need to establish a payment history with most suppliers prior to their granting you credit privileges. The advantage of revolving credit is that you can often sell your goods long before you have to pay your supplier. In effect, your suppliers are bankrolling your business, and you get access to your profits without having to use your own cash. A word of advice: Treat all supplier accounts with respect and pay on time and in full when required to do so. Credit is a privilege for those who deserve it, not a right.

Drop-Shipping Option

Another option open to buy-and-sell entrepreneurs who resell new products is not to purchase inventory for resale at all, but instead open accounts with wholesalers and manufacturers who offer drop-shipping services. Drop-shipping is simple. You sell a product to a customer and collect payment via credit card, debit card, cash, or check. You then send the order to your supplier via e-mail, fax, or courier. Your supplier fulfills the product order and ships it to your customer under your business name. Your supplier bills your account for the product shipped. You pay your account when due. The big benefits of drop-shipping for the small buy-and-sell entrepreneur are that you do not have to worry about buying inventory upfront, you do not have to rent warehouse space for inventory, and you do not have to worry about transportation and delivery issues. In short, all you have to concentrate on is finding people to buy your products. Many online retailers work with drop-ship wholesalers, but you can also work with drop-ship wholesalers and manufacturers even if you sell via mail order, in-home parties, or consumer shows. All that is required is product samples, product literature such as brochures and catalogs, and order forms. To find manufacturers and wholesalers who provide drop-ship solutions, you can refer to the directories listed below, though you will have to purchase them. The other option is to conduct online searches through Google or Yahoo. Submit Drop-Ship Wholesalers, and you will have hundreds of matches.

RESOURCES
- American Drop-Shippers Directory, ♂ www.bookservices.com
- Drop-Ship Source Directory, ♂ www.mydssd.com
- No Minimum, wholesale drop-shipping sources, ♂ www.nominimum.com

Developing a Mini-Marketing Plan

Developing a mini-marketing plan for your buy-and-sell venture is well worth the effort. Based on your research and the information revealed in the plan, you will be able to prove that there is sufficient demand for your product, that you can compete in the marketplace, and that the market is large enough to support your venture and marketing goals. Of course, your marketing plan does not have to be highly sophisticated. Even a few well-researched and documented pages covering the basics are often sufficient to reveal the information needed to identify your customers, your product's advantages, your sales goals, your marketing strategies, and your action plan. By answering the questions in the following eight subsections, you will have compiled enough information to create your own mini-marketing plan. This information can then be used to help market your products and guide your marketing decisions from where you are now to where you want to be in the future—and ultimately to profitability.

1. Your Buy-and-Sell Enterprise

The starting point is to describe your buy-and-sell venture in general terms; your business name, legal structure, owners' and partners' special skills and experiences, and key product suppliers. Also, if your buy-and-sell venture is currently in operation, use this space to recount successes, failures, and growth or decline in sales to date, and describe where your business is now versus where it will be in the future should marketing goals and objectives as set out in the marketing plan be reached.

A. What is your business name and legal structure? _____

_____

B. Where is your business located? _____

_____

_____

C. Describe your own and any business partner's relevant experience, skills, and training. _____

_____

_____

D. List key product suppliers and the products each supplies. _____

_____

_____

2. Marketplace

Describe the marketplace in which your business will operate or might expand into in the near future. The biggest benefit of conducting and recording marketplace information is that it enables you to greatly reduce your exposure to financial risk, increase your chances of capitalizing on marketplace opportunities, and prove that there is a big enough marketplace to support your business and expected sales.

A. Describe the trading area that your buy-and-sell venture will serve. (City, county, state) _____

_____

_____

B. How big is the current market? _____

_____

_____

C. How big is the potential market? _____

_____

_____

D. In what life-cycle stage is the market—growth, decline, or static? _____

_____

_____

3. Target Customer

Describe your target customers: where they live, their age range, their gender, what they do for a living, what they like to read, and what is important to them when they buy products. Having this information enables you to aim your advertising, marketing, and sales activities directly at your target customers, saving you money and time.

A. Where are your target customers geographically located? _____

_____

_____

B. What percentage of your target customers are male, and what is their age range? _____

_____

_____

C. What percentage of your target customers are female, and what is their age range? _____

_____

_____

D. What is the marital status of your target customers? _____

_____

_____

E. What level of education do your target customers have? _____

_____

_____

F. What do your target customers do to earn a living? _____

_____

_____

G. What is most important to your target customers when making purchasing decisions; price, value, service, or quality? _____

_____

_____

H. What publications do those in your target audience like to read? _____

_____

_____

4. Competition

Researching and documenting competitor information is important because it tells you who your direct competition is—that is, the other businesses that sell the same or similar products to the same target audience within the same geographical area. You can use information you gather and record to develop strategies to turn competitors' weaknesses into your strengths.

A. Describe your biggest competitors. _____

_____

_____

B. What are your competitors' strengths? _____

_____

_____

C. What are your competitors' weaknesses? _____

_____

_____

D. What do your competitors do well that you should also be doing? _____

_____

_____

5. Sales Goals

Your sales goals should be given in easily measured, quantifiable financial terms and the corresponding number of units. Be realistic, and list a firm date when each sales goal will be reached. If you are planning on utilizing more than one sales venue, you will want to separate and list sales goals for each individually.

A. What are your first-month sales goals? _____

_____

_____

B. What are your six-month sales goals? _____

_____

_____

C. What are your first-year sales goals? _____

_____

_____

D. What are your five-year sales goals? _____

_____

_____

6. Product, Price, Place (Distribution), and Promotion

Developing your marketing strategy revolves around the four marketing Ps—product, price, place (distribution), and promotion. It is the combination of the four Ps that creates your marketing mix, which is, in effect, the entire marketing process. Essentially, the four Ps are about finding the right portions of each, enabling you to create the perfect marketing mix comprised of the marketing strategies that will allow you to meet and exceed your marketing objectives.

6.1 PRODUCT

A. Describe your product(s) in detail, including packaging. _____

_____

_____

B. What special features do your products have, and how do customers benefit by purchasing and using your products? _____

_____

_____

C. What advantages do your products have over competitors' products? __

_____

_____

D. Describe your product warranties, return/refund policies, and customer-service guarantees. _____

_____

_____

6.2 PRICE

A. How much will you charge for your product(s), how did you arrive at your selling price, and what is your pricing strategy? _____

_____

_____

B. How sensitive are your target customers to pricing issues, and why? ____

_____

_____

C. How much do competitors charge for their products?   _____

_____

_____

D. List the purchase payment options that you will provide to your customers, e.g., credit cards, debit cards, electronic transfers, and the setup and ongoing fees associated with each.   _____

_____

_____

6.3 PLACE (DISTRIBUTION)

A. Describe the methods you will utilize to sell your products.   _____

_____

_____

B. Describe the inventory management system you intend on using.   _____

_____

_____

C. Describe how customers receive your products and describe your logistics system, including order fulfillment, warehousing, and transportation needs.

_____

_____

_____

6.4 PROMOTION

A. Describe what advertising mediums you will utilize in the promotion of your products, as well as marketing materials such as fliers, signs, catalogs, and business cards.   _____

_____

_____

B. Describe any direct-sales tactics you will employ, including personal selling, mail, telephone, and electronic.   _____

_____

_____

C. Describe how you will utilize public relations in the promoting of your products. _____

_____

_____

D. Describe how you will use the Internet to promote your goods, including your Web site and online marketing strategies. _____

_____

_____

7. Marketing Budget

Use a ground-up approach to calculate the cost of each marketing strategy and activity you will use to sell, advertise, and market your goods. Break down each marketing activity by individual cost, and add them together to estimate your overall marketing budget. You also may want to consider the use of a break-even analysis. Once you know how much the marketing activity will cost, you can then calculate how many product units will have to be sold to cover, or break even with, the cost of the planned activity.

A. List your main marketing activities and the cost to implement each. ____

_____

_____

B. Describe how these marketing activities will be paid for. _____

_____

_____

8. Action Plan

The action plan is nothing more than a big do-to list broken into marketing categories and timetables outlining when each promotional activity will be implemented and managed, and how results will be measured. You may also want to purchase a large wall-mounted calendar that can be written on in erasable marker, and outline promotional activities and relevant dates; this is especially handy because it enables you to look at the entire year, not just each week or month. Your action plan must also include details on how and when you will measure the progress, success, or failure of each promotional activity. By measuring results incrementally, you can make sure that the promotional activity is working and that you are on track to meet your marketing and sales objectives.

A. Describe how each marketing strategy will be implemented. _____

_____

_____

B. Outline the timetable for when each marketing strategy will be imple-mented. _____

_____

_____

C. Describe how you will track and measure the effectiveness of each market-ing strategy. _____

_____

_____

Mastering Personal Selling

Preparation is the starting point for mastering all personal selling. What are you selling? Who are you selling to? Who else is selling it? And, what tools will help you sell and close? Sales preparation can be divided into four main categories: product, customers, competitors, and sales tools.

- *Product*. You have to know what you are selling inside out and upside down. Knowledge about your product can be acquired from research, spe-cialized training, suppliers, information in books and other published for-mats, feedback from customers, and hands-on experience. The better you know your product, the more you will be able to identify potential cus-tomers and sell them what they need and want.
- *Customers*. You must know who needs what you are selling, where these people are located, how much they buy, and how often they buy. Additional customer information such as what clubs they belong to and what newspa-pers they read can also prove valuable. Perhaps more importantly, sales preparation means you know the answers to the questions your prospects and customers have, in advance of their asking.
- *Competition*. Sales preparation also means you know your competition thor-oughly—what people like and dislike about competing businesses, prices, and guarantees; how those businesses are promoted; and after promoted how competitors secure paying customers. Basically, you need to know how your business stacks up against the competition.
- *Sales tools*. The final aspect of sales preparation is to have a toolbox packed with great sales tools, which are the instruments you will use to grab your

prospects' attention, create interest and desire, and motivate them to buy. Sales tools include product literature, product samples, signage, customer testimonials, training, and purchase payment options.

Qualifying the Buyer

Qualifying the buyer is the process of asking questions and using the responses to determine if they need, want, and can afford what you are selling. The importance of qualifying cannot be overstated. The better qualified a prospect is, the greater the chance of closing the sale. You might feel uncomfortable asking qualifying questions because you think it's being pushy, nosy, or aggressive. But keep in mind that every person must ask questions in order to help others or to determine what the others need. Doctors ask questions about symptoms so they can make informed diagnoses. A fitness trainer will ask about specific goals so they can develop an exercise program that will help achieve those goals. You should focus on four issues when qualifying buyers: Do they need it? Who makes the buying decision? Can they afford it? When do they want it?

Do They Need It?

Determine right away if the person you are trying to sell even needs or wants what you have to sell. If not, you are wasting your time and theirs by continuing the conversation. If you have in-depth knowledge of what you sell and how people benefit by owning or using it, qualifying a prospect with a few simple questions should be easy: What problems need solving? What are their requirements? What needs to be improved? What is wrong with what they currently have, or alternately, what would make their job or life easier?

Who Makes the Buying Decisions?

Always make sure you are dealing with the person who makes the buying decision. Nothing is more frustrating than having a hot prospect on the line, only to discover after spending much time and energy with him that he cannot make the decision to buy, or that there are more people involved in the decision-making process. The best way to find out right upfront is to simply ask: Who will be making the purchasing decision? Will you be making the decision on your own, or will there be other people involved in the purchasing decision? If you find my _____ suitable, are you authorized to make the purchase?

Can They Afford It?

You do not want to waste time trying to sell your products to people who cannot afford them, especially in fast-paced selling venues like trade shows and flea markets where every selling moment counts. You have to be able to quickly determine if the person you are talking to has the money or access to the money needed to make the purchase. Ask your prospect if she has the money put aside to pay for the purchase, can she afford it, and is it in her budget. Regardless of how you phrase the question, you have to know they can afford to buy, or move on to someone who can.

WHEN DO THEY WANT IT?

Some people start shopping for products they want and need months or even years in advance. While you want this business, at the same time you have to know what the best use of your time is at this precise moment. Are you talking with someone who wants to buy right away or two years from now? I'll take the buyer who is ready to purchase right now every time, because too many things change with time. How soon do you need the _____? When will you be ready to have the product installed? When would you like to take delivery? These are all questions you can ask to find out when they want to buy.

Getting Past Objections

Most new entrepreneurs confuse rejection and objections. Rejection is a flat-out refusal to buy what you are selling, while objections are nothing more than prospects telling you they need more information to help them make the right buying decision. Therefore, when prospects start stating reasons why they shouldn't buy, don't turn tail and run for the hills. Instead, welcome and overcome these objections. The big three are: The price is too high, I don't have the money, and Let me think about it.

GETTING PAST PRICE OBJECTIONS

It should come as no surprise that most people automatically respond, "The price is too high" or "The price is too much" whether or not they have given it much thought. For most of us it's a natural response when asked to buy. Your first reply should be, "The price is too much in comparison to what?" This throws the majority of people off balance, especially if they have not actually considered why the price is too high. Another strategy for overcoming price objections is to simply agree that your price is more than competitors' prices, but explain why—better quality, longer warranty, more features, or some other competitive advantage that justifies a higher price. Also ask, "Is price the only objection you have to proceeding with the sale?" The answer will let you know if price is the only objection or if there are other obstacles. If price is the only objection, look for suitable solutions—cheaper model or creative financing options, for example.

GETTING PAST NO-MONEY OBJECTIONS

When prospects tell you that they cannot afford to buy, ask them why. You cannot overcome the no-money objection unless you know all the details and the reasons for their decisions. You can then develop workable solutions that might otherwise go unnoticed. Clearly demonstrate to prospects that the benefits of buying are so important to their particular situation that a no-money objection would not be wise. In other words, the cost of not buying far outweighs the cost of buying. When you receive a no-money objection, one of the first things that you should do is turnover every last stone to find suitable financing—credit cards, consumer loan, and leasing, for example. When you can show people they can purchase by using financing means they had not thought of, often the no-money objection fades and they warm up to the idea of buying because now they can.

GETTING PAST LET-ME-THINK-ABOUT-IT OBJECTIONS

When people say they want to think about it, suggest you go over things again while the details are fresh in everyone's mind. This tactic opens the door once more and enables you to flush out real obstacles to overcome. You can also try the Benjamin Franklin technique by listing the advantages of a buy decision in one column, while listing the disadvantages of not buying in a second column. When people see in black and white that the advantages of buying far outweigh the disadvantages, often it is all the persuasion they need to go ahead. Also try offering an incentive to overcome the objection—a discount, upgraded model, free delivery, or whatever you think will clinch the sale.

Negotiate Like a Pro

By its very nature, a buy-and-sell enterprise means that you will need to master the art of negotiation, because this is a skill you will use daily. You negotiate with suppliers for lower prices and better terms; you negotiate with buyers to buy more and at higher prices; you negotiate with flea market managers for lower booth rent and more space. In short, buying and selling is a constant round of negotiation.

Information is the cornerstone of mastering negotiations, and the more of it you have, the stronger your position becomes for getting what you want on your terms and conditions. Obtaining information means you have to find out as much as you can about what the person you are negotiating with wants and needs, and how these are prioritized—by benefits, budget, or by schedule. Having this information lets you know what the other person wants to achieve through negotiations, thus strengthening your position and weakening theirs.

Also keep in mind that if someone really needs what you are selling, price often becomes a secondary issue to user or owner benefits. In other words, what the product will do for them, such as solve a problem or make them healthier, becomes paramount. So before negotiations start, you must first position the value of your product in relation to the benefits the person will receive by taking ownership. This is a critical step in the negotiation process. If what you have to sell is properly positioned in terms of value, it gives you increased leverage and power to get what you want out of the negotiation process, without having to accept less money or unfavorable conditions. Never accept first offers. If you do, I can guarantee you will be leaving money on the table or, alternately, paying too much yourself. Few people walk away from negotiations when a first offer is declined, on either side of the deal. Always, counter-offer, which (depending on whether you are buying or selling) means telling the other party you want to pay less or sell for more. Finally, don't be afraid to walk away from negotiations if you are positive you have nothing to gain by continuing. When the result of the negotiations is no longer beneficial to you, walk away. If not, be prepared to sacrifice profits or waste time.

Closing Every Sale

All buy-and-sell entrepreneurs have to get in the habit of asking for the sale every time they talk to a potential customer. If not, all they will have accomplished is to educate the buyer, making them an easy closing target for the next vendor they talk to. And remember, few people will take it upon themselves to offer you the sale unless they are asked to do so. Closing is an essential selling skill, but bear in mind that no matter how much closing intimidates you, in reality it is nothing more than the natural progression in the sales cycle. You prospect, qualify, present, and close. Therefore, asking for the sale should be nothing more than a formality.

The assumption close is a good closing technique because it requires doing nothing more than assuming every person you talk to about your products will buy. Do this by making statements like, "I will have this shipped to you by the end of the week." "I just need your signature on this agreement so we can start processing your order." Or, "How would you like to pay for this?"

The alternate-choice close is also an easy one to master, often with great results. As the name suggests, this closing technique means giving your prospect more than one product option by asking a question such as, "So which choice would you prefer, the green Kevlar canoe, or the red one?" The alternate-choice close pulls your prospect into making a buying decision and selecting one of the options. Not buying is no longer an available option, based on the alternate-choice closing question. The alternate-choice questions can also be used effectively to increase the quantity of a particular product you want your customer to buy. For instance, "Would you like to buy one lifejacket to go with your new canoe, or two?" Once again, this pulls your customer into a buying decision. The question is no longer will you buy, but rather how many you are going to buy.

Once you have closed the sale, ask for a referral. Almost all small businesses survive on referral business and positive word-of-mouth advertising.

Advertising That Works

The golden rule of advertising for the buy-and-sell entrepreneur is: You do not need to spend a bundle advertising and promoting your products. Just make sure the money you do spend is on advertising and promotions aimed directly at your target audience. So how much do you spend on advertising? The answer will depend on the type of products you sell, how they are sold, and how much you can afford to spend. If you sell sunglasses at your local weekend flea market, you need not spend any money on advertising outside of promotional fliers and signs. If you sell big-ticket items like classic cars, real estate, boats, and antiques, chances are you will need a substantial advertising budget to reach your target audience and build interest in your product. If you do spend considerable money on advertising, you will need to create a system for tracking your advertising activities so you can determine the effectiveness of each. This is important to know because it allows you to allocate your advertising dollars where they have the greatest impact in terms of reaching your target audience and generating the most revenue. This section covers advertising basics, such as creating high-impact ads that sell, finding cheap and free classified advertising and publicity sources, and using two of the buy-and-sell entrepreneur's most powerful promotional tools—fliers and signs.

Creating Ads That Sell

Creating clever and convincing copy that sells is needed for advertising, fliers, presentations, signs, catalogs, newsletters, and Web site content. At the core of creating great copy is the time-tested and proven AIDA advertising formula—attention, interest, desire, and action. Your copy must grab the attention of your target audience, create interest in what you have to say, build desire for what you have to sell, and compel people to take action and buy.

The starting point is a powerful headline. In good advertising copy, the headline is king because you only have a brief moment to grab the readers' attention and pull them into your message. For instance, "Nobody beats our low prices, guaranteed" is certainly a powerful headline that will grab the readers' attention and pull them into your story.

Also, when it comes to terms of advertising effectiveness, the old adage that *a photograph is worth a thousand words* is very true. Photographs have the unique ability to showcase the best qualities of your product without saying a word, so be sure to include photographs of the products you sell in your advertisements and marketing materials.

Clever advertising copy also appeals to people on an emotional level. It uses emotional triggers of basic human feelings such as the need for friendship, the need for security, and the desire to achieve. Your copy must single out and talk directly to your target audience in the same way that they would think and speak. That is what great copy does. While reaching the masses, it makes everyone in your target audience feel as though you are talking to them directly as an individual. The final, and arguably most important, aspect of creating great copy is to always ask for the sale. You can have the best attention-grabbing headline, dazzingly descriptive photographs, a wow sales pitch, and an unbeatable offer, and all of it will be for nothing unless you ask your audience to buy, giving compelling reasons to do so and providing the tools for them to take action. Never assume that your reader will know what to do next. Tell them what you want them to do next, and give them the tools and motivation they need to take action.

Cheap and Free Classified Advertising Sources

Classified advertising is unquestionably the buy-and-sell entrepreneur's best friend because it is easy to create, cheap to run, and almost always has a higher response rate than display advertisements. People generally read the classifieds looking for a specific product to buy, not for the entertainment value they seek in other sections of the newspaper. This is good news. It enables you to sell your goods aggressively, because readers expect these types of ads. Write short, powerful copy that sells; create urgency by stating a deadline or limited availability; and most importantly, include the main benefit that a person receives by buying your products. Start with an attention-grabbing headline that jumps off the page and pay a few extra dollars to have it set in bold type, flagged with an icon, or surrounded by a border. Also, give thought to the type of publication and the classified heading or section under which your advertisement will appear. Pick publications that are read by your target audience, and choose a section they are most likely to read. Because classified advertisements are cheap and quick to post, continually look for ways to improve your results by testing new ads in various publications read by your target audience. Test your headline, your main sales message, and your special offers on a regular basis. Classified advertising costs vary by publication, number of words, number of insertions, and other factors such as the use of icons and photographs.

There are many print and online classified advertising sources, some of which offer totally free classified ads, while others you have to pay for. In addition to utilizing your own local newspaper classifieds, check out the list below for some of the more popular classified advertising services.

RESOURCES

– *Buy and Sell*, print and online classified advertising, ♂ www.buysell.com
– *My Town Ads*, online classified ads indexed geographically, ♂ www.mytown ads.com
– Penny Saver USA, print classified advertising, ♂ www.pennysaverusa.com.
– The Recycler, print and online classified advertising, ♂ www.recycler.com
– Thrifty Nickel, print and online classified advertising, ♂ www.thriftynickel ads.com
– Yahoo Classifieds, online general merchandise classified ads, ♂ www.classifieds. yahoo.com

Getting Free Publicity

Small-business owners tend to shy away from publicity, but why? When the potential to reach thousands, even millions, of people for free is a real possibility, why would anyone pass it up? The answer is simple. Most don't realize they could easily create some publicity buzz around what they sell. It just takes a bit of imagination. Start by using these simple and highly effective publicity tools.

PRESS RELEASES

The quickest and easiest way to let the media know what you sell is to create a press release outlining the details and send it to them. If you are new to writing press releases, read a few first to get an idea of what kind of information to include, formatting tips, and to whom to send it. Visit PR Web online at ♂ www.prweb.com. There you can read through thousands of press releases for free, which can help you write your own.

SPEECHES

Another great way to secure publicity is by giving speeches at seminars and work-shops. There are numerous associations, organizations, and clubs of every type in every community, and these organizations often have experts speak to members on topics related to the purpose of the club. For instance, if you sell military collectibles you can arrange to speak to members of historical societies and military collector clubs.

TALK RADIO

Talk radio is a potential publicity windfall for buy-and-sell entrepreneurs. Get started by developing a story idea. For instance, if you sell antiques, develop a show idea around teaching listeners what to look for when buying antiques. Or if you sell personal security devices, develop a show that educates listeners about how to buy and use personal security devices. Once your idea is fully developed, contact show producers to pitch your ideas. Radio Locator, ♂ www.radio-locator. com, has links to more than 10,000 radio stations, including talk radio format.

LETTERS TO THE EDITOR

Writing letters to the editor is another simple method for buy-and-sell entrepreneurs to secure publicity. If you sell fitness equipment, write a letter outlining the benefits of physical exercise, for example. The letter should be signed with your business name and telephone number. Published letters can provide you with all sorts of free advertising.

COMMUNITY PUBLICITY

Getting out and meeting people in your own community is also a way to inform the public about the products you sell, especially if you are selling from home. It's proven that people like to buy from people they know and like, as well as refer other people to these businesses. So it makes sense to get active in your community—clubs and churches, as well as charity, business, and social functions are all great places to meet new people, hand out business cards, and talk about the products you sell.

Phenomenal Promotional Fliers

The majority of buy-and-sell entrepreneurs find that printed fliers represent one of the best advertising vehicles and values available to promote their products. Fliers are a fast and frugal, yet highly effective, way to promote a wide range of products and services, especially if you take the time to learn basic design skills so you can create high-impact, promotional fliers in-house on your own computer. Graphic design is expensive, and doing it yourself saves money. Most commercial printers charge $60 to $80 per hour to design marketing materials like fliers, product brochures, and newsletters. In addition to saving money, you will also be able to save precious marketing time because you will have the ability to create promotional materials within a day, perhaps even a few hours, instead of waiting days or weeks working around the printer's schedule. Likewise, having the equipment and skills to produce your own promotional materials gives you the ability to experiment, at little cost, with various print marketing tools, messages, and special promotions until you find the right mix. Once your fliers have been created and printed, they can be copied in bulk for as little as two cents each at your local copy center, or you can invest in a high-speed laser printer for about $350 and keep the printing in-house, too.

The great benefit of printed promotional fliers is that they can be used everywhere and for everything. Hand them out at flea markets, garage sales, auction sales, seminars, trade shows, and networking meetings. You can canvas busy parking lots tucking fliers under windshield wipers and leave them in public-transit areas such as buses, subway cars, and train stations for riders to read and take home. And you can stock a supply of promotional fliers and thumbtacks in your car so you can make a weekly run posting the fliers on every community notice board in your area—at supermarkets, libraries, schools, community centers, laundries, churches, and gas stations.

RESOURCES
– Adobe, desktop publishing software, ♂ www.adobe.com
– Corel, desktop publishing software, ♂ www.corel.com

Sizzling Signage

Signs are one of the lowest-cost, yet highest-impact forms of advertising, especially for buy-and-sell entrepreneurs operating from a homebased location. Signs work to promote your products 24 hours a day, 365 days a year virtually for free once paid for. However, signs are not something you should cut corners on; they must be professionally designed and constructed. Most signs today are designed on a computer, printed, and cut on large sheets of vinyl; they're easily installed, long lasting, and very inexpensive. You always want to make a positive first impression, so keep all of your signage in tip-top condition. Faded signs, peeling paint, torn banners, or signs that require maintenance in general send out negative messages about your business and the products you sell. Also use attention-grabbing design elements, colors, graphics, and pictures of the products you sell to lend visual appeal.

Installing signs at home is tricky business because of local bylaws, which stipulate the size of signs, as well as placement and style. Often commercial signage is not even permitted in residential neighborhoods. There is no one set of regulations for home business signage. Each municipality has its own. Generally, a call to the planning department or bylaws office is all that is required to get the answers you need. Keep in mind that if you are not going to have customers visiting your home to view and buy products, you will be better off not having signs at all.

Many buy-and-sell entrepreneurs also need to obtain professional event signage and banners to use at flea markets, consumer shows, and community events. Once again, these signs and special promotional signs such as discounts, show specials, and sale on, should be professionally designed and made, attention-grabbing, and should perfectly describe the products you sell

Taking Your Buy-and-Sell Enterprise Online

If you are excited about the prospect of selling your goods online, you should be. American consumers spent more than $95 billion on online purchases in 2003, and according to Forrester Research, business-to-consumer online sales are expected to top $133 billion in 2005 and $230 billion by 2008 in the United States alone! Although there is more you need to know to start an online buy-and-sell business, the following information covering basics such as building a Web site, choosing a domain name, registering with search engines, keyword optimization, permission-based marketing, and online advertising is a good starting point. Additional information about online sales venues such as eBay and electronic storefronts can be found in Chapter 5.

Creating Your Own Web Site

The first question is, do you need a Web site? If you plan on selling online, it would be wise, although not totally necessary, because you can utilize other online venues to sell products. However, if your goal is to build a stable, long-term, and profitable buy-and-sell venture that substantially sells online, I highly recommend that you learn as much as you can about online e-commerce and make the necessary financial investment to set up a proper online shop. Alternately, if you plan to sell mainly at flea markets and other offline venues, having your own Web site is of lesser importance. Ultimately, much depends on the type of goods you sell, your marketing objectives, and your future plans. The advantages of online retailing include having your store open 24 hours a day, sending information to customers in minutes—not hours, days, or weeks—and updating or altering your marketing message and strategy quickly, conveniently, and very inexpensively.

Once you have made the decision to build a Web site and make Internet marketing an active part of your buy-and-sell enterprise, there are many decisions to be made: How much is your budget to build your Web site? Who will build it? Who will maintain it, and how much will it cost? Who will host your Web site, and how much will it cost? And what shopping cart will you use, and what purchase payment options will you offer customers?

Your first option is to design, build, and maintain your own Web site. There are a plethora of Web site building programs available to enable novice Web-masters to build and maintain their own sites. You will still, of course, need to be familiar with computers and the Internet if you choose this option, regard-less of the "no experience required" advertisements. The cost to maintain your site will vary by content needs, maintenance needs, and your sales and mar-keting objectives. Hosting costs vary, depending on the services you select—e-commerce shopping carts, payment systems, order-tracking, Web site statis-tics, and database storage options. You can expect to pay a minimum of $50 per month for basic business Web site hosting and about $250 per month for pre-mium services.

Your second option is to hire a professional to design and build your Web site. Costs here have dramatically decreased in the past few years. In fact, for less than $1,000, you can have a complete, fully functional Web site built with e-commerce, visitor interaction, and database marketing options. Regardless of how you build your site, all successful Web sites share qualities that make them popular with cus-tomers. They include products and information that appeal to the target audience, tools and information that create a sense of online community, and ease of use and navigation.

RESOURCES
- 1234 Find Web Designers, e-commerce and Web designers directory, ♂ www.1234-find-web-designers.org
- eCommerce Times, e-commerce and marketing portal providing daily news, features, advice, and links of interest, ♂ www.ecommercetimes.com
- Top Ten Web Hosting, Web site hosing directory, ♂ www.toptenwebhost ing.com

Selecting a Domain Name

Choosing a domain name, or URL (Uniform Resource Locator), for the online por-tion of your buy-and-sell business is more difficult than you might think. Short, high-impact .com designations are becoming increasingly difficult to acquire, and the domain name you select must suitably match the product(s) you sell. Your domain name should also be short, preferably 15 letters or fewer, and easily remembered and spelled. Once you have decided to launch a buy-and-sell enter-prise, start the process of choosing a domain name right away, and register a few variations as soon as you have compiled a short list. Good names are hard to come by. Ones that do become available or have not already been selected go fast. Don't worry if your Web site is not ready. Once you have paid your domain registration fee, you can park the domain until your site is ready to be added to the World Wide Web. Domain name registration fees vary greatly from a low of $10 per year to as much as $75 per year, depending on the designation and the registration service you choose. The majority of domain registration services also provide various additional Internet and e-commerce services and packages, ranging from Web site design to shopping carts, hosting and maintenance services, and Web site promotional services.

RESOURCES
- Domain Direct, ✆ www.domaindirect.com
- Network Solutions, ✆ www.networksolutions.com
- Register, ✆ www.register.com

Registering with Search Engines

The number-one way people find products on the Internet is through keyword submissions via search engines and directories. Some studies suggest that as many as 90 percent of Internet users search for what they want this way. Because you don't know which search engine or directory people will use, your Web site and pages need to be registered with many search engines. Before you start registering with every search engine and directory out there, you should know the basics.

Search engines such as Google are indexed by bots or spiders, which extract specific information and keywords from Web site pages and use this information for indexing. Search directories such as Yahoo have people called directory editors who compile the information by hand, generally indexed and grouped by relevance to the submitted search. These days the line between search engine and search directory is increasingly blurred. Most major search engines and directories use both mechanical and human power to build and index information, or they supplement each other's services, so you need to register with both.

Many entrepreneurs find registering their Web sites and pages a frustrating task because there are no standard regulations or guidelines: most search engines and directories have individual submission policies. If you do not want to register yourself, you can use search engine and directory submission services that will automatically submit or register your Web site with all major search engines and directories. Often you only have to complete one relatively basic form. Some submission services are free, but the majority charge fees if you want quick listings, regular maintenance, and other premium listing services. These services enable small-business owners with limited time to optimize their Web sites for the best search-rank results and great value for a relatively small fee.

RESOURCES
- Add Me, submission services, ♂ www.addme.com
- Google, search engine, ♂ www.google.com
- Submit It, submission services, ♂ www.submit-it.com
- Submit Express, submission services, ♂ www.submitexpress.com
- Teoma, search engine, ♂ www.teoma.com
- Yahoo, search directory, ♂ www.yahoo.com

Keyword Optimizing

Because 90 percent of Internet users conduct searches using keywords and key-word phrases, you need to optimize your Web site for keyword searches. Most online marketing specialists suggest that you aim for a keyword density of about 5 percent, meaning that keywords will comprise 5 out of every 100 words of site content, and include keywords in your page titles, headers, meta tags, and hyper-links. And because each Web page is unique in terms of the information featured and its marketing objective, be sure to select different keywords for each. Be descriptive when selecting keywords and phrases, keeping in mind that few peo-ple type in single search words, so combining keywords into short descriptive phrases is wise. A good starting point is to make lists of words describing the products you sell and conduct search engine and directory searches using these words. The top ten results will help you pinpoint the best and most descriptive keywords to use when optimizing your site. There are also keyword generators and even keyword creation services that will optimize your keyword selection for a fee. Finally, always include the maximum number of keywords the search engines allow, but keep in mind that directories base ranking more on the quality of the content than just on keywords. So also concentrate on quality content to improve search results.

RESOURCES
- 1st Position, keyword creation service, ♂ www.1stposition.net/keyword-generator.html
- Keyword Creator, keyword creation service, ♂ www.keyword-creator.com
- Keyword Handbook, keyword creation service, ♂ www.keywordhandbook.com
- Word Tracker, keyword creation service, ♂ www.wordtracker.com

PERMISSION-BASED MARKETING

Permission-based marketing is a term used to describe asking for and securing per-mission from your Web site customers and visitors to send them information via e-mail. Providing they agree, information you send can range from simple e-special offers to elaborate e-newsletters and e-catalogs, depending on your marketing objectives. Regardless of the information you send, gaining permission brings three benefits. First, if people ask to be included in your electronic mailings, in all likelihood they have an interest in the products you sell. Second, by securing permission, you won't be spamming—that is, sending e-mail messages without the recipient's permission. Third, you will be building a very valuable inhouse mailing list, which can be used for any number of research and marketing purposes. On that note, you will need to purchase customer database software so you can compile, store, and manage your subscriber base.

Online Advertising

You also have to create an online advertising and linking strategy to help drive traffic and buyers to your Web site, all the while keeping your sales and marketing objectives and budget in mind. Once you have mapped out a strategy and developed a budget, your options for advertising and promoting your Web site and products are almost unlimited, especially if you combine online and offline options. In fact, there are far too many online advertising opportunities to discuss here, so this information focuses on the basics: advertising banners, advertising in electronic publications, and pay-for-hits programs.

BANNER ADVERTISING

Advertising banners have recently become popular again as more and more Internet marketers fight to grab the attention of online consumers. Costs range from a few dollars per thousand impressions to a few hundred dollars per thousand impressions, depending on the target audience you wish to reach. The idea of cheap banner advertising might be alluring, but your results can suffer dramatically by not presenting your advertising message to your primary target audience. Also, bigger is not always better. Brand-name Web sites may attract untold numbers of visitors, but once again, that does not necessarily mean they are comprised of your target audience.

ADVERTISING IN ELECTRONIC PUBLICATIONS

Many buy-and-sell entrepreneurs have found advertising in electronic publications to be a highly effective way to reach their target audience at a very modest cost. There are an estimated 100,000 monthly electronic publications to choose from, but before committing to advertising, you will want to know the basics: audience size, demographics, and costs. A larger subscriber base is not necessarily better, because these publications often contain more advertisements. Your main focus should always be on reaching your target audience. E-zine Listings, ♂ www.ezinelistings.com, and E-zine Directory, ♂ www.newsletter- directory.com, list thousands of electronic publications indexed by subject.

Pay-for-Hits Advertising

Another form of advertising on the Internet is through pay-per-click programs. Google's AdWord program, ♂ www.adwords.google.com, and Overture's Pay-for-Performance program, ♂ www.overture.com, are the biggest and most effective. Pay-per-click programs involve bidding on choice keywords you believe your target audience uses to search for the products you sell. Although each has different requirements and rules for keyword selection, both programs are similar in the way you bid for the keywords you want. For instance, you can bid one dollar for a specific keyword. If yours is the highest bid, you win and get top search results rankings. On the other hand, if you bid 20 cents and other Web marketers bid more for the same keywords, your ranking would be greatly diminished.

WHERE YOU CAN BUY
THINGS CHEAPLY

The mantra of every successful buy-and-sell entrepreneur is the same—buy low and sell high. Your ability to buy cheap is of paramount importance; after all, it makes up 50 percent of the success equation. The objective of this chapter is clear—to show you where and how you can buy valuable new and used merchandise for dirt-cheap prices. Once you have decided what type of product(s) you will sell, the next decision is where you will buy these products at prices low enough that you can resell them for a profit.

If you plan to buy and sell new products, your buying sources will include manufacturers, sales agents, craftspeople, wholesalers, importers, distributors, and liquidators. Deciding whom you will buy from will be largely based on criteria relative to your specific needs, and revolve around product price, supplier reliability, product quality, product and supplier guarantee, supplier terms, and supplier fulfillment. For instance, if you are short on storage space and adequate transportation, then suppliers who drop-ship orders directly to your paying customers will be a far more attractive supply source, even if their unit costs are higher than suppliers who do not offer drop-shipping options.

Buying previously owned items for resale is an entirely different ball game because the product sources are much different. There are no wholesalers, manufacturers, and sales agents to supply you with cheap products for resale. Instead, you have to rely on your detective abilities and negotiation skills to track down the best items to purchase cheaply. These sources will include private sellers, auctions, flea markets, online marketplaces, garage sales, and thrift shops. In this chapter, buying sources for both new and used products are discussed at length. You will discover the tricks and tips professional buyers use to get the best products at the best prices.

Buying Wholesale

Traditional channels of distribution have greatly changed. At one time, all levels of distribution served an important function in the marketplace. Importers scoured the globe, visiting manufacturers for specific products, which they bought in large quantities and imported to their own countries. National wholesalers would then sell to local distributors, who sold to dealers or retailers, who in turn sold directly to businesses or consumers. It was not uncommon for a product to pass through four or five levels of distribution on its way from factory to end consumer, with each level adding a markup to cover expenses and profit. These traditional channels of distribution changed in the late 1970s when national retailers began to buy in large quantities direct from importers and manufacturers. This change in the distribution system really exploded with the arrival of the Internet. Every level of distribution, including retailers regardless of size, had access all at the click of a mouse from their office or home to a worldwide base of manufacturers, importers, exporters, wholesalers, and agents.

Today, distribution roles are somewhat blurred, and there is overlap among wholesaler, distributor, importer, and liquidator. But the end game of each is the same—sell products in volume to resellers at less than retail, enabling the resellers to sell to consumers and businesses for a profit. The information below focuses on three wholesale buying sources: wholesalers, liquidators, and importers. I must stress, however, that when you buy from these sources, you are not buying wholesale, but rather from a discount retailer, if they do not require a sales tax ID number. I mention this because recently there has been an increase in online businesses claiming to sell wholesale, when in fact they are discount retailers advertising as wholesalers. So always remember that if you are not asked for your sales tax ID number, you are not buying from a legitimate wholesale source. True wholesalers do not sell to the general public—only dealers, retailers, and resellers—and are referred to as business-to-business (B2B) wholesale sources. I have endeavored to only include true wholesale buying sources in the Resources, and not discount retailers. Information about sales tax ID numbers and permits may be found in Chapter 2.

Wholesalers

Your first option for buying new products at less than retail is from wholesalers, who generally offer a broader range of merchandise than importers and manufacturers. General-merchandise wholesalers are the most common, and they stock and sell a vast range of household products. The next type of wholesaler is industry-specific, such as food wholesalers, tools and equipment wholesalers, or clothing and textile wholesalers.

There are really no tricks to buying from wholesalers as the process is pretty straightforward—find one who carries the type of merchandise you want to sell, open an account, and start buying wholesale. That's about all there is to it. But again, your choice of which wholesaler you choose to buy from will be determined by your own specific needs and additional factors such as price, reliability, terms, product quality, and extended services offered, like drop-shipping and warranties. Given that there are many factors to consider, you will want to talk to a few wholesalers before deciding to buy from one. It is always a good idea to open accounts with more than one so you can shop for lowest price, take advantage of the specials each offers, and ensure that you always have a reliable supply in case one runs out. In addition to the wholesale sources, directories, and associations listed below, you will find hundreds more featured in Chapter 6.

RESOURCES
- Buck Wholesale, general merchandise wholesaler, ♂ www.buckwholesale.com
- Buy N Save, general merchandise wholesaler, ♂ www.buynsavedirect.com
- Crazy Discounts Wholesale, general merchandise wholesaler, ♂ www.crazydiscounts.com
- Dollar Days, general merchandise wholesaler, ♂ www.dollardays.com

 – Hot Dandy Wholesale Superstore, general merchandise wholesaler, ♂ www.hotdandy.com
 – JD Wholesale, general merchandise wholesaler, ♂ www.jdwholesale.com
 – National Association of Wholesaler-Distributors, ☎ (202) 872-0885, ♂ www.naw.org
 – Open Box USA, general merchandise wholesaler, ♂ www.openboxusa.com
 – Wholesale 411, online B2B wholesaler directory, ♂ www.wholesale411.com
 – Wholesale Hub, online B2B wholesaler directory, ♂ www.wholesalehub.com

Liquidators

Next to factory direct, buying merchandise from liquidators will generally be your cheapest wholesale source of new products. Liquidators differ from wholesalers, distributors, and importers in that they do not carry a steady supply of the same items all the time. They purchase many types of merchandise from various sources, including retailers trying to unload out-of-season goods, returns, and slow-moving inventory; manufacturers selling seconds and end-of-run; insurance companies disposing of damaged and recovered merchandise; and inventory of all sorts from bankrupt retailers, wholesalers, distributors, and manufacturers. The variety of products that can be purchased from liquidators knows no limits—clothing, electronics, dollar-store items, sporting goods, kitchen and bath accessories, toys, books, and the list goes on. However, all merchandise is new, though it may be slightly damaged, seconds, store returns, out-of-season, or discontinued. In some instances it is possible to purchase products with warranties, which adds value to the goods when you're reselling. But never assume that any merchandise purchased from liquidators is covered by any type of warranty or guarantee unless it is in writing. There is little chance of trying to negotiate better prices with liquidators. This can be accomplished only through volume buying, or by becoming a liquidator and buying the above-mentioned types of merchandise from the above-mentioned sources, which necessitates deep pockets.

If you buy frequently and in large quantities, it is possible to arrange incremental discounts, so be sure to arrange this from the outset. Also, there are auctions for liquidated merchandise, which is one way to buy for less. Liquidators are a great buying source for good, easily saleable merchandise at very low prices, provided you do not need a regular supply of exactly the same products. If you do, buy from wholesalers, distributors, or manufacturers who can provide the same products on a regular basis.

RESOURCES

- 1 AAA Wholesale Liquidators, general merchandise and surplus inventory liquidators, ✆ www.1aaawholesaleliquidators.com
- Buyers Guide, directory of liquidators and surplus merchandise dealers indexed alphabetically, ✆ www.buyersguide.net
- Liquidation Online, general merchandise liquidators, ✆ www.liquidation.com
- Merchandise USA, general merchandise liquidators, ✆ www.merchandiseusa.com
- Quitting Business, inventory liquidation portal, ✆ www.quittingbusiness.com

Importers

Importers are another source of new merchandise at wholesale prices. As a rule of thumb, however, importers are usually product- or industry-specific. There are general merchandise importers, but they are not common. Most deal in specific products and sometimes very highly specialized products such as surgical rubber hose, or in specific subsections of industries such as hand tools. All importers deal in new merchandise, although some import items such as antiques. But these are usually referred to as import dealers. Likewise, importers only bring products into the country. Those who ship products out are referred to as exporters or importers/exporters if they do both.

Buying from importers is the same as buying from wholesalers, distributors, or manufacturers. Source one or more and open a buying account. However, don't be surprised if more than one importer refuses to supply you. This is because some importers only work with large-volume clients. In time and with a little legwork, you will find an importer who will sell you the type of product you want to buy and sell. You will, of course, also want to consider factors such as price, quality, and reliability before choosing an importer.

RESOURCES

- American Importers Association, ☎ (727) 724-0900, ✆ www.americanimporters.org
- Canadian Association of Importers and Exporters, ☎ (416) 595-5333, ✆ www.importers.ca
- Global Importers Directory, directory listing worldwide importers indexed geographically, ✆ www.export-import-companies.com
- Import-Export Internet Advertising, worldwide import/export portal, indexed geographically, ✆ www.importers-exporters.com

– World Trade AA, directory listing worldwide importers, ♂ www.worldtrade
   aa.com

Buying from Manufacturers

Another buying source for new products is manufacturers, who also include
farmers, producers, craftspeople, growers, and sales or manufacturers' agents. But
I have chosen to concentrate on buying factory direct, manufacturers' agents, and
craftspeople because they are the most likely buying sources. When buying from
manufacturers, the inevitable questions arise: Should you buy from local or
domestic manufacturing sources and support your own economy, or should you
shop overseas manufacturers in hopes of lower prices? The answer is that each
person will have to make that decision individually, but there is a strong argument
for supporting your own economy, especially in light of labor laws and practices
in some foreign countries. It is no mystery that products generally cost less from
foreign manufacturing sources than domestic sources. On the other hand, domes-
tically manufactured and produced goods are generally of much higher quality.
Ultimately, your target audience will play a large role in determining where you
buy. In addition to the manufacturing directories, associations, and sources listed
here, there are hundreds more listed in Chapter 6.

Buying Factory Direct

The first option is to purchase directly from the factory—no middlemen,
agents, distributors, importers, or wholesalers of any kind. Buying factory
direct for the small operator was not an easy or very accessible option as
recently as five to ten years ago. Tracking down a manufacturing source often
meant spending time and money on research, calls, and domestic and even
international trips to find suppliers and reach equitable agreements. For the
most part, much has changed with the wide use of the Internet. What took
days, weeks, and even months and considerable expense to track down can
now be accomplished in a few hours or less online, and all with the simple click
of a mouse. With the aid of the Internet, you can source product manufacturers
from around the globe and buy direct.

Even with the assistance of the Net, however, the fact remains that you often
have to buy in large quantities, especially from overseas manufacturers who
need to sell by the container load to justify expenses and their competitive pricing. The Internet has not changed this. Still, there are thousands, perhaps hundreds of thousands, of manufacturers nationally and internationally who
welcome new customers with open arms, regardless of their current buying

power. It will just require a little more homework by you to flush them out. For many of the products featured in this book, purchasing directly from the factory is the best and least expensive option. And I have listed hundreds of manufacturer sources for specific products in Chapter 6.

Still, you do need certain things for the relationship with the manufacturer to be successful, especially when starting out, including:

- *Fair pricing*. You need the ability to buy from manufacturers at a price level that enables you to resell competitively while still retaining the ability to profit. Never assume manufacturers will not negotiate on their list or catalog pricing. All manufacturers will negotiate to a certain degree. They are like any other businesspeople, and need paying customers to remain viable.

- *Quality products*. You need quality products, within reason, to sell. They do not have to be the best, but they must be able to stand up to consumer scrutiny. A super-low price is of no benefit to you if the product quality is so poor people won't buy.

- *Reliability*. You need a reliable buying source. The manufacturer(s) you choose to work with must be able to supply the products you need when you need them, and in a timely fashion. Buying and selling is very much a now, or impulse, business. You cannot ask customers to wait days or weeks for products.

- *Terms*. You need manufacturers who will offer you payment terms on purchases. Initially, in most cases you will have to apply for and be approved for credit or establish a payment record by paying in full for your first few orders. However, beyond this you should expect manufacturers to extend 30-, 60-, and even 90-day payment terms. The longer the better, from your perspective. Payment terms enable you to resell inventory and pay suppliers with your customer's money, not your own.

Additional information about working with suppliers and establishing trade accounts can be found in Chapter 3. Next to working with manufacturers in your own area, the best way to find a manufacturing source for the type of product(s) you want to buy and sell is to use online and print manufacturers' directories, like the ones listed below.

RESOURCES
- Alibaba, billed as the world's largest database of suppliers. B2B manufacturers' directory for sourcing suppliers and products from around the world, ✄ www.alibaba.com

- Asian Products, B2B manufacturers' directory for sourcing suppliers and products from Asia, ✆ www.asianproducts.com
- Canadian Manufacturers' & Exporters Association, ☎ (613) 238-8888, ✆ www.cme-mec.ca
- Global Sources, B2B manufacturers' directory for sourcing suppliers and products from around the world, ✆ www.globalsources.com
- India Mart, B2B manufacturers' directory for sourcing suppliers and products from India, ✆ www.catalogs.indiamart.com
- National Association of Manufacturers, ☎ (202) 637-3000, ✆ www.nam.org.
- Online International Business, B2B manufacturers' directory for sourcing suppliers and products from around the world, ✆ www.b2b-bestof.com
- Taiwan Products Online, B2B manufacturers' directory for sourcing suppliers and products from Taiwan and China, ✆ www.manufacture.com.tw
- *Thomas Register*, B2B manufacturers' directory for sourcing suppliers and products from around North America, ✆ www.thomasregister.com
- *Webster's* Online, online business directory and product search engine including manufacturers and wholesalers, ✆ www.webstersonline.com

Manufacturers' Agents

Many manufacturers, especially small ones, enlist the services of sales agents, otherwise known as manufacturers' agents, to find new customers for their product(s) in new geographic markets, nationally, and internationally. This is especially true of manufacturers who do not have the financial resources or people inhouse to undertake establishing distributorships in far-flung locations, or who currently have a limited product line, too small to grab the interest or attention of major wholesalers and distributors. The job of the agent is to prospect for new business for the manufacturer, often establishing accounts with retailers to buy products on a frequent basis. Buying through a manufacturer's agent generally means you will be paying slightly more for the product on a per-unit basis, but over time, as your buying volumes increase, incremental discounts will reduce unit costs. The best way to source manufacturers' agents is to harness the power of the Internet and search manufacturers' agents directories, or to contact manufacturers' agents associations.

RESOURCES

- Find A Sales Agent, manufacturers' sales agent directory, ✆ www.find-asalesagent.com
- Manufacturers' Agents National Association, ☎ (949) 859-4040, ✆ www.manaonline.org

Craftspeople

Talented craftspeople across North America make everything from custom furniture to woodcraft decorations, garden ornaments, stained-glass items, and everything imaginable in between. According to the Craft Organization Directors Association (CODA), the crafts industry generates $14 billion in sales annually. Needless to say, crafts are very big business in America. But how do craftspeople distribute their goods? Once again, according to CODA, approximately 60 percent of them retail their goods directly to consumers through craft shows, mail order, and online marketplaces. A further 10 percent place their products on consignment with retailers, such as gift shops, furniture stores, and fashion retailers. And the remaining 30 percent wholesale their crafts to retailers and resellers of all sizes. This 30 percent wholesale market adds up to a whopping $4 billion-plus worth of wholesale crafts up for grabs every year for resale!

Keep in mind that most craftspeople who do retail direct to consumers are the first to admit they are not the best marketers of their own goods, and miss out on a lot of profit because of their lack of sales and marketing skills. Therefore, persuading them to sell to you wholesale should not prove difficult. Start by talking with craftspeople right in your own area to inquire about the goods they make and their wholesaling policies. You can also contact craft guilds and associations to track down people who make specific products you would like to buy and sell. And rather than buy crafts wholesale for cash, consider working out a revenue split arrangement for all goods sold. This way, you'll to minimize the amount of start-up investment needed to get rolling. They supply, you sell, and both of you profit.

Resources

- Arts and Crafts Association of America, ☎ (616) 874-1721, ✐ www.artsand craftsassoc.com
- Canadian Crafts & Hobby Association, ☎ (403) 291-0559, ✐ www.cdn craft.org
- Crafts Shows USA, provides visitors with a free online directory listing crafts shows nationally, indexed geographically by state, ✐ www.craft showsusa.com
- Indian Arts & Crafts Association, ☎ (505) 265-9149, ✐ www.iaca.com

Buying at Auction Sales

Live or offline auction sales provide a host of excellent buying opportunities for entrepreneurs who are willing to spend time researching and attending sales. These efforts are usually rewarded with incredible buys, which can be resold for two, three, or even four times as much as cost. In this section you will learn auction terminology and buying tips, as well as information about the four main types of offline auction sales—public auction sales, police auction sales, government surplus and seized-items auction sales, and estate sales. There are other types of offline auctions, such as charity auctions and retailer inventory-reduction auctions, but these seldom provide many buying opportunities with resale potential. Likewise, seldom will you find new merchandise being offered at auction sales, unless it is a retailer or manufacturer bankruptcy sale. For the most part, live auctions are for the purpose of selling secondhand goods, such as cars, homes, furniture, antiques, tools, and equipment. Therefore, buy-and-sell entrepreneurs dealing in the sale of new products would do well to focus their buying efforts on sources that are better suited, such as wholesalers and manufacturers.

Auction Terminology

Before bidding at an auction, you first have to know auction terminology. The following are a few of the more common auction terms:

- *Conditions of sale.* Conditions of sale are the terms under which the auction will operate, including buyer's premium in effect, reserves in place, payment options and terms, and date by which items must be removed from the sale site. These sale conditions are generally printed on the registration agreement, announced by the auctioneer at the beginning of the sale, and printed in the auction lot catalog.
- *Bidder number.* Before being able to bid on items, you must first obtain a bidder's number, which is issued at the registration desk. The bidder's number is boldly printed on a paddle or piece of cardboard and is large enough to be seen by the auctioneer or bid spotter during the sale. When you have successfully purchased an item, the auctioneer will ask for your bidding number and assign this number to the item purchased, so you can claim it at the end of the sale.
- *Bid.* A bid is the amount of money you offer on a particular item you wish to purchase. Low-value items will generally increase by dollar increments, while higher-value items can increase in hundred or thousand-dollar increments.
- *Opening Bid.* The auctioneer usually opens bidding, at which point bidders can wait as the opening bid drops, or begin to bid, driving the price higher.
- *Absentee bid.* People who are not physically at the auction sale can bid on items by telephone, by e-mail, by predelivered letter stating the lot and bid price, or through the auctioneer's Web site.

- *Reserve.* A reserve is the minimum price a seller is willing to accept for an item. For instance, if bids top out at $200 for a desk, but the reserve is $250, the desk will not sell because the reserve price was not reached. The auctioneer informs bidders that the reserve was not met, though he will not disclose the reserve amount, and moves on to the next lot for sale.

- *Buyer's premium.* To increase revenues many auctioneers now add a buyer's premium to the total value an item has sold for, which can be represented as a flat fee or a percentage of the total value. For instance, if a desk sells for $200 and the buyer's premium is 10 percent, then the buyer must pay $220 for the desk, plus applicable taxes. As a rule of thumb, buyer's premiums are generally 5 to 10 percent of the total sales value of items purchased.

- *Preview.* A preview is the opportunity for bidders to inspect items before the sale. Larger sales generally have a preview day or half-day preview time anywhere from one week before the sale to the day of the sale; smaller sales generally have the preview an hour or two prior to the sale. Some auctioneers also list sale items on their Web sites for preview prior to sales. The purpose of the preview is to give bidders the opportunity to closely examine the items for condition and details prior to bidding.

- *As-is.* As the term suggests, when you purchase items at auctions as-is, where-is, these items are sold absent of any warranties. You get what you see, with no guarantee it will work or as to the overall condition.

- *Lots.* The term lot(s) has two meanings. First, every item being auctioned receives a number, which is referred to as a *lot*. Second, often a number of small items, such as hand tools, are grouped together in one lot and sold to the highest bidder. So a lot can be one item, or a number of items grouped together.

- *Pick.* When more than one identical item is being auctioned, such as six computer monitors of the same size and age, the first successful bidder will get to choose which one they want and how many they want at the same price. The buyer may choose to buy one, some, or all. He or she gets "The pick of the lot." The items not purchased by the first successful bidder are auctioned once more until all have sold, or the auctioneer has moved on to the next lot.

Auction-Buying Tips

Remember, the greatest auction-buying tip you will every get is simply this: *Caveat emptor*, which is Latin, meaning *Let the buyer beware*. Seldom are auction items covered by a warranty or guarantee of any kind. There are the occasional exceptions to the rule, but for the most part, you get what you buy. Therefore, the onus is on you and no one else to ensure that you know what you are buying, its condition, and its value before you make the bid. The following are a few indispensable tips for buying at auction sales:

- Go to the preview to inspect items of interest, and be sure to take your auction toolbox, which should include a flashlight, magnifying glass, camera, and mirror. These items will help you to properly examine an item to determine its condition before bidding. Also, recheck items you intend to bid on the day of the sale to ensure no damage occurred during the preview.

- Do your homework and know the value of what you want to purchase before bidding. Make sure to factor in all costs, including buyer's premiums, time, transportation, repair or alterations if required, plus a return on investment. You have to buy cheaply enough that you can add in all related expenses and still be able to resell the item(s) at a profit. It is a good idea to keep a logbook and list expenses for each individual sale, along with items purchased, and what they were later resold for.

- Don't get carried away in all the excitement and bid on items you did not intend on buying. Also, never bid higher than your preset limit on any one item, not even if it is only $10.

- Once the auctioneer has said "Sold!" you cannot retract your bid if you were the successful bidder, but you can at any time up until that point. If you are feeling uneasy about the item or the price, get out of the bidding by telling the auctioneer or bid spotter you are dropping out before the gavel drops.

- If you are an absentee bidder, submitting by phone, fax, e-mail, or online, make sure you know the currency the sale is dealing in before you bid.

- If possible, try to attend midweek auctions as opposed to weekend auctions because there are generally fewer people in attendance, which usually means less pressure to drive bids into the stratosphere.

- Look for auctions listing "fish out of water" items because these items can usually be bought for a song. For instance, if you deal in antique furniture and you notice an auction selling mainly computer and office equipment but listing a few pieces of antique furniture, then at least go to the preview to examine the antiques. Dealers generally shy away from these sales because of the limited number of items of interest, and the other people in attendance are more likely to be interested in the computers than the antiques.

- Get to know auctioneers in your area so they can keep you informed about items of interest to you prior to sales. Also ask to be included on their auction notification and schedule lists, which are generally sent by fax or e-mail, and list forthcoming auction sales and the items available.

- On items that interest you and are within your preset price range, enter the bidding late, as this often discourages other bidders from continuing because they feel the item will go out of their range. Last-minute bidders coming into the game can even force the most determined bidders to give up.
- Come to the sale with suitable transportation and equipment, such as loading dollies so you can leave with your purchases. Trips back to pick up purchased items cost time and money, driving up the prices of items that must be resold to make a profit.
- Look for deals in need of a little elbow grease or minor repairs. Some of the most profitable auction finds are ones that require a little TLC to bring them back to their former glory.
- If you are interested in items that did not sell because the reserve was not met, be sure to give the auctioneer your business card with the lot number of the item and the maximum price you would spend for the item printed on the back of the card. The auctioneer can easily present your card to the seller, who may accept the offer after the sale and contact you.

Public Auctions

The most common type of auction sale is a public auction. As the name suggests, these sales are open to the general public. Items available for sale vary greatly—cars, real estate, furniture, business equipment, restaurant equipment, antiques, collectibles, tools, machinery, and anything else imaginable. Items being auctioned can be supplied by private sellers, estates, businesses, and trustees, or any combination of these supply sources. Auction sales featuring household items are generally conducted on weekends and evenings, when the largest number of the target audience is available to attend. Business and bankruptcy sales are typically held Monday through Friday during normal business hours.

Regardless of the type of auction you attend, you must plan and think big. Make the experience worth your while in order to justify your time and expenses. Buying an item for $20 and reselling it later for $40 might be doubling your money, but if it was the only item bought at the sale, a $20 gross profit hardly justifies the time and expense. In fact, you would be losing money. Only attend sales that have the potential to make you money. Buy items that are $100, $1,000, and more, and look to double or triple these amounts when reselling. Calculate your total fixed costs for the day including an hourly rate for your time, and factor in your costs to market and resell items. Chances are you will come up with a figure in the range of $250, which means if you cannot earn $250 in gross profit from the items you intend to purchase at the sale and then resell, in all probability it would be best for you to skip the sale. Depending on your overhead and other factors, the $250 minimum gross-profit base may be less or more; nonetheless, you still need to know in advance how much profit you have to generate from each sale before attending.

RESOURCES

- Auction Guide, billed as the Internet guide to auctions and auctioneers worldwide, indexed by country, ♂ www.auctionguide.com
- Auctioneers Association of Canada, ☎ (866) 640-9915, ♂ www.auctioneerscanada.com
- National Auctioneers Association, ☎ (800) 662-9438, ♂ www.auctioneer.org
- Net Auctions, directory listing online and offline auction sales by type and auctioneers by specialty, ♂ www.net-auctions.com
- 📖 *Price it Yourself: The Definitive, Down-to-Earth Guide to Appraising Antiques and Collectibles in Your Home, at Auctions, Estate Sales, Shops, and Yard Sales*, Joe L. Rosson and Helaine Fendelman (Harper Resource, 2003)

Police Auctions

Police auctions represent an excellent opportunity to purchase a wide variety of secondhand products at very low prices. Many police forces in the United States and Canada host quarterly, semiannual, or annual auction sales to sell stolen items they have recovered, but were never claimed by owners, (that is, the people the thieves ripped off in the first place). At police auctions you will find a vast array of products for sale, including bicycles, tools, car parts, home electronics, computers, jewelry, and shoplifted merchandise, much of it for a mere fraction of the original retail value and current resale market value. There are several levels of police forces—city, county, state, and federal. So the best way to find out about police auctions in and beyond your area is to log on to police Web sites, or call and ask who conducts sales and how the organizer can be contacted. Most forces hire auctioneers. As noted below, some are starting to utilize online auction services to sell recovered property. Online or off, police auctions are conducted in the same manner as any auction; you bid on the items you wish to purchase, and, providing your bid is the highest, you will get it. As always, preview items of interest first, stick to your preset bid amounts, don't impulse-buy, and have the right transportation.

– Property Room Police Auctions, provides online police auctions and listings for offline live police auctions, ♂ www.stealitback.com.

Government Auctions

Government surplus and seized-items auctions and tender sales are other excellent buying sources, especially for large-ticket items that can often be purchased for 10 percent of their original value, making them extremely profitable for resale purposes. Many government agencies routinely hold auction sales or sealed-bid tenders to dispose of government surplus assets and equipment, foreclosed property, seized property, and unclaimed property. A few of these agencies include:

- Internal Revenue Service (IRS)
- U.S. Department of Housing and Urban Development (HUD)
- U.S. Justice Department
- U.S. Marshals Service
- U.S. Postal Service
- U.S. Small Business Administration (SBA)
- U.S. Treasury Department

There are many more government agencies at the federal, state, county, and city level that also routinely hold auction sales to dispose of surplus, foreclosed, and seized property. Most of these sales are conducted like traditional auction sales, but sometimes the sale is by sealed tender, which means you complete a tender form and submit the amount you are willing to pay for a specific item. Tenders are opened after the closing date and the item is awarded to a bidder, mostly, but not always, the highest. Tender forms are available directly from the government agency holding the sale, or the auctioneer conducting the sale.

To find government auctions in your area, contact city, county, and state offices to make inquiries and ask to be included on the auction-sale notification and schedule list. Items routinely auctioned include computers, real estate, automobiles, machinery and tools, jewelry, furniture, electronics, and boats. Depending on the agency and type of items auctioned, sales can be conducted live, online, or both. Most are still live at present, but this is rapidly changing because the Internet offers exposure to a broader audience of buyers.

RESOURCES
– Public Works and Government Services Canada–Crown Assets Distribution, sales of government surplus and seized property by auctions, tenders,

and public sales, including real estate, equipment, automobiles, furniture, boats, jewelry, clothing, furniture, and electronics, ☎ (905) 615-2025, ♂ http://crownassets.pwgsc.gc.ca/text/index-e.cfm

- SBA–Property for Sale Auctions, includes residential and commercial real estate, machinery, equipment, and inventory, ♂ http://appl.sba.gov/pfsales/dsp_about_us.cfm
- U.S. Department of Housing and Urban Development–HUD Home Sales, real estate, ☎ (202) 708-1112, ♂ www.hud.gov/homes/index.cfm
- U.S. Department of the Treasury, seized-property auctions, including automobiles, boats, jewelry, electronics, and furniture, ☎ (202) 622-2000, ♂ www.ustreas.gov/auctions/customs
- U.S. General Services Administration, government-owned asset sales, ☎ (800) 473-7836, ♂ www.gsa.gov
- U.S. Marshals Service, seized-property auctions including real estate, automobiles, jewelry, and electronics, ☎ (888) 878-3256, ♂ www.usdoj.gov/marshals/assets/assets.html
- U.S. Postal Service, damaged and unclaimed items auctions, ♂ www.usps.com/auctions

Estate Sales

Estate sales can be conducted in a similar fashion to an auction, as buyers bid on items live or by sealed bid to purchase one or more items from the sale. Or the organizer of the estate sale may elect to price items individually and hold the sale over a number of days or weeks, until all or most items have been sold. Estate sales can be organized and conducted by auctioneers, estate sales specialists, family members, lawyers, or executors. Regardless of who organizes the sale and how it is conducted, one thing remains constant: Due to the need to settle accounts and inheritances and to dispose of property, it is very possible to purchase items at well below their true market value. Your ability to buy cheaply will be enhanced further if you are prepared to purchase more than one item, or even all of the items for sale. Estate sales are typically advertised in the newspaper classifieds and on Web sites, as well as in newsletters of companies that organize such sales. To find these companies, search under Estate Sales in your Yellow Pages directory. You yourself can also advertise in the classifieds and other publications, advising that you purchase entire estates or household contents. Combining both approaches will serve your buying interests best. Keep in mind that, regardless of who organizes the sale or how the sale is conducted, your ability to resell for a profit rests on your ability to out-negotiate the seller, buy at well below market value, and buy items that are in demand.

Buying Through Online Marketplaces

Almost all wholesale buying sources of new products, such as wholesalers, distributors, importers, and manufacturers, now have a Web site, or some sort of online presence. This section, however, focuses on three other buying sources: eBay, electronic auctions, and electronic classified ads. Individuals and businesses both utilize these online forums to sell new and used merchandise. The advantages of buying online are obvious: You save time because it can be accomplished from home, and you save money because there is no need to travel in most cases. Of course, there are also a few disadvantages, such as sifting through junk to find what you are looking for, and scammers. When I say scammers, I am really talking about thieves who are more than willing to take your money in exchange for new and used goods that never arrive, even though you paid. The Internet is full of them, so due diligence is of paramount importance. Know who you are dealing with and try to pay with a credit card, because there is recourse for buyers using plastic, but cash leaves no fingerprints.

EBay

Most people think of eBay as a great place to buy products for personal use or a great place to sell products, not necessarily as a venue to buy new and used products for resale purposes. But eBay provides opportunities for both buying new products wholesale for resale and buying used products cheaply to resell for a profit.

New products in bulk are listed under the *Wholesale* link in the navigation bar on the eBay home page. The wholesale lots page is segmented into numerous product categories, including electronics, home furnishings, jewelry and watches, clothing, health and beauty, and sporting goods, each with its own subcategories of products. Via the wholesale lots page you can purchase new products, liquidated merchandise, seconds, pallet lots, remainders, and returns posted by wholesalers, liquidators, and manufacturers. Some products are available by way of no-reserve and reserve-bid auctions, while others have volume pricing through individual eBay stores.

If you are going to troll no-reserve auctions to steal merchandise at super cheap prices, I suggest you use one of the auction-bidding software programs available, mainly because constantly checking before the auction closes to see if your bid is the highest can be very time-consuming, especially if you are tracking numerous items in numerous auctions. Automated bidding software is often referred to as sniping software. Sniping is waiting until the last moment to place your bid. The software enables you to do this automatically, and generally you get products at a lower price than if you tried the same tactics yourself without the software. This is because sniping software swoops in at the last moment to make bids slightly higher than those already placed; when I say last moment, I mean within the last couple of seconds, which does not give other bidders a chance to increase their bids.

Three of the more popular auction-bidding software programs and services are Auction Stealer, ♂ www.auctionstealer.com; Auction Sleuth, ♂ www.auction sleuth.com; Auction Sniper, ♂ www.auctionsniper.com. The price of software for the service can be a monthly fee of $8, or free, but with a 1 percent commission added to all successful purchases, or a flat fee of $20 for the software and a yearly fee to upgrade. Aside from using bidding software on eBay USA, keep in mind that eBay has established marketplace portals around the world—Canada, Australia, England, France, Germany, South Korea, and many other countries.

E-Auctions

In addition to eBay, there are hundreds of online auction sites. Some are general auction sites with numerous categories ranging from collectibles to cars and clothing, while others are product-specific auction sites such as fine art, boats, antiques, and sports memorabilia. EBay is the undisputed king of online, multi-venue buy-and-sell marketplaces. But you do not want to limit your buying and selling options to one single venue, especially if you can combine others with eBay to increase your revenues and maximize profits. If you are going to specialize in buying and selling new products, there are better buying sources than online auction sites, but if you are going to specialize in buying and selling previously owned products, then spending time online at various auction sites can be very worthwhile. When there are no reserve bids on products, great deals can be had. It's all about being in the right place at the right time. Get started by visiting numerous online auctions daily to get a feel for the types of products listed, selling prices, and turnover of goods. Time spent researching will enable you to know what auction sites typically have the best buying deals specific to the product(s) you buy and sell.

Resources
– Auction Fire, general auction site, ♂ www.auctionfire.com
– Bid 4 Assets, general auction site, ♂ www.bid4assets.com
– Buy Sell Trades, general auction site, ♂ www.buyselltrades.com
– The Internet Auction List, directory listing over 2,000 Internet auction sites and auction companies, ♂ www.internetauctionlist.com
– Net Auctions, directory listing online and offline auction sales by type and auctioneers by specialty, ♂ www.net-auctions.com

202

Things You Can Buy and Sell for Big Profits

- Online Auction Users Association, ♂ www.auctionusers.org
- On Sale, general auction site, ♂ www.onsale.com
- Sell Whatever, general auction site, ♂ www.sellwhatever.com
- Yahoo Auctions, general auction site, ♂ www.auctions.yahoo.com

E-Classifieds

E-classifieds can also be a source for tracking down previously owned items to buy for resale. The best e-classifieds are those that also have a print version, such as your local newspaper or buy-and-sell-style publications. The downside to shopping for deals in online classified ads is there is often a lot of junk to sift through, a lack of descriptive ads with photographs, and the geography can be problematic on larger items because of travel needed for inspections, unless you are searching strictly in your area. The upside is that there are deals to be found, and it is quick, easy, and free to scan thousands of ads every day right from home. The rules for buying from e-classified private sellers are the same as the rules for buying from private sellers advertising in print classifieds, and are outlined in the next section.

Resources

- *Adpost*, online classified ads, indexed geographically, ♂ www.adpost.com
- *Buy and Sell*, online general merchandise classified ads, ♂ www.buy sell.com
- *My Town Ads*, online classified ads, indexed geographically, ♂ www.my townads.com
- *The Recycler*, online general merchandise classified ads, ♂ www. recycler.com
- *Sell.com Classifieds*, online general merchandise classified ads, ♂ www. sell.com
- *Thrifty Nickel*, online general merchandise classified ads, ♂ www.thriftynickel ads.com
- *Trader Online*, online automotive classified ads, ♂ www.traderonline.com
- *Yahoo Classifieds*, online general merchandise classified ads, ♂ www.classifieds. yahoo.com

Buying from Private Sellers

People who sell items through auction sales, flea markets, or online, as well as through other methods, can also be private sellers, but for the sake of simplicity, this section deals with five private-seller sources for buying previously owned items such as cars, furniture, jewelry, antiques, and sporting goods. These five private-seller buying sources are garage sales, moving sales, print classified advertisements, bulletin board advertisements, and for-sale signs. All can become excellent ways to buy items for resale purposes, providing you know the success secrets of each, which you will discover in this section.

Just as you qualify a buyer for your products, you also have to qualify private sellers and the items they are selling, mainly because your first contact with private sellers will usually be on the telephone. You do not want to waste time and money going to see items for sale unless they meet your buying criteria. Depending on what types of product(s) you decide to specialize in buying and selling, these criteria could include size, age, overall condition, price, make and model, and any other information that will help you decide if an appointment to inspect the item and possibly purchase is warranted.

Once an appointment has been set, you must then be comfortable in asking questions, lots of questions. You want to know the history of the item for sale, especially if it is mechanical, such as a car, boat, riding lawn mower, and shop tools. You want to know if any work or repairs have been done, and if so, look at the receipts for a description of the work and warranty information. Remember, sellers have reason to embellish the truth on occasion—they want to sell. You, on the other hand, must work like a detective, uncover any telltale signs of a fishy story, and satisfy yourself that the item meets your buying criteria. Find out as much as you can about the item from the seller, how long they have owned it, what changes have been made, what is the overall condition, and why they are selling. Through careful questioning, you will also be able to determine their level of motivation to sell. Remember, it is the person asking the questions (you) who stays in control of the buying process and negotiations.

Here are a few more helpful tips when buying from private sellers:

- Only buy what you know and, more importantly, what you know can make a profit on resale.
- Get a receipt for every purchase, including the date, product description, any guarantees the seller is willing to provide, the seller's complete contact information, the selling price, and the method of payment. Once you pay, ask the seller to sign their name beside *Paid in Full*. Professional buyers carry their own carbon copy receipt books.
- Always insist that the seller include the extras. For instance, you need a helmet to ride a motorcycle, so get the seller to include the helmet(s), leather jacket, and any other accessories. Or if you are buying a computer system, make sure you get the printer, scanner, software, and monitor. Or

if a pool table, then get the balls, racks, cues, and cover. Some sellers may not want to give in because they might be selling to move up to a better model and need the accessories, but hold firm and insist the extras be included. Having the extras is very valuable when it comes time to resell. First, you can charge extra for the extras and increase your profit. Second, people prefer to buy a package because it is more convenient and represents a better value.

- Always make your first offer half of what you are really prepared to pay. If you want to become a professional buyer, you have to get comfortable with making lowball offers. It is simply part of the business and without this ability, the chances of success are slim. Flush out the seller's reason for selling. What is their true motivation? Financial problems, divorce, health, moving, item doesn't work, or lack of interest, it has to be one or a combination of these. Once you know, you can use this information to support your offer. "Look, you told me you really need the money. I only can offer you this much because it is all I have." "You told me your bad back keeps you from using your kayak. I wish I could offer you more, but at least it is better than just letting the kayak sit there unused. Besides, you can use the money to pay the chiropractor." Don't laugh! When you can explain to people why they should accept your offer, based on their own reasons and motivations for selling, it will make logical sense, and most will bite.

Garage Sales

Most people who attend garage sales, do so for fun and entertainment, and to find simple treasures for their homes. But be aware: there are an increasing number of people who have discovered garage sales can be a gold mine of buying opportunities. Just like you, they want to find highly valuable merchandise for a song and resell it in the right marketplaces and to the right consumers for huge profits. It is not difficult to spot the professional buyer—they arrive early, are pushy, drive the hardest bargains, and are the ones snapping up the true treasures, leaving all the junk in their wake. If you do not like the description, then look for alternative buying sources. The world of the professional garage sale hunter can be furiously competitive. Buying previously owned merchandise for resale at garage sales starts with the advertisement. Carefully examine the ad, because you can often tell a good sale from a bad, based on the advertisement. The best garage sales tend to be estate sales, moving sales, multifamily or block sales, and "first sales in 20 years" ads. Basically, the aforementioned tend to have lots of great merchandise, and sellers who have reason and great motivation to dispose of it, at any reasonable offer. The worst garage sales are those at the same addresses week after week (telling you they are professional garage sale sellers), charities (because people will donate junk just to feel good), and those that list the best items as used tires. Here are a few more garage sale buying tips. (Information about garage sale selling can be found in Chapter 5.)

- Garage sale hosts generally don't like it, but be sure to show up early to the most promising sales so you get the pick of the litter so to speak. The best items always sell on the first day, in the first hour, and to the first shoppers on site.

- If possible, try to buy items more than one at a time. Purchasing a number of items at once can often save you 50 percent or more of the individual selling price. If the seller does not want to budge on price, say you'll pay full price, but that you want whatever other item interests you for free. Buying in volume, regardless of the items or place, always nets lower purchase prices.

- Cash talks, plastic and paper checks walk. There is only one currency at garage sales—cash, so bring lots of small bills and stash it in various pockets, so that when you are negotiating you do not pull out a wad that would choke a horse while trying to cry poor mouth with the seller.

- Follow the in-and-out rule. Get in quick, check the merchandise for what you want. If it isn't there, get out quick and go on to the next sale. Remember, this is your business, so there is not time for idle chitchat or browsing.

- Prioritize the garage sales you intend to visit, starting with the most promising. After the most promising, group the rest together geographically so you can get to more sales in less time.

- Always avoid impulse buying, and stick to your specialty. If you specialize in antiques, don't buy toys, no matter how good the deal seems. Only buy what you know and what you know you can resell for a profit.

- Always go shopping with suitable transportation—a van, a truck, or towing a trailer. Larger items such as machinery, tools, and furniture can often be purchased for a song because many people garage sale shopping simply do not have the ability to transport the item. Most sellers frown on buyers who say they'll come back with suitable transportation, never showing up and leaving the seller with leftover items they do not want. Besides, making trips back to pick up items is a waste of time and fuel, cutting into profits.

- It is okay to buy items in need of a good cleaning or basic repair, but never buy anything in need of a major overhaul. And always look for reasons to offer less—chipped paint, scratches, no owner's manual, and so forth.

- Don't be afraid to make super-duper lowball offers. Remember, most people holding garage sales are doing so to rid their homes of clutter, not pay off their mortgage with the proceeds. Ten bucks for an antique rocker might seem like a ridiculously lowball offer to you, but to the seller it may seem reasonable for something that was collecting dust in the attic just one day earlier.

RESOURCES

– Garage Sales Daily, directory listing U.S. garage sales indexed by state, plus garage sale information and forums, ♂ www.garagesaledaily.com
– Garage Sale Planet, directory listing U.S. garage sales indexed by state, plus garage sale information and forums, ♂ www.garagesaleplanet.com
– Local Yard Sales, directory listing Canadian garage sales indexed by province, plus garage sale information and forums, ♂ www.localyard sales.com
– Yard Sales Search, directory listing U.S. garage sales indexed by state, plus garage sale information and forums, ♂ www.yardsalesearch.com

Moving Sales

Like garage sales, moving sales can also be an incredible buying source for previously owned items that can be resold for a profit. There are basically two ways to locate moving sales. One, you can wait for people to advertise their moving sale in the newspaper classifieds or with bulletin board fliers. Two, you can be proactive and create your own ads stating that you buy partial or entire household lots, everything from furniture to books. Option one requires you to scan your local classified ads and community bulletin boards. Option two requires you to place classified ads and post flier ads on bulletin boards.

Most entrepreneurs engaged in buying partial or entire household lots opt to combine both options to maximize buying potential and profit. The majority of people who hold a moving sale do so over the course of a few days or a week, and as a general rule, most items will be displayed in the seller's home and individually priced. The same rules apply here as at other sales—know what you want, what it's worth, and negotiate a hard bargain every time. Driving a hard bargain and getting products for the price you want to spend is usually not difficult because the seller is moving and, depending on how soon, she may be very motivated to liquidate personal belongings at any price.

Classified Ads

Private-seller print classified ads represent a wealth of buying opportunities for previously owned merchandise, especially when dealing with motivated sellers.

Their motivation or reason for selling could be based on any one of a number of considerations. Regardless of the motivation, under pressure sellers are more apt to take much less than asking price and market value, and of course, these are the types of sellers you want to find. Look for ads that give selling reasons such as "moving" or have statements such as "must sell," "best offer by a certain date," or "will accept offers." The best two approaches to buying from classified ads are first in or last in.

First in means you scan the classifieds each morning, circling ads of interest, and call right away. When talking with the seller, try to gauge their level of motivation to sell, and make sure the item for sale meets your buying criteria. If so, set an appointment to inspect right away. Remember, what separates the professional buyer and the average person selling is the fact that you do this for a living and they do not. All they want or need to do is dispose of an item. Sellers often accept first-but-low offers because they worry they might not get any other offers, especially if they are motivated to sell and need the money.

Last in means you cut out classified ads of interest and wait a week to ten days before calling to see if the item is still for sale. If yes, and it meets your buying criteria, there is a good chance the seller will accept considerably less than the asking price because they have not been able to sell yet. In addition to your local newspaper classifieds, there are also a host of classified-advertising-only newspapers such as the *Thrifty Nickel, Penny Saver*, and *Buy and Sell*. All are excellent places to find great items to buy for resale. And, don't overlook specialty publications relevant to the specific products you deal in, such as boating publications if you buy and sell boats or antique publications if you buy and sell antiques. Almost all specialty publications have classified advertising sections. (Information about using classified advertising to sell items can be found in Chapter 5.) The steps for purchasing items from private sellers using classified ads include:

- Scan newspaper and specialty publication classified ads daily for items of interest.
- Qualify sellers and the items for sale over the telephone before setting an appointment to view. If items do not meet your buying criteria, don't bother wasting your time with an appointment.
- Carefully inspect items, and ask sellers for the complete history of the product. Also be sure to take along your inspection and buying tools. Depending on the item(s) you specialize in, these tools will include a camera, flashlight, pricing guides, receipt book, magnifying glass, and angled mirror.
- Negotiate like a seasoned pro, and never pay full asking price. Look for reasons to offer less—chips, repairs needed, out-of-season, and a host of others.

Factor in all costs, including highest-possible purchase price, which will still leave you a reasonable return on investment when resold. If you cannot meet your profit needs and expectations because the purchase price is too high, do not buy.

- Get as much original documentation as possible, including repair receipts and warranties, original purchase receipts, and owner's or operator's manuals. All are valuable marketing tools for reselling.

- Get every available extra you can with the product you are buying. For example, if you buy a bicycle, request that the seller include any extras like a helmet, rack, tool kit, and spare parts. All can be resold separately or as a package to increase sales value and profits.

- Always take your own receipt book, and list a full description of products purchased, including serial and model numbers. Date the receipt, list purchase price and payment method. Complete the seller's full contact information as well as your own, and have the receipt signed by the seller. If the seller is offering any type of guarantee, warranties, or return options, make sure these are also included on the receipt.

Resources

- *Penny Saver USA*, print classified advertising newspapers, ♂ www.penny saverusa.com
- *The Recycler*, print classified advertising newspapers, ♂ www.recycler.com
- *Thrifty Nickel*, print classified advertising newspapers, ♂ www.thriftynickel ads.com
- *Trader Classified Media*, publishers of numerous classified advertising newspapers, including *The Bargain Finder*, *The Buy and Sell*, *Auto Trader*, and *Wheels & Deals*, ♂ www.trader.com

Bulletin Boards

People often utilize community bulletin boards to pin up fliers advertising things they have for sale—furniture, cars, jewelry, electronics, computers, and tools. Typically, these bulletin boards are found in grocery stores, public markets, gas stations, convenience stores, libraries, laundries, fitness clubs, universities, and colleges, and community centers. There are really two approaches you can use when purchasing items from private sellers who use bulletin boards to advertise the items for sale.

The first approach is to call right away on items of interest, get all the information you need, set an appointment to view, and then use all of your sales and negotiation skills to get the item for the lowest possible price. If you choose this route, do not try to prenegotiate over the telephone before you see the item. Instead, make sure you ask the right questions to ensure the item meets your buying criteria, and save the price negotiations for the face-to-face meeting. When people are made cash offers in person, they are far more likely to get excited and take your offer seriously than when one is made over the telephone. The old adage, Money talks, BS walks, is very true.

The second approach is to start a bulletin board logbook, which is nothing more than a 50-cent spiral notepad. Make a weekly run to all bulletin boards in your area and record items listed for sale that interest you, including product description, price, date posted, and seller's contact information. Wait a week to ten days, and then begin to call to inquire if the items are still for sale. The reason you wait is because many businesses and organizations that provide bulletin board space require all ads to have a posting date on the flier so ads older than one week can be taken down, making space for new ads to be posted. Otherwise, the bulletin boards would become an overcrowded mess of items, many no longer for sale. If the item is still for sale after a week to ten days, there is a better than average chance you will be able to negotiate a substantially lower purchase price.

It is also useful to create your own fliers listing the products you are looking to purchase—antiques, cars, furniture, electronic devices, or whatever—to post when you make your bulletin board runs.

For-Sale Signs

Out for a walk or a drive, you always see lots of for-sale signs pinned to cars, boats, houses, bicycles, and the like. It is very possible to buy some of these items low and resell them for a profit. In fact, I have firsthand experience in this type of buying and selling. Some years ago, on my way to and from home, I passed a sailboat on a trailer for sale. A number of months passed and the boat was still for sale. It was now fall, and having sold my own sailboat the year previous, I decided to stop in and inquire. After some hard negotiations, I purchased the boat for approximately half of the $10,000 asking price. I used the boat the following season, stored it for the winter, and the following spring sold it through a boat broker for $8,500. I had use of the boat for an entire season, and even after broker commissions and a few minor cosmetic changes, I still netted about $2,200 on the deal. The reason I was successful on both sides of this transaction was timing and condition. I purchased the sailboat off-season, and though otherwise a good boat, it was dirty and needed some attention. When it came time to sell the boat, I received top dollar for it because it was the beginning of the boating season, it was in immaculate condition, and, more important, the boat was in the water and could be taken for a test sail by interested parties. So it just goes to show you: do not be afraid to negotiate hard, and buy products that are in need of some elbow grease, but otherwise sound. You never know a person's reason for selling or their level of motivation to sell at any price until you ask or make an offer.

Additional Buying Sources

In addition to the buying sources already mentioned, there are others such as flea markets, thrift shops, storage companies, hotels replacing furnishings, contractors for reclaimed building materials, including lumber and architectural antiques, and landowners for cedar rail fencing and rocks used in landscaping. Any Penny Saver-type publication (♂ www.pennysaverusa.com) will have a freebie or recyclers section, where many very saleable items can be picked up absolutely free. For instance, in my local Buy and Sell publication (♂ www.buysell.com), here are examples of three of the 67 freebie listings in one issue: "Three church pews, good condition, you pick up." "Solid wood executive desk, free." "Hot tub, works great, you move." A few hours of work and a bit of elbow grease would probably net the innovative entrepreneur $700 to $1,000 from just these three freebie sources alone! But because of space constraints, we will focus on the best buying sources for previously owned merchandise: flea markets, secondhand shops, and moving and storage companies.

Flea Markets

In spite of the fact that dealers are there to make a profit, flea markets do provide ample buying opportunities for previously owned merchandise, especially for antiques, collectibles, and items in need of some spit and polish. You need to practice the same shrewd negotiations you would for any other buying source. Simply do not buy if you are not sure you can resell for a profit. Also, whenever you make a purchase, always ask for a receipt and the vendor's full contact information. Thieves often use flea markets as a front to fence stolen merchandise, so you want (and perhaps may even need) proof that all items in your possession have been purchased.

The following are a few great tips for buying low at flea markets. (Information about flea market vending is found in Chapter 5.)

- To strike the best deals shop early, or shop late in the day. Flea market vendors have the most power in terms of negotiations at the busiest time of day, which is usually mid-day. If you find something early and the vendor refuses to budge on price, return later in the day to see if it is still for sale. If so, restate your offer, but no more. Some might bite because it beats having to reload and transport.

- Never pay full asking price, if for no other reason than it goes against the nature of a buy-and-sell enterprise. Always start low and hesitantly work your way up incrementally, if need be. If the dealer still won't budge, suggest he throw in another item for free. If he still won't budge, walk away unless you are absolutely sure you can resell it for purchase price, plus fixed costs, plus time, and still generate a profit. If not, there is no sense in wasting your time just to trade dollars.

- Cash speaks volumes at flea markets, so leave the plastic and checks at home and take only cash, preferably small bills stashed in various pockets so it appears you are short on cash, which supports your need to negotiate and buy low.

- Don't judge a book by its cover. A busy flea market is fantastic for selling, while a slow flea market is great for buying. A lack of customers equals hungry vendors, ready to make deals.

- You know the products you are looking for, so don't get sidetracked and buy things on impulse, especially if you are clueless in terms of value, condition, and how and where they can be resold for a profit.

- Have suitable transportation when you go flea market buying. A truck, van, or trailer means you may be able to purchase larger items others cannot, and negotiate a lower price because of it. Also, having to make multiple trips wastes time and gas and cuts into your profitability.

- Look for dealers with items that seem out of place in their inventory. For instance, a dealer selling mainly tools, but with a couple of antiques, or a dealer selling household goods, but with a few bits of vintage clothing. Like any retailer of used goods, when they sell something out of their normal range, there is a good chance the item will be undervalued, especially in the case of antiques and collectibles.

- Take a flea market toolbox stocked with the tools of the buyers' trade, including a magnifying glass, flashlight, retractable search mirror, camera, price guides, and tape measure, all of which can be used to closely examine items prior to buying.

- Go shopping in poor weather when other shoppers are likely to stay home. When customers are few, dealers get hungry and are willing to make deals.

- Look for items that are otherwise sound, but in need of a little TLC. These items can generally be bought at bargain-basement prices, and a few repairs and a bit of elbow grease will go a long way to greatly increasing resale values.

RESOURCES
- *Collectors*, directory listing flea markets in the United States, indexed geographically, ✍ www.collectors.org/FM
- *Flea Market Guide*, directory listing flea markets in the United States, indexed geographically, ✍ www.fleamarketguide.com
- *Flea USA*, directory listing flea markets in the United States and Canada, indexed geographically by state and province, ✍ www.fleamarkets.com
- *Keys Flea Market*, directory listing flea markets in the United States, indexed geographically, ✍ www.keysfleamarket.com
- The National Flea Market Association, ☎ (602) 995-3532, ✍ www.fleamarket.org

Secondhand Stores

Junk shops, secondhand shops, thrift shops, and pawnshops also provide potential buying opportunities, though not generally as good as other buying sources listed in this chapter. Because the retailer needs to generate a profit to stay in business, products tend to be priced at true market value. But with that said, it is still possible to find valuable hidden treasures, which can be bought for a song and resold for a profit. As mentioned in the introduction, a teen working part-time is earning $5,000 a month buying secondhand T-shirts from thrift shops and secondhand stores and reselling them online, so the potential is there.

The key to success when looking for bargains in these shops is twofold. First, try to stick with shops that are run by or aligned with local or national charities. Most items coming in are donated by people within the community. Because of this, there is a much higher chance neither the person donating nor the volunteer in the shop will have any idea of the item's true value. After all, why should they? They are simply people helping out by donating merchandise or time to help run the charity. It is not their business to know junk from treasure, as owners of specialty secondhand shops should. Second, if you can't deal only with charity shops, look for fix-it-upper items in all secondhand shops, though not ones in such poor condition that you end up spending too much time fixing and not enough selling. Preferably, items should need no more than basic repairs and a good cleaning to quickly transform them into valuable, resalable merchandise.

RESOURCES
- *Consignment Shops Online*, directory listing thrift shop locations, indexed geographically by state, ✍ www.consignmentshops.com
- National Association of Resale & Thrift Shops, ☎ (800) 544-0751, ✍ www.narts.org

– National Pawnbrokers Association, ☎ (817) 491-4554, ♂ www.national pawnbrokers.org
– Pawnshops Online, directory listing pawnshop locations, indexed geographically by state, ♂ www.pawnshops.net

Moving and Storage Companies

Moving and storage companies, as well as towing companies, can represent a wealth of incredible buying opportunities for the innovative entrepreneur. When people do not pay their moving, storage, or towing storage bills, companies often sell any goods stored or still in their possession to recover all or some of the monies owed. Typically, the personal belongings stored at public storage centers will include furniture, clothes, antiques, sporting goods, books, and records. Occasionally business owners who fall behind in their rent will have equipment and inventory seized that can often be purchased for less than wholesale value. Larger yard-stored items such as boats, cars, RVs, motorcycles, and trailers can also be purchased. Registered items such as cars, however, require owner transfer. A bailiff or another official is typically brought in to seize and sell the items so they can be legally transferred to new owners. It is best to contact moving, storage, and towing companies directly to inquire about how they sell or dispose of goods seized for nonpayment of rent. Each company will have its own disposal methods and policies.

RESOURCES

– American Moving and Storage Association, ☎ (703) 683-7410, ♂ www. moving.org
– Self Storage Association, ☎ (703) 921-9123, ♂ www.selfstorage.org
– Towing and Recovery Association of America, ☎ (800) 728-0133, ♂ www. towserver.net

5

WHERE YOU CAN SELL
THINGS FOR BIG PROFITS

I f buying low represents 50 percent of the equation required to succeed in a buy-and-sell enterprise, selling high represents the other 50 percent. The objective of this chapter is to show you where and how you can resell items for top dollar to maximize revenues and profits. There are a vast number of ways and places to sell, certainly more than are featured here. This chapter is not simply a list of all the ways to sell, but explains the best selling venues for the vast majority of buy-and-sell entrepreneurs. You will learn how to utilize the following venues and methods to sell your goods at big profits.

COMMUNITY RETAILING
- Flea markets
- Arts and crafts shows
- Live auction sales
- Kiosks
- Farmers' and public markets
- Street vending
- Community events
- Trade shows, consumer shows, and seminars
- Selling direct to business (B2B)

ONLINE MARKETPLACES
- eBay
- Your own e-commerce Web site
- e-storefronts and malls
- e-auctions
- e-classifieds

HOMEBASED SALES
- Homebased showrooms and exterior displays
- Garage sales
- In-home sales parties
- Selling direct to collectors

Most of the ideas and concepts detailed in this chapter work in conjunction with information from other chapters. For example, information about personal selling in Chapter 3 can be applied to flea market vending in this chapter. Keep in mind that most tips featured for one type of retailing are portable, and can be used in other retailing venues.

Community Retailing

Beyond traditional retail storefronts, there are numerous retailing opportunities in every community for the innovative entrepreneur. Selling tools at a weekend flea market, selling flowers from a rented mall kiosk, selling antiques at auction, or selling organic vegetables at the local farmers' market, are examples. Although there are many community-retailing opportunities, this section focuses on what I consider the best: flea markets, arts and crafts shows, live auctions, kiosks, farmers' and public markets, street vending, community events, trade shows and seminars, and direct-to-business sales (B2B). Depending on the items you sell and your objectives, you might select only one of these community-retailing options or perhaps combine two or more to maximize the potential for success and profits.

Flea Markets

There are an estimated 750,000 flea market vendors peddling their wares in the United States and Canada at more than 1,000 flea markets, bazaars, and swap meets, some of which attract crowds in excess of 25,000 a day. These flea market vendors are comprised of professional and amateur sellers working full-time, part-time, seasonally, or only occasionally, and it is not unusual for vendors to earn as much as $50,000 a year working only a few days a week.

LOCATING THE BEST FLEA MARKETS

Good flea markets are everywhere. But don't judge a flea market by size alone. Instead, conduct research by visiting a few before deciding which one to set up shop at. Check out other vendors—what do they sell, how much are they charging, how much are they selling, and how many are selling the same things as you? Also check out people in attendance—are they buying or browsing, how many are there, and do they meet your target-customer profile? You have to get a feel for the venue, vendors, and customers prior to setting up to truly know which is the right flea market for you. There are also many types of flea markets—weekends only, every day, summer only, outside under tent, open air, and inside swanky building resembling mall retailing, more than flea market vending.

All have advantages and disadvantages. For instance, outside flea markets are subject to weather: wind, rain, sun, heat, and cold. Booth rentals also widely vary from a low of $5 per day, to as much as $100 for single-day events. You can also reserve space for a month or longer at a time, and while this method secures your cheapest rent, be sure to test it out for a few days before getting locked into a long-term lease. Other considerations include customer and vendor parking, electricity, phone lines for credit card and debit card terminals, on-site ATM machine, washrooms, food services, and overall organization. Online flea market directories such as the ones listed in Resources offer the best way to find flea markets. Most directories are indexed geographically.

THE PRODUCTS THAT SELL BEST

There are exceptions, but generally the best *new products* to sell are dollar-store items, toys, hand and power tools, crafts, costume jewelry, sunglasses, auto parts, and novelty products. The best *previously owned products* to sell are glassware, antiques, collectibles, toys, tools, children's clothing, vintage clothing, and books.

EQUIPMENT FOR VENDORS

In most cases you will need a vendor permit and sales-tax ID number, and some flea markets also require vendors to have liability insurance. You will also need to supply your own transportation and equipment, such as dollies to load and unload merchandise and displays. Some flea markets provide merchandising tables, canopies, and displays, with cost built into booth fees. Others rent these items separately, and still others do not supply anything except for the booth. Therefore, you have to clarify equipment and merchandising needs with managers upfront. You will also want to be sure to bring along a few creature comforts such as comfortable shoes, lots of water and food, a stool instead of a chair to sit on because it looks more professional and keeps you up higher, an umbrella for outside events, and a radio. A basic first-aid kit and tool kit is a good idea too.

Because you can never have enough tricks up your sleeve when it comes to flea market vending, here are 15 more great tips to get you started on your way to earning huge profits.

1. Create a flea market vendors' tool box stocked with lots of handy items such as tape, string, receipt books, calculator, pens, fliers, business cards, credit card slips, magic markers, price gun or label marker, scissors, cleaning products and rags, and supplies such as newspaper, plastic bags, and cardboard boxes to pack customer purchases.

2. Buy small inexpensive items related to your main product line, and boldly advertise and resell these at low cost to draw shoppers to your tables. For instance, if you sell new hand and power tools, fill up a box with assorted screwdrivers for $1 each. The idea is to grab the attention of people, draw them into your booth, and once you have their interest try to sell higher-priced merchandise.

3. Offer numerous ways for customers to pay by getting a merchant account and wireless terminal for debit cards and credit cards. Most customers will pay cash, but accepting plastic increases impulse buying by as much as 50 percent. Let shoppers know you accept credit cards by posting a large sign. Don't accept checks, even with proper ID; it's not worth the risk of being returned NSF. Also, make sure you have an ample supply of small bills. You do not want to risk losing sales because you cannot change a $20 bill.

4. Invest in professional displays and sales aids to help boost revenues and profits. Have bold and colorful professional signs and banners made, purchase high-quality and attractive display units and devices on wheels

for easy loading and transportation, keep your merchandise and sales area clean and organized, and even consider uniforms, such as silkscreen T-shirts, hats, or golf shirts with an identifier like Jim's Gas Station Collectibles emblazoned across them, for example.

5. Hand out fliers to everyone passing, even if they did not buy. The fliers should describe your products and list ways for people to buy—Web site, telephone number, and mail order address. To increase the effectiveness of this simple marketing trick, print tips on the back of the flier so people have reason to hang on to it rather than toss it in the trash once home. For instance, if you sell fishing tackle, list 20 tips for catching, cleaning, or preparing fish on the back of the flier.

6. Develop a system for capturing names and addresses so you can utilize this information for direct marketing purposes—mail, e-mail, and telemarketing. Hold a contest and use the information on the entry ballot to build a database, or ask people to subscribe to your free electronic or print product catalog, for example.

7. Everyone shopping at flea markets expects to bargain and wants to flex their negotiation muscle, so be ready to haggle. Price items 10 to 20 percent higher than you expect to get so you will have some negotiating room and still be able to get your price. Also, there are pros and cons to pricing each item individually. The pro is that if each item is tagged with the price, you will not have to continually repeat the price each time someone asks. The con is that if people think the price is too high, they may move on to the next vendor and not try to negotiate. Personally, I think you should strike a balance and price some items, but not all.

8. Stand out in a sea of vendors by using colorful banners, balloons, lights, music, and flags; basically any and all types of attention-grabbing devices. Large markets have hundreds, sometimes thousands, of vendors all vying for the attention of shoppers, so you need to be creative and stand out from the crowd.

9. Flea market vendors cannot afford to be wallflowers; there are far too many competitors chasing the same consumers. You have to be creative. Develop ways to engage people and get them into your booth, or use product demonstrations to pull them in. You can't sell to people if they don't stop and check out your goods. Therefore, you need to create a hook and provide reasons for people to stop and shop.

10. You will need to consider your return and refund policy. I suggest you do not offer any refunds or returns, especially on new items because you will

not be able to resell them for full retail. If you do offer returns on used items, only offer exchanges for items of equal or greater value. Ideally, there should be no returns or refunds and you should post signs stating "ALL SALES FINAL" and have this printed on receipts.

11. Whenever possible, try to sell items with their original packaging, manuals, and accessories, such as a remote control with the television or a key chuck with a drill. Doing so greatly increases the value and makes the item much easier to sell.

12. Always keep more expensive items grouped together, so they are easier to watch to prevent theft. Always look inside of larger items to make sure smaller ones are not hidden. Likewise, keep your cash with you, in a lockbox, or a safe.

13. Never hold items for people who say they will be back to pick it up unless they have left a substantial deposit. Many shoppers say they will return later to pick up items after they have browsed the event or have suitable transportation to carry larger items, but they often never return. All merchandise must remain for sale unless paid for in full or a substantial deposit has been obtained.

14. Price products according to competition and demand, but aim for at least a 50 percent markup on new products. Price used products as a percentage of new cost, perhaps 70 percent of the cost of new for perfect condition, down to 20 percent of new for poor condition.

15. Only sell items in good working order and free of rips, rust, and excessive wear (unless antiques). Also, if power is available on-site, have an electrical cord so people can test electronics and appliances, and have batteries for battery-powered items. Clothing should be cleaned, neatly pressed, and displayed on hangers.

RESOURCES

- *Collectors*, directory listing flea markets in the United States, indexed geographically, ♪ www.collectors.org/FM
- *Flea Market Guide*, directory listing flea markets in the United States, indexed geographically, ♪ www.fleamarketguide.com
- *Flea USA*, directory listing flea markets in the United States and Canada, indexed geographically by state and province, ♪ www.fleamarkets.com
- *Keys Flea Market*, directory listing flea markets in the United States, indexed geographically, ♪ www.keysfleamarket.com
- The National Flea Market Association, ☎ (602) 995-3532, ♪ www.fleamar ket.org

Arts and Crafts Shows

Providing you have the right products to sell, arts and crafts shows and fairs can deliver excellent selling opportunities. These shows come in different styles and sizes, from the church-run crafts shows leading up to Christmas to international fine arts and crafts shows that last for a week and attract buyers from around the globe. Most, however, are small events lasting a day or two and take place in community centers, exhibition buildings, hotels, convention centers, and school gymnasiums. Often arts and crafts shows are also held outdoors, but vending at these shows can be greatly affected by weather. Rent also widely varies—from $5 to $500 per day. The key to success is the same as for any vending opportunity: select shows based on reaching your target audience and not necessarily for show size or total attendance. Other factors to consider include admission fees, parking, competition, rent, operating history, and attendance statistics. You should visit larger, more expensive shows before signing on to vend to make sure the show and audience meet your exhibiting criteria. Whenever possible, try to talk to other vendors to get firsthand feedback about the show and audience.

Here are a few more helpful tips.

- Create a checklist a week before any show, and check off each item or task as completed so you are 100 percent ready to sell come showtime.
- If you are the artist or you make your own crafts, try in-booth demonstrations as a way to draw a crowd. Booths and displays alive with activity always grab more attention than static ones, and a busy booth equals more selling opportunities.
- Keep your booth, displays, and inventory clean and organized, and use mirrors and clamp-on lighting to brighten your booth and displays. Also bring along a basic toolbox for last-minute changes or emergencies. Stock the toolbox with a hammer, screwdrivers, flashlight, wrench, extra light bulbs, cleaner, rags, stapler, and garbage bags.
- Stock lots of materials for packaging purchases, including newspaper, plastic bags, boxes, tape, string, and scissors, and offer free gift wrapping as a way to distinguish yourself from competitors.
- Also consider cash management and purchase payment options. Ideally, you will want to accept credit cards and debit cards because it boosts impulse buying by as much as 50 percent. You will also need a receipt book, credit card slips, calculator, pens, price gun or blank price tags, and a cash lockbox.
- You should bring 50 percent more inventory than you expect to sell, especially if you are traveling far from your home base. You do not want to chance losing sales and profit because you are out of stock.

- Because shows can be very busy, make sure you price all items to save the time of repeating prices to everyone who asks. Also, make sure you create a couple of worthwhile *show specials* to really grab attention and pull shoppers into your booth. A 50-percent-off show special may seem excessive, but what profit you lose on one or two items can be made up in volume sales and through up-selling opportunities.

RESOURCES

– Arts and Crafts Association of America, ☎ (616) 874-1721, ✎ www.artsand craftsassoc.com
– Canadian Crafts & Hobby Association, ☎ (403) 291-0559, ✎ www.cdn craft.org
– Crafts Shows USA, provides visitors with a free online directory listing crafts shows nationally, indexed by state, ✎ www.craftshowsusa.com
– Indian Arts & Crafts Association, ☎ (505) 265-9149, ✎ www.iaca.com

Live Auction Sales

Live auction sales are great for selling specialized and high-value products such as boats, antiques, and power equipment. The downside is that you have to pay commission, which is generally 10 percent. But think of the commission as the cost of marketing. For instance, if you were to advertise the item for sale in the classifieds, you would have to pay for the ad and pay yourself for the time to answer the telephone and show the item to prospective buyers. There are always costs associated with the marketing of any product. The true downside associated with auction selling is that you have no guarantee of how much the product will sell for, although there are two ways to combat this. First, make sure you are consigning your item for sale at the right type of auction, one that will attract the right types of buyers. About half of all auctioneers specialize in one particular field, such as auctioning cars, real estate, heavy equipment, or antiques. The main advantage of consigning with specialist auctioneers is their contact list. Before sales, auctioneers send out a catalog of available items to people who have purchased similar items in the past. This marketing practice assures that qualified buyers will attend the sale, which usually equates to higher bid prices.

Second, you can place a reserve bid on the product, which means if no one bids at least the minimum acceptable price, the item will not be sold, and you take the item home after the sale or leave it with the auctioneer for the next sale. Be aware that most auctioneers charge a fee for items with reserve bids that do not sell. The fee can be a flat rate or a percentage of the reserve-bid amount, so be sure to check with the auctioneer.

The following are a few more helpful tips for selling through auction services.

- Not all auctioneers are the same. Some are masters of merchandising and at driving up bids, while others are not. Attend sales to get a good feel for the type of auctioneer before consigning.
- Before consigning items, receive the following information in writing: commission charges, reserve-bid charges, length of time to process and payout for items sold, and any storage and transportation issues.
- If you are selling expensive items, find out how much insurance the auctioneer carries in the event your property is damaged or stolen before, during, or after the sale, up until you get paid out.
- Before consigning items make sure they work, are clean, and include all manuals and documentation.
- It is illegal to bid on your own merchandise in the hope of driving up the price. The best way for you to get top dollar is to make sure you have an excellent item for sale, and you are selling it through the right auction service, and the right bidders are in attendance.

RESOURCES

- Auction Guide, billed as the Internet guide to auctions and auctioneers worldwide, indexed by country, ♂ www.auctionguide.com
- Auctioneers Association of Canada, ☎ (866) 640-9915, ♂ www.auctioneers canada.com
- National Auctioneers Association, ☎ (800) 662-9438, ♂ www.auction eer.org
- Net Auctions, directory listing online and offline auction sales by type and auctioneers by specialty, ♂ www.net-auctions.com

Kiosks

Kiosks and pushcarts also represent great selling opportunities for vendors with the right products. I am sure that many of you think hot dogs, ice cream, and popcorn when you think of pushcarts or kiosks. But kiosks and pushcarts can actually be adapted for selling any number of items: costume jewelry, clothing, electronics, leather goods, gifts, music and movie disks, flowers, and souvenirs. There are both interior and exterior styles, though the focus here is on interior kiosks and pushcarts that you would find in malls, office buildings, government buildings, and airports and train stations. Many of these carts and kiosks are available to rent on a short- and long-term basis, from one day to a year. Generally speaking, it is the building or property management company that rents vending space, so these are the people you should contact. In addition to a vendor's permit, most locations also require you to have liability insurance. Locations such as the ones mentioned above can be lucrative in terms of revenues, but vendors who specialize in selling from mall kiosks tend to fare the best and produce the highest sales, especially during the Christmas shopping season.

Farmers' and Public Markets

Farmers' and public markets come in many shapes and sizes—open air, under tent, inside buildings, summer only, weekends only, or seven days a week year round. Public markets tend to be more formal and have more long-term merchants selling from upscale booths and kiosks. Farmers' markets tend to be more laid-back affairs, but also can be strict and want only vendors who sell food products. Others allow food-related items such as cookware. Still others have a more open-door policy, allowing vendors to sell just about anything, and resemble a flea market more than a traditional farmers' market.

Mostly, you will only find new products for sale at farmers' and public markets, with the occasional exception of antiques and collectibles. Best-selling food products at both include seafood, baked goods, vegetables, herbs and spices, organic foods, and candies. Best-selling nonfood items include cookware, recipe and food books, clothing, flowers, crafts, antiques, gifts, costume jewelry, and souvenir items.

To maximize your potential for success, concentrate on three areas: the market, merchandising, and sales. Start by visiting farmers' and public markets in your area. Don't judge by size, organization, or types of vendors, but rather on the number of shoppers, how much they buy, and what they buy. You want to know you are vending at a market that attracts buyers, not sightseers. In terms of merchandising, offer good-quality products at fair prices, and keep your booth, displays, and products clean and organized. Place your best-selling merchandise in plain view, and always have a special offer announced using professional signage—discounts, two-for-one, or free upgrades.

Markets are generally loud and busy, and you will want to stand out from the crowd and grab attention, so be sure to use lights, loudspeakers, and other attention-grabbing devices. Finally, you must be outgoing and persuasive. Don't wait for people to stop in; instead, engage everyone, and give them reasons to buy—coupons, free samples, and contest giveaways are all good reasons.

Booth or kiosk rentals vary from a low of $10 per day to more than $100, depending on location. Public markets prefer long-term tenants, as opposed to farmers' markets, which usually have vending space available by the day, week, or season.

RESOURCES
- Farmers' Market Online, directory listing farmers' markets, indexed geographically by state, ✆ www.farmersmarket.com
- The North American Farmers' Direct Marketing Association, ☎ (413) 529-0386, ✆ www.nafdma.com

Street Vending

There are also street-vending opportunities in many cities across North America, but obtaining a street vendor's permit can be difficult. City or municipal street vendor permits are usually issued and renewable yearly, or they can be issued in a lottery-type drawing and range in price from $25 to $1,000 annually. Contact your local city or municipal government to inquire about street-vending opportunities. Vending from federally owned lands and buildings is regulated by the U.S. General Services Administration, which can be contacted at ☎ (877) 472-3779 ✆ www.gsa.gov to inquire about opportunities. In addition to a vendor's permit, you may also have to obtain liability insurance, a health permit, and a fire permit, depending on goods sold. It is not uncommon for people to disregard regulations and street-vend without a permit, mainly because to some people, the lure of big profits justifies the occasional fine. But this is no way to build a long-term successful business and reliable revenue stream. Take the time, and go to the expense necessary to obtain all of the required street-vendor permits. Vending permits are, however, usually not required if you operate from a privately owned location such as lumberyard or car wash parking lot.

The best-selling products include hot dogs and ice cream, T-shirts, sunglasses, costume jewelry, wristwatches, souvenirs, umbrellas, hats, and flowers. Before you decide what type of product(s) to sell, do the rounds. What are other vendors selling? Who is the busiest? Which days are they busiest? Who are their customers? Duplicating a successful business model is one of the easiest ways to eliminate or substantially reduce financial risk.

Street vendors can work from portable kiosks and pushcarts or right from a suitcase, depending on what they sell. Depending on your budget, you can rent, lease, or purchase new and used pushcarts and kiosks, which come in many styles and price points. Some can be towed behind vehicles or placed on a trailer for transport, some are motorized, and other are pedal-powered.

Invest in wireless payment processing technology so you can accept credit cards and debit cards on-site. This gives you a huge competitive advantage over vendors who do not offer these payment options, greatly increases impulse buying, and reduces the risk of theft because you have little cash on hand. Remember, street vendors are never wallflowers. You must love what you do, what you sell, and be extremely comfortable talking with people.

RESOURCES

– Carriage Works, pushcart and kiosk manufacturers and sellers of used kiosks and pushcarts, ☎ (541) 882-9661, ♂ www.carriageworks.com
– Cart Owners' Association of America, ☎ (559) 332-2229, ♂ www.cartowners.org

Community Events

Once on the decline, community events have rebounded in a big way and are more popular than ever. Parades, fairs, holiday celebrations, rodeos, music festivals, and swap meets—every community has numerous events and celebrations throughout the year. Many of these events provide a host of vendor opportunities to sell candy, clothing, gifts, helium-filled balloons, crafts, small flags, souvenirs, costume jewelry, and everything imaginable in between. As a general rule, community events are organized by local associations such as the chamber of commerce, charities, community social or sports clubs, churches, or by a department within local government.

You can contact the organizers of the event to inquire about available vending opportunities. Rent, booth fees, and permit costs vary depending on the type of event, anticipated crowd, and duration of the event. Some are free, but most charge. The most expensive are usually fairs and exhibitions, which can cost as much as $500 a day. Selling at community events is like any other retailing opportunity—think location within the event, signage, professional displays, first-class merchandise relevant to the theme of the event, fair pricing, quick service, and a smile. Combine these with your natural outgoing personality, and you cannot help but sell and make lots of profit in the process. Never assume your merchandise will sell itself. Get involved, chat with the crowd, show them what you've got, and have fun. Also, print a few hundred fliers describing your products and how people can contact you after the event. The fliers should be given to customers and noncustomers alike. Even if they did not buy from you during the event, that does not mean they won't sometime later.

Trade Shows, Consumer Shows, and Seminars

Trade and industry shows, consumer shows, and seminars are all fantastic venues for buy-and-sell entrepreneurs to collect leads and sell their goods. Trade and consumer shows are a personal favorite. I have used them many times to promote and sell products and services, always with great success. As you read through the information below, keep in mind that many of the sales and marketing ideas in this chapter are portable. This means most merchandising and selling techniques that work for flea market and craft show vending, for example, will also work at trade and consumer shows.

Trade and Consumer Shows

The only real difference between trade shows and consumer shows is that trade shows are generally businesses exhibiting for, and selling to, other businesses, while consumer shows are for the general public to attend, browse, gain information, and shop. For the buy-and-sell entrepreneur, few offline marketing venues can match the effectiveness of trade and consumer shows as a way to showcase and sell your products to a large audience at one time, in one place, and in a cost-effective manner. Over the course of one day to a few weeks, depending on the show, you can make personal contact with hundreds, if not thousands, of qualified prospects, affording you hundreds, if not thousands, of opportunities to sell your products.

These days there is a trade or consumer show for every type of product. There are home and garden shows, food shows, industry-specific shows, sports and recreation shows, car shows, antique and collectible shows, and the list goes on. In fact, there are in excess of 10,000 trade and consumer shows hosted annually in North America. Fortunately, you can click through hundreds of show listings online in no time, gain valuable insights into each show, and, more importantly, learn about the people who attend to make sure they match your target audience. As in other types of retailing, considerations for selecting the right show include costs, competition, audience, duration, and geographic location.

I strongly suggest that you attend shows first to get a feel for the vendors, management, and audience before making the commitment to exhibit. When designing your booth and displays, keep in mind that booths alive with exciting product demonstrations draw considerably more interest and larger crowds than static booths. The show pace can be fast and furious, and time is a commodity that is always in short supply. So it is important to have an effective and well-rehearsed sales plan ready to put into action. Your sales plan should revolve around four key elements—engage prospects, qualify prospects, present your products, and close the sale. Rarely will your booth, exhibits, or displays do the selling. This job is left up to you.

Seminars

Seminars provide yet another selling opportunity, although a bit limited because certainly not every product is suited to this type of marketing. Best products to sell in the seminar or workshop environment include information in print or electronic format, health products, educational products, and security products. It is especially productive for the sale of goods that can be easily demonstrated, revealing all of the benefits to a live audience. Product sales at seminars are often referred to as back-of-room sales, because tables displaying your merchandise are located at the back of the room near the entrance and exit so that before and after the seminar, guests must pass by your merchandise. Seminars and workshops do not have to be formal—they can be held in a banquet room, living room, supplier's warehouse, or at a local restaurant. The specific place will depend on the audience, the objective of the event, and the topic or subject matter. Fortunately for small-business owners with tight marketing budgets, seminars can be promoted effectively and with success for little cost. Design a basic, yet informative, promotional flier on your personal computer. List the details of your seminar or workshop event, print a few dozen copies, and post the fliers on free bulletin boards throughout your community.

RESOURCES
- Trade Show Exhibitors Association, ☎ (312) 842-8732, ✄ www.tsea.org
- Trade Show Exhibits Sales & Rentals, free online quotes for display and exhibit sales and rentals, ✄ www.trade-shows.org
- Trade Shows Online, directory listing trade and consumer shows, conventions, and expos worldwide, indexed by country, ✄ www.tradeshows.com

Selling Directly to Businesses (B2B)
Selling your goods directly to businesses is another sales option, provided you have the right products such as office equipment, restaurant equipment, candy for vending, arts and crafts items for decorations, new books, and gift and promotional items. The downside to B2B sales is that business owners are bombarded daily by people who want to sell them everything imaginable, and because of this, most become hardened to even the most professional sales pitches. This sales method is not suitable for people who are easily put off by rejection, because you will get lots. You have to be innovative in your approach, professional, and respect people's time. Know your product inside and out, especially user benefits; know what your prospects need, and know the reasons they should buy from you and not competitors.

One of the best ways to mingle with business owners and prospective customers is to join business and nonbusiness clubs and associations so you can network with members. This is a grassroots approach to building your business through personal contacts and word-of-mouth. Groups such as the chamber of commerce provide many valuable networking and business-building opportunities. Additional information about personal-contact selling can be found in Chapter 3. In addition, because B2B selling is such an all-encompassing topic, you may also want to drop by your local library. Check out *The Ultimate Small Business Marketing Guide*, (Entrepreneur Press, 2003), which features over 1,500 sales and marketing ideas for small-business owners.

RESOURCES
- Canadian Chamber of Commerce, ☎ (416) 868-6415, ♂ www.chamber.ca
- United States Chamber of Commerce, ☎ (202) 659-6000, ♂ www.uschamber.com

Online Marketplaces

The innovative entrepreneur can take advantage of a nearly unlimited number of selling opportunities in a nearly unlimited number of online marketplaces. You can sell products on eBay, through electronic classified ads, by developing your own electronic storefront, and by building and publishing an e-commerce Web site. And these are just a few of the ways to get started in online product sales. Selling online means you can reach consumers around the globe quickly, easily, and at very modest costs. The Internet enables you to specialize in selling your own niche product even when your local market cannot support it, because you can reach greater numbers of your target audience wherever they reside. In short, buy-and-sell entrepreneurs who decide to sell their products online can strike it rich! In addition to the information featured here, additional information about taking your buy-and-sell enterprise online can be found in Chapter 3.

EBay

Online auction and retail marketplace giant eBay has more than 100 million registered users around the globe, and the company has set up camp in more than 20 countries. Even more amazing, and a testament to the strength of the buy-and-resell boom, is that 450,000 of eBay's registered users report that selling products through various eBay venues is their sole source of income. Not part-time, but their full-time sole source of income. EBay's sales, number of registered users, and the number of people operating eBay buy-and-sell businesses continues to grow by double-digit percentages annually. So if you are worried that you might have missed out on the eBay boom, don't. As they say in Hollywood "You ain't seen nothing yet, baby." While there is no telling how big eBay will get, at the same time it is not likely to reach critical mass any time soon, and in all probability, never.

Volumes can, and have, been written on the subject of profiting from an eBay business. Because this book is not really about eBay, space does not permit a detailed explanation about its workings. And eBay itself supplies information to all buyers and sellers. All you have to do is sign up, and it's all there for the taking. The following information, however, will give you a basic understanding of how eBay works, with a focus on eBay Auctions, eBay Stores, and eBay Motors. EBay is as wide as it is deep, so I strongly suggest you spend lots of time at its sites, take advantage of its sponsored workshops, and read books about eBay selling to further your knowledge before you get started. Listed below are a few of the more popular books on operating an eBay business. They can be purchased at bookstores, bought online through Amazon, ♂ www.amazon.com, and Barnes & Noble, ♂ www.bn.com, or checked out from your local library.

RESOURCES

- 📖 *eBay Timesaving Techniques for Dummies*, Marsha Collier (Evangelical Press, 2004)
- 📖 *How to Sell Anything on eBay and Make a Fortune*, Dennis Prince (McGraw-Hill, 2003)
- 📖 *The Official eBay Bible*, Jim Griffith (Gotham, 2003)
- 📖 *Sell It on eBay: Teck TV's Guide to Creating Successful eBay Auctions*, Jim Heid and Toby Moline (Peach Pit Press, 2003)
- 📖 *Start Your Own Business on eBay*, Jacquelyn Lynn (Entrepreneur Press, 2004)
- 📖 *Starting an eBay Business for Dummies*, Marsha Collier (Evangelical Press, 2004)

EBay Auctions

EBay offers sellers numerous types of auctions to meet individual marketing needs, including traditional, reserve-price, Dutch, private, and restricted-access auctions. EBay also offers a *Live Auction Service* with real-time bidding, but to qualify, a seller must be a licensed auctioneer, or use the services of a licensed auctioneer to conduct the sale. Find out more about eBay Live Auctions at ♂ www.ebayliveauctions.com.

TRADITIONAL AUCTION

Still the most popular and common type of eBay auction is the traditional or classic auction. In this type of auction there is no reserve price set, and at the end of the 1-,3-,5-,7-, or 10-day auction, the highest bid wins. The advantage of a short auction is that it may enable you to generate more heat and bidding excitement than a longer auction in which bidders can take their time to bid, which might eventually lead to diminished interest as time passes. On the other side of the coin, a longer auction means your item will be exposed to more potential buyers and might fetch a higher price. Ultimately, you will have to play around with auction lengths a bit to find what works best for what you sell. EBay also offers sellers a Buy It Now option, which simply means you can set a price for your item and a buyer can purchase the item for the set price without having to wait for the auction to end. But once you receive a bid, the Buy It Now icon disappears and the sale reverts back to a traditional auction.

Traditional Auction Sellers' Fees
Sellers pay a nonrefundable insertion fee to list an item on eBay with the fee based on the starting price value.

Starting Price	Insertion Fee
$0.01–$.99	$.30
$1.00–$9.99	$.35
$10.00–$24.99	$.60
$25.00–$49.99	$1.20
$50.00–$199.99	$2.40
$200.00–$499.99	$3.60
$500 and up	$4.80

Sellers also pay a final-value fee, a percentage based on the final sales value of the item.

Final Sales Value	Final-Value Fee
$0–$25	5.25% of the final sales value
$25–$1,000	5.25% of the initial $25
	2.75% of the balance
$1,000 and up	5.25% of the initial $25
	2.75% of the initial $25–$1000
	1.50% of the balance

RESERVE-PRICE AUCTION

Sellers have the option to set a reserve price for the item on sale. A reserve price is the lowest possible price a seller is prepared to take for the item, but buyers do not know how much the reserve price is, only that there is a reserve. Once a bid exceeds the reserve price, the item sells to the highest bidder. If the reserve price is not met before the auction expires, the item does not sell and the seller can choose to relist or not. Often sellers like to set a reserve price that matches their cost price as a way to protect their investment and not sell for less than cost. Reserve prices can be set for all auctions discussed here, with the exception of Dutch auctions.

Reserve-Price Auction Sellers Fees

Sellers using a reserve-price bid option pay the same fees as for a traditional auction, with two exceptions: One, the insertion fee is based on the reserved price. And two, in addition to the insertion fee you also pay a reserve-price auction fee, which is refundable if your item sells for the reserve bid or higher. If it does not sell, the reserve-auction price fee becomes part of the insertion fee and is nonrefundable.

Reserve Price	Reserve-Price Auction Fee
$.01–$49.99	$1.00
$50.00–$199.99	$2.00
$200 and up	1% of the reserve price to a maximum of $100.00

Dutch Auction

A Dutch auction is a good choice when you have multiple units of the same products for sale, such as 50 pairs of identical sunglasses, or 200 identical wristwatches. There is no upper limit to how many items you can list using a Dutch auction—10 or 10,000, it's up to you. Bidders also have the option of selecting how many of the items they want to purchase, one, some, or all. Sellers start by listing the number of items for sale, along with the starting bid. Bidders enter the amount they are willing to pay along with the number of units they want to purchase. The winning price is determined by the lowest successful bid at the time the auction closes, and all winning bidders receive this price even if their bid was higher. The idea is that if you receive bids for more items than you have for sale, then the lowest bids drop off, raising the price. Bidders can rebid a higher amount to stay in the game if they choose. A Dutch auction is a great way to move large quantities of products, quickly and efficiently, especially products in high demand.

Dutch Auction Sellers' Fees

The insertion fee is the same as for a traditional auction, but is based on the opening price you establish times the number of items you have to sell, to a maximum insertion fee of $4.80. Final sales value fees are once again the same as traditional auction final sales value fees per item, times the number of items sold. For instance, if you sold ten watches for $10 each, the final sales value fee is $10 multiplied by 5.25% = $.0525 multiplied by 10 items = $5.25 total sales value fee.

PRIVATE AUCTION

A private auction protects the identity of the buyer by not listing any e-mail address in the bidding history screen, and when and if the item is sold, only the seller knows the buyer's identity. You can use the private-auction feature on any of the auctions listed here, with the exception of a Dutch auction. Sellers may choose to use the private-auction option when selling very valuable or controversial items, once again to protect potential buyers who may not wish to be identified.

Private Auction Sellers' Fees

The fees are the same as traditional-auction insertion and final sales value fees, plus a reserve-rice auction fee if this option is selected.

RESTRICTED-ACCESS AUCTION

If you sell adult-themed products, your only selling option on eBay is through restricted-access auction services. Be aware, however, that eBay offers sellers limited promotional tools, and only visitors with credit cards and visitors who have agreed to the terms and conditions are granted entry into restricted-access auctions.

Restricted-Access Auction Sellers' Fees

The fees are the same as traditional-auction insertion and final sales value fees, plus a reserve-price auction fee if this option is selected.

EBay Stores

EBay also offers sellers who qualify an opportunity to open their own eBay storefront. At present they offer three packages ranging from the basic, to featured, to the granddaddy of them all: the anchor store. Depending on the program you choose, some of the features could include 24-hour customer service, 5 to 15 customizable Web pages to feature products for sale, traffic reporting and administration, in-site advertising, and keyword promotion programs. There are many benefits to having your own store, including the opportunity to build repeat business with customers, longer listings so you can spend more time selling and less time listing, your own Web address and linking programs, listing in the eBay store directory, and an internal in-store search engine enabling customers to conveniently browse through your products. According to eBay, sellers who have upgraded from selling through standard auction services to their own storefront have realized a 25 percent increase in sales, on average, after a three-month period, which is a very impressive figure. At this writing, eBay was offering a free one-month trial subscription for all new customers. To find out more and to get started, go to ♪ http://pages.ebay.com/storefronts/start.html.

EBAY STOREFRONT FEES

EBay offers three levels of participation—basic service at \$9.95 per month, featured service at \$49.95 per month, and anchor service at \$499.95 per month. To learn the features and benefits of each go to ♂ http://pages.ebay.com/storefronts/featuredstores.html. You will also pay insertion fees ranging from \$.02 to \$.08 per item, depending on sale duration. Final sales value fees when sold are the same as traditional auction fees. More information about eBay Storefront sellers' fees can be found at ♂ http://pages.ebay.com/storefronts/pricing.html.

EBay Tools and Resources

- *EBay Learning Center*. The eBay Learning Center is your first stop to register to open an account and to learn everything you need to know about buying and selling on eBay. ♂ http://pages.ebay.com/education/index.html
- *EBay University*. Across the country in classroom settings, or online from the comforts of home, eBay offers numerous classes and workshops taught by experts on every imaginable eBay topic and category. ♂ http://pages.ebay.com/university/index.html
- *EBay Live*. EBay Live is an annual conference organized and hosted by eBay that is open to all registered users. The conference features a number of educational workshops, classes, and events for both buyers and sellers at all skill levels, beginners through advanced. The 2005 eBay Live conference will be held in San Jose, California, June 23–25. Find out more by visiting the following link. ♂ www.ebay.com/ebaylive/
- *Seller's Guide*. In the Seller's Guide, you will find answers to the most common questions asked by sellers, such as how to list items for sale, eBay sellers' fees, and how to revise listings. ♂ http://pages.ebay.com/ help/sell/index.html
- *EBay Promotional Tools*. Learn how to boost sales and revenues by using promotional tools such as a picture gallery, bold text, subtitles, and keyword optimization. ♂ http://pages.ebay.com/sellercentral/tools.html
- *Financing Center*. If you sell expensive equipment, eBay offers financing solutions via third-party lenders. Providing buyers with financing options often means your items will sell faster and for more money. ♂ http://financing-center.ebay.com/ebaybusiness/
- *Opinions, Authentication, and Grading*. Selling antiques and collectibles? EBay provides links to companies that will value and authenticate one-of-a-kind antiques and collectibles, helping you secure top dollar from buyers

who can shop in confidence knowing they are bidding on the real McCoy. ♂ http://pages.ebay.com/help/community/auth-overview.html

- *Shipping Center.* Using the Shipping Center, you can calculate shipping costs to worldwide destinations, purchase U.S. postage, track shipments, and print UPS shipping labels. ♂ http://pages.ebay.com/services/buyand sell/shipping.html

- *Selling Internationally.* In addition to selling in your home country, there are also opportunities to sell internationally through eBay. Here you will discover how to trade internationally, receive payments, ship products, and communicate with buyers. ♂ http://pages.ebay.com/help/sell/ia/selling_ internationally.html

- *Security Center.* All the information you need to know about safe buying and selling, as well as protecting your eBay account, online payments, and financial transactions can be found in the eBay Security Center. ♂ http:// pages.ebay.com/securitycenter/index.html

- *PayPal.* Sign up for a PayPal account so you can send and accept electronic money payments from customers buying your products on eBay. ♂ https://www.paypal.com/ebay/buyer

- *EBay Insider.* The *eBay Insider* is a free monthly newsletter loaded with tips, tools, tricks, and stories for and from eBay users. You can also access past newsletter issues in the archives using the link below. ♂ http://pages. ebay.com/community/life/ebay-life-pA1.html

EBay Motors

For the most part, eBay and eBay Motors operate in a very similar fashion in terms of buyer and seller services and functions. The big difference is that eBay Motors categories revolve around vehicles, marine transportation, aviation transportation, and all related parts and accessories. If you sell cars, trucks, boats, planes, scooters, motorcycles, automotive parts and accessories, marine parts and accessories, recreational vehicles, trailers, and so on, then eBay Motors is a venue for you to list and sell through. Categories also extend to automotive collectibles and antiques such as gas station memorabilia. The popularity of eBay Motors continues to grow, mainly because they offer so many security tools aimed at protecting both buyers and sellers. Programs like eBay's Assurance Program, Financing Center, Shipping Center, and Insurance Center really do make purchasing vehicles online as easy as from any offline dealer or private seller. With eBay you will need to open an account and spend some time researching all of the tools they offer sellers for listing-promotion purposes. In short, check out everything the site and service has to offer before you get started because there is lots of helpful information there.

EBAY MOTORS SELLERS' FEES

- *Passenger and Other Vehicles.* Cars, trucks, recreational vehicles, and large power and sailboats pay a fixed listing fee of $40, plus a $40 transaction fee, but only if the vehicle receives a bid. No bid, no transaction fee.
- *Motorcycles and Power Sports Equipment.* Sellers of motorcycles and power sports equipment such as snowmobiles, all-terrain vehicles, scooters, and personal watercraft pay a $30 listing fee, plus a $40 transaction fee, but only if the vehicle receives a bid. No bid, no transaction fee.
- *Parts and Accessories.* Sellers of all categories of parts and accessories, including automotive, aviation, and marine, pay fees that are the same as for normal items on eBay, including insertion fees, reserve-price fees (if applicable), multi-item insertion fees (if applicable), and final sales value fees.

RESOURCES

- EBay Assurance Program: offers short-term power-train warranties and vehicle inspection services, ♂ http://pages.ebay.com/ebaymotors/services/ assurance.html.
- EBay Motors, ♂ www.ebaymotors.com.
- EBay Motors "How To" Center: learn how to sell cars, boats, motorcycles, recreational vehicles, and automotive accessories, ♂ http://pages.ebay.com/ ebaymotors/howto/overview.html.
- Financing Center: increase sales values by helping buyers secure financing, ♂ http://financing-center.ebay.com/.
- Insurance Center: provides free online insurance quotes and links to insurance agents and brokers, ♂ http://pages.ebay.com/ebaymotors/services/ insurancecenter.html.
- Vehicle Shipping: use the instant-quote feature to calculate vehicle shipping costs anywhere in the country, ♂ http://pages.ebay.com/ebaymotors/ services/das-shipping.html.

Your Own E-Commerce Web Site

You can also develop, build, and publish your own e-commerce Web site on the Internet, so you can sell your goods to a worldwide audience of consumers. The advantages of Internet marketing include having your store open 24 hours a day, sending information to customers in minutes—not hours, days, or weeks—and you can update or alter your marketing message and strategy quickly, conveniently, and very inexpensively.

However, I do not suggest an independent Web site as your sole means of selling products online. Instead, your Web site should be used in combination with other online sales and distribution methods such as eBay, e-storefronts, and Internet malls, as well as offline selling venues such as homebased sales, and mail order. Once you find the right marketing mix, then you can pour more resources into that area, but in the meantime, if you are going to sell online, eBay has to be included in your marketing plans.

Other considerations in posting a Web site include who will build, maintain, and host your site, and how much will all this cost? Also, you will need shopping carts, online payment systems, content, Web tools, and a strategy for promoting the site and your products. More information about building and promoting a Web site can be found in Chapter 3.

RESOURCES
- 1234 Find Web Designers, e-commerce and web designers directory, ♂ www.1234-find-web-designers.org
- eCommerce Times, e-commerce and marketing portal, providing daily news, features, advice, and links of interest, ♂ www.ecommercetimes.com.
- Top Ten Web Hosting, Web site hosting directory, ♂ www.toptenwebhosting.com

E-Storefronts and Internet Malls

The premise behind Internet malls is the same as that behind bricks-and-mortar shopping malls—create a central location comprised of many product and service retailers, and in doing so, offer consumers a one-stop shopping opportunity. In the bricks-and-mortar world, this means consumers can go to one location and purchase many of the goods and services they need. In cyberspace, the same holds true. Consumers can visit one online mall and buy many of the goods and services they need and want. There are a number of companies and services offering Internet mall and e-storefront programs. The big players in this arena are eBay, Amazon, and the Internet Mall, but there are also hundreds of smaller outfits offering numerous online retailing opportunities for the small e-tailer, and some of these I have listed in Resources.

Most Internet malls or e-storefront programs offer two basic types of services. One, they operate as a directory service listing product and/or service categories, and for a fee your business can be listed under one or more appropriate categories. This option means you already have or you are building your own Web site so you can link to the mall's directory. Two, the Internet malls and e-storefront services offer a more complete package, which can include one or more of the following: domain name registration, Web site building, hosting, e-commerce tools, back-end administration tools, and promotion. Of course, there are also programs that blend the two types according to your needs and budget. Fees vary widely depending on your level of participation and the services you sign up for, but they generally start at a few hundred dollars in development fees and with ongoing monthly fees ranging from $20 to $500.

If you will be selling from a homebased location, also check your local area because often you will find online malls that service specific cities or geographic regions comprised of local merchants and service providers. These community Web sites and Internet malls are a good option for selling focused on a specific geographic region. Moreover, you will probably have to combine many online retailing venues, as most online sellers do, to meet sales and marketing goals.

RESOURCES

- Active Plaza, e-storefront programs, ♂ www.activeplaza.com
- Amazon, e-storefront programs, ♂ www.amazon.com
- American Internet Mall, e-storefront programs, ♂ www.aimone.com
- Canadian Internet Mall, e-storefront programs, ♂ www.cdn-mall.com
- Internet Mall, e-storefront programs, ♂ www.internetmall.com
- Mall Park, e-storefront programs, ♂ www.mallpark.com
- Web Square, e-storefront programs, ♂ www.websquare.com

E-Auctions

In addition to eBay, there are many other online auction sites. They are listed in online auction directories, such as The Internet Auction list. Some of these sites are general auction sites with numerous categories ranging from collectibles to cars to electronics. Others are product-specific, such as fine art, boats, antiques, and sports memorabilia. Likewise, some operate on a highest-bid, reserve-bid, and/or Dutch auction format, depending on the site and products offered for sale. Most of the same marketing and promotional techniques you use on eBay to receive top dollar for your goods are portable, and can be applied to other online auction sites. People selling very specific items are encouraged to explore alternate auction services because they attract targeted buyers, which generally means you get a higher price. Without question, eBay is the undisputed king of all online multi-venue buy-and-sell marketplaces. But at the same time, you do not want to limit your buying and selling options to one single venue, especially if you can combine other options to complement eBay sales, thereby increasing your revenues and maximizing profits.

RESOURCES

- Auction Fire, general auction site, ✆ www.auctionfire.com
- Bid 4 Assets, general auction site, ✆ www.bid4assets.com
- Buy Sell Trades, general auction site, ✆ www.buyselltrades.com
- The Internet Auction List, directory listing over 2,000 Internet auction sites and auction companies, ✆ www.internetauctionlist.com
- Net Auctions, directory listing online and offline auction sales by type and auctioneers by specialty, ✆ www.net-auctions.com
- Online Auction Users' Association, ✆ www.auctionusers.org
- On Sale, general auction site, ✆ www.onsale.com
- Sell Whatever, general auction site, ✆ www.sellwhatever.com
- Yahoo Auctions, general auction site, ✆ www.auctions.yahoo.com

E-Classifieds

Advertising products for sale in online or electronic classifieds is the same as for print classifieds—you want descriptive ads that jump off the page and grab the attention of readers, are exposed to the right target audience, and include a call to action. That is, it motivates readers to contact you to buy. Just about every print newspaper now has an electronic edition with classified advertising opportunities. There are also a number of e-classified advertising opportunities that are available exclusively online. One of the biggest benefits of online classified advertising is you can include a link in your ad to direct readers to your Web site, eBay auction, e-storefront, or any other online location you want to send them to for further information or to buy. Additional benefits are: e-classifieds are cheap, and sometimes free; your ad can be posted in minutes instead of days; ads can be changed, altered, or deleted in minutes; and you can reach consumers worldwide. Here are a few tips:

- Pay a few dollars more to flag your ad with a bold border, animation, or other attention-grabbing devices. This will help your ad stand out from others.
- Get creative with your headline so you can catch the attention of skimmers.
- Advertise only in e-publications and classified-only sites frequented by your target audience.
- Use photographs whenever possible. They are invaluable.

RESOURCES

- *Adpost*, free and paid online classified ads, ✆ www.adpost.com

 – *Buy and Sell*, paid online classified ads, ✆ www.buysell.com
 – *Classifieds for Free*, free online classified ads, ✆ www.classifiedsforfree.com
 – *My Town Ads*, free and paid online classified ads, ✆ www.mytownads.com
 – *The Recycler*, free and paid online classified ads, ✆ www.recycler.com
 – *Sell.com Classifieds*, paid online classified ads, ✆ www.sell.com
 – *Thrifty Nickel*, free online classified ads, ✆ www.thriftynickleads.com
 – *U.S. Free Ads*, free online classified ads, ✆ www.usfreeads.com
 – *Yahoo Classifieds*, paid online classified ads, ✆ www.classifieds.yahoo.com

Homebased Sales

All across North America, signs are popping up in front of homes. But they are not for-sale signs; they are signs advertising home businesses and the products and services these homebased entrepreneurs sell. Almost all buy-and-sell ventures are operated or substantially managed from a homebased location. This section focuses on selling goods directly from home by utilizing interior showrooms, exterior display, garage sales, in-home sales parties, and selling direct to collectors, as well as simple and cost-effective advertising methods, such as classified advertising and fliers to promote homebased sales. One of the advantages of selling goods from home is that you can combine this method of distribution with so many others—online sales, flea markets, auctions, and vending at community events. There are also a great number of other advantages of selling from home, including no commute, tax advantages, and making the most out of existing resources. Of course, not every home is suited for sales, and some communities do not allow homebased businesses or sales at all. But for entrepreneurs who have suitable homes and products, homebased businesses have the potential to generate enormous revenues and profits.

Homebased Showrooms and Exterior Display

There are two basic methods to display and sell merchandise from home: an interior showroom or an exterior display. Depending on what you sell, you might choose to utilize both.

INTERIOR SHOWROOM

You can convert your garage, basement, den, or just about any room of your home into a well-stocked showroom. Ideally, the space you choose will have a separate entrance to afford privacy for your family. Display and merchandise your products just like a traditional retailer, taking advantage of display cases, racks, lighting, mirrors, and signage. Perfect products to sell from a homebased interior showroom include clothing, arts and crafts, jewelry, antiques, sporting goods, cookware, and computers. Be open daily, with fixed operating hours, weekend hours, or occasional hours—whatever suits your sales and marketing objectives.

EXTERIOR DISPLAY

Displaying products for sale outside your home is the second option, and a good one because you can receive a fair amount of interest from passing motorists and pedestrians. Perfect products to display outdoors include cars, small boats on trailers, RVs, patio furniture, greenhouses, sheds, and weathervanes. What you sell will determine the best places around the home to display items—cars in the driveway, patio furniture right on your own sundeck, greenhouses in the garden, and weathervanes adorning your roof line. Theft may become an issue, so be sure to install motion lights, fencing, and gates as required. Information about setting up a homebased workspace and additional homebased business issues can be found in Chapter 3. You might also want to visit your local library to check out *The Ultimate Homebased Business Handbook* (Entrepreneur Press, 2004). That book contains everything you need to know about starting and growing a homebased business venture.

Promoting Homebased Sales

If you are going to sell from home, consumers have to know what you sell, where you are located, and how they can contact you. Consequently, you will need to advertise, but wisely and on a small budget. For budget-minded entrepreneurs, the best and least expensive ways to promote homebased sales are with attention-grabbing signage, classified advertisements, fliers, and word-of-mouth. Detailed information about these and other sales and marketing topics can be found in Chapter 3. You might want to also visit your local library to check out *The Ultimate Small Business Marketing Guide* (Entrepreneur Press, 2003). That book contains over 1,500 sales and marketing ideas.

Providing local bylaws permit them, exterior signs are one of the best promotional tools for homebased sales. You can advertise what you sell, business hours, and regular specials for zero costs outside of routine maintenance once you have paid for your signs. Get started with two types of exterior signs; one stationary backlit sign to advertise your business and what you sell, and a portable sign with interchangeable letters so you can promote new products, sales, and special events.

Next in effectiveness is promoting your business and goods utilizing cheap and free classified advertisements. People seldom search the classifieds for entertainment purposes; they are usually looking to buy, which make them the buy-and-sell entrepreneur's best friend. Your ads should include a product description, contact information, a price, and an attention-grabbing device such as a border.

Fliers are the ultimate fast and frugal promotional tool for advertising your homebased sales and products. Providing you have a computer and basic design savvy, you can create your own fliers at home and have them copied for pennies each at your local copy center. Pin fliers to community bulletin boards, tuck them under parked cars' windshield wipers, or have them delivered door-to-door.

Finally, word-of-mouth advertising is the ultimate cheap source of highly effective advertising because it costs nothing. But how do you get it? Get out in the community, network, and tell people about your products. Sell high-quality products at fair prices. Provide incredible customer service. And never stop looking for innovative ways to deliver the types of goods your customers need and want.

Garage Sales

An estimated 60 million people go garage sale shopping annually in the United States. If each spent $20, total sales would rack up more than $1 billion dollars a year.

If you plan on hosting garage sales from home, the first step is to make sure you can do so legally. Most communities permit garage sales, but some don't. A call or visit to your municipal planning or bylaws office will supply the answer. Sometimes there are no regulations governing garage sales, other times you have to purchase a permit. Some communities don't allow signs, or they may limit them; some restrict the size, duration, and frequency of sales; and still some others have banned garage sales altogether because of parking and neighborhood traffic concerns.

You don't want neighbors calling city hall complaining every time you have a sale. This is best avoided by keeping sales professional, noise to a minimum, and not holding one every Saturday and Sunday. Of course, if neighbors can profit from your sales, all the happier they will be, so let them consign items. If sales are not permitted or if your home is not suitable for garage and yard sales, you can still participate by renting space at larger community sales. Charities, schools, churches, and sports clubs all routinely hold sales to raise revenues for any number of reasons, and most happily accept vendors willing to pay a small rent or a portion of their sales to the cause. Or you can partner with a friend or family member who does have a suitable location and share the work and profits.

A recent poll conduct by GarageSalePlannet.com asked garage sale enthusiasts what day of the week they liked best to go garage sale shopping. It was no surprise that Saturday was number one by a landslide, but Friday beat out Sunday for the number-two spot. Good information to keep in mind when planning your sale.

Of course, you want to know "What sells best at garage and yard sales?" First, all products in good clean working order, but more specifically power tools, hand tools, toys, sporting goods, kitchen items, glassware, things for babies, lawn and garden equipment, crafts and decorations, collectibles, books, music and movie disks, kids clothing, and adult designer clothes. Professional merchandising is also important, and if you are going to regularly hold garage sales, I suggest you invest in folding display tables, display cases with casters for easy transportation, and even a portable gazebo tent to keep both rain and sun off you, customers, and the merchandise. Skip having a sale every weekend. Instead, collect great items over time and hold a sale once a month. It won't take long for garage sale enthusiasts to spread the word about your monthly sales with great merchandise. Also, ask customers for their e-mail addresses so you can keep them informed when the next sale is taking place, as well as about the items for sale. Event promotion is also crucial to success, so have signs professionally made in the shape of an arrow pointing in the direction of your home with *"Garage Sale Today"* and your address printed on them. On the morning of the sale, attach balloons and streamers to your signs to make them stand out. Install the signs in a two-block radius around your home as well as around major intersections close to your home, but be sure to remove them immediately following the sale.

Many newspapers also allow free garage sale ads, so take advantage of these. Also print fliers promoting the event and post on community bulletin boards at supermarkets, gas stations, sports arenas, and libraries. Read other garage sale ads to get an idea what to write, but always include all the particulars such as date, time, place, and a description of a few of your best items for sale. Also add special instructions like *"Sale on, rain or shine"* or *"No early birds."*

Because you can never have enough tricks up your sleeve to aid in organizing and managing super garage and yard sales, here are 15 more great tips to get you started on your way to earning huge profits at your next sale.

1. Have one central checkout table stocked with tools that will speed purchase transactions and streamline your entire operation, making management a snap. These tools should include a calculator, a receipt book for customers who request a receipt, and packaging materials like string, rope, scissors, tape, boxes, newspaper (glassware), and plastic bags.

2. Garage sales can attract hundreds of shoppers during the course of a day, so give some thought about traffic flow and congestion. You want enough space so people do not feel crowded and leave without making a purchase.

Think wide aisles, big items displayed on the ground, smaller items displayed higher up, and two long lines of tables or a grid pattern to keep traffic flowing.

3. Garage sales also attract lots of drive-by shoppers who slow down to see what you have, and stop only if they see something of interest. Therefore, it is a good idea to display some of your best merchandise nearest the road—tools and outdoor power equipment to grab the attention of men, and kitchen items, antiques, and crafts to grab the attention of women.

4. Hold back some of the better merchandise to put out as the day goes on. This way you will always have stuff that will appeal to people coming late, so they will stay longer and browse and, with luck, impulse buy.

5. Whenever possible, try to sell items with their original packaging, manuals, and accessories, such as a remote control with the television. Doing so greatly increases the value and makes the item much easier to sell.

6. Always keep more expensive items grouped together so they are easier to watch to prevent five-finger discounts. Likewise, look inside items to make sure smaller items have not been hidden there. This is a favorite trick of thieves.

7. Never hold items for people who say they will be back to pick it up later unless you get a 50 percent deposit upfront. Most don't return, especially if they have not paid a deposit.

8. Create a sliding *scale of condition* for pricing: high-demand products in excellent shape should be priced at 50 to 70 percent of new costs, dropping to 20 to 30 percent for items not particularly indemand or in poor condition.

9. Don't hold your sale on a holiday weekend because there are generally too many other events going on that will keep shoppers away—unless you live in a resort area. Then holiday weekends are the best times to hold your sale.

10. To avoid sounding like a parrot and repeating prices all day long, price all items individually, unless you have many of the same, like records. Then you can create one sign—for example, "All records $5."

11. Only sell items in good working order—bicycle tires should be full of air, and upholstered furniture should be free of rips and stains. Have an electrical cord and batteries handy so people can test items and see them working. Televisions, radios, and similar items are best left on during the sale to prove they work. Items with engines should be working and easy to start.

12. Clean and press clothing before displaying and hang it on hangers. (Make up a sign advising that hangers are not included.) Also, check pockets to make sure nothing is inside.

13. When pricing, anticipate that people will want to haggle, so price items 10 to 20 percent higher to give you room to negotiate while still getting your price.

14. Don't accept checks, even with ID. Work on a cash-only basis, keep your money in a fanny pack or the like, and each time you reach $100 take it inside and put it in a safe.

15. Have an "ALL SALES FINAL" sign posted at your checkout table and printed on your receipts. You do not want people showing up at your door a day, week, or month later, trying to return something.

RESOURCES
   – Garage Sales Daily, directory listing U.S. garage sales, indexed by state, plus garage sale information and forums, ♂ www.garagesaledaily.com
   – Garage Sale Planet, directory listing U.S. garage sales, indexed by state, plus garage sale information and forums, ♂ www.garagesaleplanet.com
   – Local Yard Sales, directory listing Canadian garage sales, indexed by province, plus garage sale information and forums, ♂ www.localyardsales.com
   – Yard Sales Search, directory listing U.S. garage sales, indexed by state, plus garage sale information and forums, ♂ www.yardsalesearch.com

In-Home Sales Parties

Home sales parties are an excellent selling option for the right products. In a nutshell, you hire contract salespeople to organize and host parties right in their own homes to sell your products. You can also organize and host your own in-home sales parties. Salespeople can be paid a commission based on total sales; they can buy product from you wholesale and resell at retail, keeping the profit; or they can receive free products based on their total sales. There are numerous remuneration options. The biggest advantage of home party sales is zero competition. Salespeople have the undivided attention of party guests. In a few short hours sales agents can earn hundreds in profits, and so can you from their hard work. The best products to sell at home sale parties are clothing, books, cookware, jewelry, gifts, aromatherapy products, gourmet foods, and health products. Perfect candidates to recruit to your sales team are stay-at-home parents, students, retired folks, and anyone else looking to make extra money working from their home. Sales agents can take orders for products, which you can later ship from your central location. Or they can have product on hand for customers to take home. You will need to supply each with product samples, sales brochures, and a sales and operations manual that includes how they can organize and host the event.

Here are a few ways sales agents can boost sales and profit.

- Design and print $10 gift certificates and distribute one to each guest attending. But mark void if not used that night. Many people feel compelled to buy rather than risk losing a freebie.
- Offer additional savings at various purchase levels. For example, buy $50 worth of product and receive a $5 credit; $100 receives a $12 credit; and $200 receives a $30 credit toward the purchase of more product.
- Display your entire product line, not just a few items, and offer guests multiple ways to pay: check, cash, credit card, and debit card. Both will greatly increase impulse buying.
- Tell each guest that if they bring a friend, both will receive a 10 percent discount on all purchases.
- Offer free gift-wrapping at the party so people will feel compelled to purchase product as gifts for others not in attendance.
- Hold a contest and give away a prize at each party. Have guests complete an entry form, including full contact information, and draw for the prize. The entry forms may then be used to build a database of potential customers, who can be routinely contacted with special offers via e-mail, mail, and telephone.

Selling Direct to Collectors

If you are going to specialize in antiques and/or collectibles, you can also sell direct to collectors by exhibiting at collectible shows and sales, joining associations and clubs to network, and by consigning items to live and online antique and collectible auctions. More times than not, selling direct to collectors will garner the highest price, provided that you plan, are patient, and choose the right sales venue. Collectors are a fickle bunch. What's hot today is not necessarily hot and valuable tomorrow. Antique furniture seems to be the most stable in terms of value and gradual appreciation.

There are many factors determining how much you can sell antiques and collectibles for, including condition, rarity, special history (famous owners, etc.), and above all, what the marketplace will bear. Let's face it, few consumers have an extra $15,000 lying around to buy a 150-year-old Pennsylvania Dutch sideboard. Selling antiques and collectibles is as much about choosing the right sales venues and target audience as it is about the actual item, perhaps more so. Success comes to antique and collectible traders who pay close attention to what's going on in the marketplace at all times. Professional appraisals and authentications also help to substantiate and support asking prices. In many situations, having antique, collectible, and memorabilia items appraised and authenticated will greatly increase the value, especially authentication.

RESOURCES

- Antiques Central, directory featuring antiques shops, auctions, and individual collectors, ♂ www.antiques-central.com
- Collector Online, directory listing more than 1,100 collectors' clubs, indexed by category, ♂ www.collectoronline.com
- World Collectors, collectible links directory, ♂ www.worldcollectors net.com

6

THE BEST 202 THINGS YOU CAN BUY AND SELL FOR BIG PROFITS

In getting here, you have learned about business structure and registration, legal and financial issues facing the buy-and-sell entrepreneur, how and where to buy new and used products at low prices, and how and where to resell products for fantastic profits. But now the real fun begins. In this chapter you will discover the best 202 things to buy and sell. Actually, the title is misleading, because there are many more than 202 things featured. Some products have been grouped together under a single heading—for example, antiques, boating electronics, and sporting goods.

The criteria used to select the best things to buy and sell were based on a number of factors, including:

- Widely available new and used products
- In-demand products
- Products currently selling the best on eBay, and at flea markets and other sales venues
- Products with excellent profit potential

Keep in mind that you do not want to reinvent the wheel. There are no new inventions or innovative twists on current products. All items listed in this chapter are time-tested, proven best-sellers. That said, however, what will distinguish you from competitors are the hundreds of sales, marketing, and merchandising ideas found throughout this book. But in addition to knowing the best things to buy and sell, you also have to know what you might be best suited to buy and sell.

What "Things" Should You Buy and Sell

Not every person has the resources or knowledge needed to buy and sell all products listed in this chapter. Some are better equipped and better suited than others to buy and sell specific items. For example, if you have no interest or knowledge about outdoor power equipment, such as riding lawn mowers or chainsaws, you are well advised not to start a buy-and-sell enterprise specializing in these products. But don't worry. This chapter clearly illustrates that there is something for everyone to buy and sell. Ultimately, you will be the best judge of what things you are best suited to buy and sell, but there are five key issues to consider: knowledge, investment, location, health, and interest.

1. *Knowledge.* Knowledge is one of your biggest and most marketable assets in a buy-and-sell venture. The more you know about the product, industry, and people who are most likely to buy, the better off you will be. Capitalize on your knowledge by selling stuff you know about.
2. *Investment.* You need to have, or have access to, enough investment capital to get your buy-and-sell enterprise rolling and profitable. Some items listed are cheap to buy and very inexpensive to market, like sun-catchers, for example. Other things, like classic cars, will require you to have or have access to a substantial amount of investment capital to get started.
3. *Location.* Where you live will also have a bearing on the type of product(s) you sell. Obviously, if you live in Florida, buying and selling snowmobiles would not be a wise choice. Your home or apartment will also be a factor, especially if you plan to sell from a homebased showroom or need considerable storage space.

4. *Health*. Buying and selling can be strenuous work, and your health must be good enough to withstand the demands this enterprise will place on it. Buying and selling online is the easiest in terms of physical work, providing you are not packing and shipping heavy items. On the other hand, flea market vending can be very physically demanding work with all of the loading and unloading of merchandise.

5. *Interest*. You can have all of the aforementioned, but if you do not have an interest in the product(s) you intend to sell, then in all probability the venture will fail. It is tough to stay motivated when you do not like what you are doing, regardless of profit potential. Only buy and sell items that you have an interest in.

Use the Information in This Chapter

The information presented in this chapter is in brief synopsis format. The product is explained, along with the best buying and selling options, and helpful resources such as wholesaling sources, associations, price guides, and listing directories are provided. None of the resources presented in this chapter are meant to promote or endorse any company, association, product, or service. All resources are included simply as helpful tools to get you to the next level, should you decide to pursue any item(s) to buy and sell. You may elect to contact and even do business with sources listed, or you may choose not to. The decision is entirely up to you. However, I did endeavor to select only reputable companies, associations, products, and services to list as resources.

At the end of the day, you must be comfortable in the knowledge that you are doing business with reliable and honest sources. The only way this can be accomplished is through research. Learn everything you can about any company or organization you intend to do business with. All should be happy to answer questions and supply references. If not, look for companies that will. It is your time, money, and energy—all very valuable assets. Do your homework to protect these assets!

The Best 202 Things You Can Buy and Sell

Antiques

The potential to profit from buying and selling antiques is as great as the potential to lose money. Replicas, paying too much, and purchasing items in poor condition are just three of the hazards you need to hone your knowledge and skills to guard against if you choose to buy and sell antiques. However, those who do take the time required to become antique experts are usually rewarded with big profits and gratifying work. Antiques is a broad subject, so pick an area in which to specialize—furniture, art, farm implements, or architectural antiques. The best places to dig up antique treasures include garage sales, auctions, estate sales, and advertising placed by private sellers in the classifieds. Secondary buying sources will include flea markets, secondhand shops, and online marketplaces. Always take along your antiques-hunter toolbox, which should include antique value guides, camera, flashlight, magnifying glass, angled mirror, and measuring tape. The best way to sell for top dollar is directly to collectors via clubs, associations, and shows. Next to selling to collectors, list on eBay and online antique buy-and-sell marketplaces, sell at flea markets, and sell directly from a home showroom supported by local advertising.

 BUY
Auctions, Flea Markets, Garage Sales, Estate Sales, Classified Ads

 SELL
Collectors, B2B, Auctions, Homebased Sales, eBay, Flea Markets

 RESOURCES
—Antique and Collectibles Dealers Association, ✆ www.antiqueandcol lectible.com/acda.shtml
—Antiques Roadshow, advice and industry information, ✆ www.pbs.org/roadshow
—Go Antiques, buy-and-sell marketplace, ✆ www.goantiques.com
—Kovels Online, antique and collectibles information and resources, ✆ www.kovels.com
—The National Association of Antique Malls, ✆ www.antiqueandcol lectible.com/naam.shtml
— 📖 *Kovels' Antique & Collectible Price List*, 37th Edition, Ralph Kovel and Terry Kovel (Random House, 2004)

Entire Household Lots

Buying partial or entire household lots is a very interesting proposition. You get lower pricing because you are buying in quantity, paying less than you would for each piece bought individually. The downside is that you may end up purchasing items you would otherwise not normally bother buying, leaving you with slow-moving inventory. There are many reasons why a person would sell all or most of their personal belongings, including moving, downsizing after the kids leave, financial problems, or illness. Often when people are faced with liquidating belongings, it is easier to sell everything as one lot than it is to sell each item individually or hold a prolonged sale waiting for everything to sell. You can advertise in your local newspaper in the classifieds, informing readers that you purchase partial or entire household lots, everything from furniture to clothing and computers. Or wait for people to advertise, usually in the classifieds, all of their belongings for sale. You can also bid on entire household lots through estate-sales services. Regardless of the buying method you choose, you will need to have, or have access to, suitable means of transporting items purchased, along with sufficient storage space. Because your inventory will be varied, you can sell in a number of ways, including direct from a homebased showroom, flea market vending, online marketplaces such as eBay, and by holding monthly or quarterly auctions for selling all inventory at one time in one place.

BUY
Estate Sales, Classified Ads, Moving and Storage Companies

SELL
Flea Markets, Garage Sales, eBay, Auctions, Homebased Sales

RESOURCES
—Team Estate Sales, ☎ (901) 758-2659, ♂ www.teamestatesales.com
—📖 *Garage Sale & Flea Market Annual* (Collector Books, 2004)
—📖 *The Official Guide to Flea Market Prices*, Harry Rinker (Collector Books, 2004)

Major Appliances

I have sold or assisted in the marketing of everything from franchises to home improvements to recreational products, and many things in between. Two products stick out in my mind for having met with little resistance—roofing and household appliances. Both are things that people seldom think about until the inevitable happens and the roof leaks or an appliance goes kaput. Then it is not a question of how much, but how soon, because the need is urgent. I mention this because buying and selling used major appliances such as refrigerators, stoves, washers, and dryers is very much a game of patience, which when played correctly can be very profitable. Buy used appliances from private sellers through classified ads and auctions, and basically name the price you are willing to pay.

Used appliances are simply not products that people shop for unless there is an urgent need, and low demand equals low price. The same holds true for reselling these appliances at a profit. But there is one major difference—because you want to generate a profit, you must be patient and wait until the right buyer comes along with an urgent need for your goods. Then price will not be an obstacle. It also helps if you have basic mechanical aptitude, so that if minor repairs are needed, you have the ability to make them and to also sell all used appliances with a 30-day warranty, which greatly increases the value.

Buy
Auctions, Classified Ads, Wholesalers, Manufacturers

Sell
Homebased Sales

Resources
—Overstock B2B Wholesale, ☎ (800) 273-6063, 🖋 www.overstockb2b.com
—Lun Dar Manufacturing, ☎ 886-6-2328133 (Taiwan), 🖋 www.general-electric-appliance.com

New Furniture

Because new furniture is a broad category, including many types, styles, construction materials, and uses, you may want to specialize in one or two specific types. An entrepreneur in my area specializes solely in selling new pine furniture and only from his home, which he has set up as a showroom utilizing many rooms in the house for specific furniture, such as the living room for couch and chair sets, the dining room for dining room sets, and so on. He refers to the business as *The King of Pine*. He purchases from local manufacturers, and judging by the large amount of advertising he does, the business appears to be thriving. In addition to homebased sales, also sell online and at home-and-garden shows. Wholesale purchasing sources include United States and overseas furniture manufacturers, wholesalers, and local craftspeople.

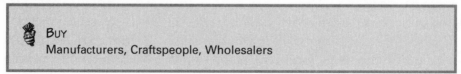

Buy
Manufacturers, Craftspeople, Wholesalers

SELL
Consumer Shows, Homebased Sales, Temporary Locations

 RESOURCES
—American Furniture Manufacturers Association, www.afma4u.org
—Custom Design Manufacturing, ☎ (323) 234-6810, www.custom designfurniture.org
—Hansen Wholesale, ☎ (800) 365-3267, www.hansenwholesale.com
—Indonesian Furniture Manufacturers Directory, www.eastjava.com/furniture

Secondhand Furniture

You can still cash in on the big bucks selling furniture, but greatly reduce your investment by buying and selling only secondhand furniture. As with new furniture, your selling options will include a homebased showroom, flea market vending, auction sales, and even eBay if you happen to purchase a rare, cool, retro, or otherwise valuable piece of secondhand furniture you know will command top dollar when exposed to a global audience of consumers. Buying sources for secondhand furniture include private sellers advertising in the classifieds, ads on notice boards, estate sales, garage sales, moving sales, and moving and storage companies. To maximize your profits, make sure all furniture is fit to sell by thoroughly cleaning before selling. The investment made in furniture polish, the odd repair, and an upholstery steam-cleaning machine will be well rewarded by increased selling prices and overall profitability.

 BUY
Garage Sales, Classified Ads, Auctions, Estate Sales, Moving and Storage Companies

 SELL
Homebased Sales, Flea Markets

 RESOURCES
—Best Consignment Shop Inventory Software, www.best consignment shopsoftware.com
—Flea Market USA, national flea market directory, indexed by state, www.fleausa.com

Home Electronics

Great profits can be earned buying and selling new and used home electronics equipment, such as DVD players, amplifiers, speaker systems, home theater systems, and even commercial electronics such as DJ equipment and PA systems. New electronics equipment can be purchased from wholesalers, and the larger the quantity you purchase, especially pallet lots, the lower your individual unit cost goes. Used electronics equipment can be bought from classified ads, at garage sales, and auctions. Advertise in the classifieds and on community bulletin boards, rent flea market vendor space, and list your items for sale in numerous online marketplaces and auctions. There are two things to remember when selling your equipment live at venues like a flea market: have access to power and a cord to prove equipment works, and give all of your inventory a good cleaning before displaying. Clean merchandise in good working order sells fast, and for top dollar.

 BUY
Wholesalers, Manufacturers, Classified Ads, Auctions

 SELL
Flea Markets, eBay, Kiosks, Homebased Sales

 RESOURCES
—1 AAA Wholesale Liquidators, ☎ (800) 661-9430, ♂ www.1aaawhole saleliquidators.com
—Dollar Days Wholesale, ☎ (877) 837-9569, ♂ www.dollardays.com
—Open Box USA Wholesale, ☎ (877) 673-6872, ♂ www.openbox usa.com

Specialty Rugs

Specialty-area rugs and runners with an international flavor are hot home décor accessories, and you can make a small fortune in your spare time purchasing Oriental, Indian, and Persian rugs wholesale, direct from the factory, or secondhand, and reselling them for top dollar to savvy collectors, interior designers, and homeowners. A word of caution, though: if you are new to specialty carpets, make sure that you educate yourself about the product before jumping in with both feet. Specialty carpets are available in many designs, quality levels, and price points; it requires knowledge of the product to spot and buy a great carpet from among the duds, especially when you consider that a Persian Gabbeh-area rug retails for over $5,000.

BUY
Manufacturers, Classified Ads, Auctions, Wholesalers

 SELL
Collectors, Online Marketplaces, Home Shows, Homebased Sales, B2B

 RESOURCES
—Floor Biz, directory of worldwide rug manufacturers and distributors,
⚲ www.floorbiz.com
—Laodica Manufacturing, ☎ 90-332-332-1211 (Turkey), ⚲ www.laod
ica.com
—Maqsood Oriental Rug Manufacturing, ☎ 92-42-7569195 (Pakistan),
⚲ www.maqsrug.com
—📖 *Instant Expert: Collecting Oriental Rugs*, Joyce C. Ware (Collector
Books, 2003)

Lighting

At first glance, lamps and lighting products may seem to be a strange item to buy and sell. But when you consider the wide variety and the numerous uses of lighting products, it quickly becomes apparent why this opportunity is exciting. Think of the range of products, ordinary and specialized—emergency lighting, ceiling lighting, table lamps, track lighting, rope and tube lights, patio lighting, underwater lights, fiber optics, holiday and decorative lighting, grow lighting, monorail light systems, and floodlights. Not to mention collectible lighting, where even a reproduction Tiffany Studio lamp sells for as much as $1,000, and the real thing from the Stickley era for ten times that amount. There are also large numbers of potential customers—homeowners, architects, renovators, retailers, restaurateurs, interior designers, contractors, electrical contractors, collectors, spa owners, and more. New lighting and lamps can be purchased from wholesalers and manufacturers, while used collectible lighting fixtures and lamps can be purchased at garage sales, flea markets, auctions, and online.

 BUY
Manufacturers, Wholesalers, Garage Sales

 SELL
EBay, Flea Markets, Collectors, Kiosks, B2B

RESOURCES
—Build Direct Wholesale, ☎ (877) 631-2845, ♂ www.builddirect.com
—Hansen Wholesale, ☎ (800) 201-1193, ♂ www.hansenwholesale.com
—National Association of Independent Lighting Distributors, ♂ www.naild.org

Real Estate

Many savvy entrepreneurs earn seven-figure incomes buying and selling real estate. As a rule they look for three types of buying opportunities: foreclosures, motivated sellers, or paint, putter, and profit opportunities. That is, the best real estate buys occur when you can purchase a foreclosed property for far less than market value; you negotiate an incredibly low buying price because the seller is very motivated by health, financial, or another reason(s); or you buy the worst house on the best street, well undervalued, and carry out minor repairs and cosmetic fix-ups so you can flip the property for a profit.

There are also things these same savvy entrepreneurs do not do. They never buy vacant land because it can not generate income (rent) until resold. They use everyone's money but their own, through mortgage takeovers, vendor financing options, equity leverage, and 100 percent financial institution options. And they never sell for less than they have invested, because they do the required homework before buying, negotiate the lowest price, and prepare the house to be sold for top dollar.

There are literally hundreds of real-estate-buying books, programs, and training seminars available to show you how to buy and sell for a profit. Some are good, while others are a waste of money. However, what does hold true is that you cannot just simply jump in with both feet and hope for the best. You have to acquire the knowledge needed to make smart investments, which can be easily resold to return your investment and a profit. This takes time, research, and education to accomplish, but is well worth the investment of time and money.

 BUY
Foreclosure Sales, Classified Ads, Estate Sales

 SELL
Classified Ads, Auctions, Real Estate Brokers, Online Marketplaces

RESOURCES
—Foreclosure Free Search, online database listing REO, HUD, VA, Fan-
nie Mae, Bank, and mortgage company real estate foreclosures
indexed by state, ♂ www.foreclosurefreesearch.com
—Real Estate Foreclosures, online database listing REO, HUD, VA, Fan-
nie Mae, Bank, and mortgage company real estate foreclosures
indexed by state, ♂ www.realestateforeclosures.net
—Real Estate Investing, online community serving small real estate
investors with industry information, resources, and links, ♂ www.
realestateinvesting.com
— *Flipping Properties: Generate Instant Cash in Real Estate*, Robert
Dahlstrom and William Bronchick (Dearborn Trade, 2001)
— *Making Big Money Investing in Foreclosures*, David Finkel and
Peter Conti (Dearborn Trade, 2003)

Vacation Timeshares

Buying and selling vacation timeshares is not for everyone. It requires incredibly sharp negotiation skills, liberal use of high-pressure sales tactics, and strong closing proficiency. There is no shortage of timeshares to purchase—an estimated 200,000 timeshares are for sale at any one given time in the United States alone, not including developer sales of new timeshares. In fact, it is more than possible to buy timeshares for nothing, zip, not a dime outside of deed transfer costs, and sometimes not even that. Why? Simply because timeshares are difficult to resell, and many people want to get out from under the ongoing membership or maintenance fees charged to manage and maintain resorts, buildings, and units.

When buying, there are a few key issues to keep in mind. Only buy units with prime weeks (Red)—generally December through March—in prime areas such as Florida, California, and Hawaii. The closer to beaches and major tourist attractions the better. In terms of price negotiations, if you have to pay, drive a hard bargain and request that owners pay all transfer fees. There are a number of online timeshare marketplaces where you can buy and sell. I recently read an article about a very clever entrepreneur who was taking over for free, buying up low-cost timeshares, and trading them for antiques, cars, boats, and basically anything else people were willing to trade. He would then resell the traded items, which are easier to sell than a timeshare.

BUY
Online Marketplaces, Real Estate Brokers, Classified Ads

 SELL
Web Sites, Online Marketplaces, Specialty Publications, Real Estate Brokers

 RESOURCES
—Sell My Timeshare Now, buy-and-sell marketplace, ♂ www.sellmy timesharenow.com
—Timeshare Resales, buy-and-sell marketplace, ♂ www.timesharesre sales.com
—Timeshare Transfer, legal services, ☎ (877) 414-9083, ♂ www.time sharetransfer.com
—The Timeshare Users' Group, buy-and-sell marketplace, ♂ www. tug2.net
—Timeshares, buy-and-sell marketplace, ♂ www.timeshares.com
— 📖 *The Timeshare Beat*, daily online e-newspaper with a circulation of two million, ☎ (808) 946-2800, ♂ www.thetimesharebeat.com
— 📖 *Timeshare for Beginners*, Michael Strauss (Vantage Press, 2001)

Vacuum Cleaners

New and used vacuums are terrific buy-low, sell-high items. Built-in, canister, upright, portable, workshop, backpack, and cordless vacuum cleaners are available for a wide range of uses. The best buying sources for new vacuum cleaners include wholesalers and liquidators. Used vacuum cleaners are generally available for purchase at auctions, through classified ads, and at garage sales, though some legwork will be needed to track down the best bargains. Sell from a homebased showroom, on eBay, at home-and-garden shows, and at flea markets. Residential models that hold their value best, and not surprisingly also the easiest to sell, are Electrolux and Kirby. Both have great reputations and are always in demand by consumers willing to pay top dollar for models in good working order with all the bells and whistles.

 BUY
Wholesalers, Manufacturers, Garage Sales, Classified Ads

SELL
Homebased Sales, Online Marketplaces, Flea Markets

 RESOURCES
—1 AAA Wholesale Liquidators, ☎ (800) 661-9430, ✂ www.1aaawhole
saleliquidators.com
—Liquidation Merchandise, ☎ (800) 574-5304, ✂ www.liquidationmer
chandise.com
—Shop-Vac ® Industrial Manufacturing, ☎ (570) 326-0502, ✂ www.shop
vac.com

Air-Filter Systems

Indoor air quality is a major concern for many people, especially those suffering from allergies and other breathing ailments. The Environmental Protection Agency says it is possible for air inside homes and offices to be as much as five times more toxic than outdoor pollutants, because of the energy-tight construction of many new homes and buildings. The solution is air purifiers and filters to clean the air and kill bacteria, mildew, pollen, and dust. There are basically two types of air-filter systems—fixed models attached to furnaces and air conditioning units, and portable units that can be plugged into any wall outlet and placed on the floor or tabletop. I would suggest you buy and sell portable units, so you need not be concerned with installation issues. Portable air-filter systems are available in many sizes, styles, and price points, and serve many different purposes. They are available from a number of manufacturing and wholesale sources, including the ones featured below. Sell from a homebased showroom supported by local advertising and networking, as well as directly to businesses and offices in your community, online through eBay and other e-commerce portals, and by displaying at home shows.

 BUY
Wholesalers, Manufacturers

 SELL
B2B, eBay, Consumer Shows, Kiosks

RESOURCES
—Comtech Research Manufacturing, ☎ (417) 452-2237, ♂ www.negative
iongenerators.com
—Hansen Wholesale, ☎ (800) 365-3267, ♂ www.hansenwholesale.com
—Heaven Fresh Wholesale, ☎ (866) 625-1857, ♂ www.heavenfresh.ca
—National Air Filtration Association, ♂ www.nafahq.org

Water Purifiers

Selling water purification and filtering systems from home, online, and at home shows is a fantastic way to supplement your income or even replace your current income altogether. Twenty years ago if someone had told you bottled water would one day cost the same as gasoline, I am sure you would have thought this person was crazy. Here we are in the 21st century and spring water does cost as much as gas and soon, no doubt, more. Next to natural spring water, the best way to provide safe and clean drinking water for the family is to install a water purification system in your home. Water purifiers can be costly inline systems or inexpensive under-counter or countertop filters. There are also portable filters for camping and the cottage, marine and RV water purifiers, and water filters for the bath, showerhead, and even the garden hose. Buying sources at up to 50 percent off retail include factory direct from the manufacturer and through wholesalers and distributors of water purifiers. Selling methods include direct-to-businesses for commercial filter systems, exhibiting at home-and-garden shows for residential, a homebased showroom supported by local advertising, and online sales via your own Web site and online marketplaces. If you have the skills and tools, extra money can be earned by installing the under-counter and inline systems, offering customers a convenient, one-stop shopping package.

 BUY
Wholesalers, Manufacturers

 SELL
B2B, eBay, Consumer Shows, Kiosks

 RESOURCES
—Aquasana Manufacturing, ☎ (817) 536-5250, ♂ www.aquasana.com

—Crystal Quest Wholesale, ☎ (888) 363-9842, ✆ www.crystalquest.com

—Pure Earth Technologies Wholesale, ☎ (800) 669-1376, ✆ www.pure-earth.com

Houseplants

In addition to buying houseplants from wholesale nurseries or direct from growers, you can also set up your own interior or exterior greenhouse and grow your own plants for sale. Of course, this is provided you have a green thumb, space, and available investment capital. Regardless of whether you buy wholesale or grow your own, great profits can be earned selling houseplants at home -and-garden shows, flea markets, mall kiosks, and directly from home, supported by local advertising and word-of-mouth referrals. If you decide to grow plants, you can also sell to plant wholesalers, and directly to retailers such as convenience and grocery stores on a wholesale basis. To help boost revenues and profits, also sell plant accessories such as pots and containers, plant stands, hanging baskets, fertilizer, soil, peat moss, and perlite.

🐛 BUY
Wholesale Nurseries, Growers, Grow Your Own

🤝 SELL
Kiosks, Flea Markets, Homebased Sales, B2B

🏚 RESOURCES
—The Plant Ranch, ☎ (800) 344-8733, ✆ www.plantranchco.com
—Specimen House, ☎ (760) 944-1193, ✆ www.specimen-house.com
—Z Plants, ☎ (800) 226-2336, ✆ www.zplantsinc.com

Cookware

Clever entrepreneurs can earn big bucks buying and selling kitchen cookware, especially if you enlist contract salespeople to organize and host cookware sales parties in their own homes. Buy cookware at low discount prices from wholesalers, liquidators, and directly from North American and overseas manufacturers. In addition to in-home sales parties, cookware can also be sold on eBay and other online marketplaces, at flea markets, home-and-garden shows, mall kiosks, and via mail order. If you specialize in commercial cookware, you can sell directly to restaurants. Join cooking clubs in your area to network for business, and participate in online cooking forums, and consider Web rings to network for business from around the globe. It is not uncommon for cookware to be marked up by 50 to 100 percent for retail sale. Aim to sell $10,000 worth per month and your profit will be in the $3,000 to $5,000 range.

 BUY
Manufacturers, Wholesalers

 SELL
Home Parties, Kiosks, Online Marketplaces, Flea Markets

 RESOURCES
—The Cookware Manufacturers Association, ✆ www.cookware.org
—Dollar Days Wholesale, ☎ (877) 837-9569, ✆ www.dollardays.com
—Liquidation Merchandise, ☎ (800) 574-5304, ✆ www.liquidationmer chandise.com

Pottery

European, Mexican, Asian, American, and British pottery varies by style and quality, depending on production region. However, what does not vary is the huge demand for functional and decorative pottery, regardless of origin. Planting pots, window boxes, picture frames, stoneware, jugs, plaques, vases, candlesticks, decorative tiles—the list goes on and on because just about any product can be made from pottery. Buying sources for new pottery include manufacturers producing mass quantities, wholesalers and liquidators, and local and overseas craftspeople. Sources for buying used pottery include the usual suspects—garage sales, flea markets, online marketplaces, estate sales, and auctions. New or used, sell on eBay, through home-and-garden shows, at flea markets, and right from your own home pottery showroom promoted by local advertising.

 BUY
Wholesalers, Manufacturers, Auctions, Garage Sales, Craftspeople

 SELL
Collectors, Flea Markets, Kiosks, Home Shows, eBay

RESOURCES
—Arizona Pottery Manufacturing, ☎ (800) 420-1808, ♂ www.arizona
pottery.com
—The Polish Pottery Shop Manufacturing, ☎ (888) 254-2119, ♂
www.polishpotteryshop.com
—Pottery Auction, new and used buy-and-sell marketplace, ♂ www.pottery
auction.com
—Pottery Bali Exports, ☎ 62-22720-8772 (Indonesia), ♂ www.pottery-
bali.dodcraft.com
— 📖 *Antique Trader: American & European Art Pottery Price Guide*,
Kyle Husfloen (Krause Publications, 2002)

Tableware

Selling new and vintage table and glassware is inexpensive to get started and has great income potential. Vintage tableware by Wedgwood, Royal Doulton, Homer Loughlin, and colorful Fiestaware can be purchased at garage sales, flea markets, estate sales, and auction, though a little detective work will be required to unearth the true treasures. Investing in glass and tableware price guides would be wise and prove an invaluable tool for establishing buying and selling prices. Once acquired, resell directly to collectors via the numerous online collectibles Web sites and list on eBay. The lowest price source for new table and glassware is factory direct, right from the manufacturer in large quantities, and wholesalers and liquidators for smaller quantities and super deals on end-of-pattern runs. New tableware can be sold through eBay, at flea markets, and consumer shows. You might also consider hiring salespeople to organize and host table and glassware sales parties right in their homes.

BUY
Manufacturers, Wholesalers, Garage Sales, Auctions

SELL
Home Parties, eBay, Kiosks, Flea Markets, Web Site

RESOURCES
—Fiesta Discounts Wholesale, ☎ (507) 427-3852, ♂ www.fiestadis
counts.com
—Image Imports, ☎ (877) 676-8222, ♂ www.imageimports.com

> —International Housewares Association, directory listing tableware manufacturers, sales agents, importers, and wholesalers, ☎ (447) 692-0109, ♂ www.housewares.org
> —Vance Kitira International Wholesale, ☎ (800) 646-6360, ♂ www.vance kitira.com
> —📖 *Fifty Years of Collectible Glass 1920-1970, Easy Identification and Price Guide: Tableware, Kitchenware, Barware, and Water Sets*, Thomas H. Bredehoft and Neila M. Bredehoft (Krause Publications, 1997)

Crystal

Waterford, Swarovoski, Wedgwood, Hallmark, and Faberge are producers of some of the world's finest crystal ornaments, picture frames, toasting glasses, figurines, server sets, candleholders, bells, and more. New or used, crystal is always in demand and a super hot seller. Buy from wholesalers and producers if you want to focus on selling new crystal, and buy at garage sales, collectibles shows, online marketplaces, and auctions if you want to focus on buying and selling used and antique crystal collectibles. Sales of both can be conducted on eBay, at consumer and collectible shows, mall kiosks, and flea markets, and through online wedding gift registries.

 BUY
Auctions, Wholesalers, Manufacturers, Garage Sales, Classified Ads

 SELL
Kiosks, Collectors, Auctions, Flea Markets, Consumer Shows, eBay

 RESOURCES
—Austrian Crystal Wholesale, ☎ (412) 795-1671, ♂ www.austrian-crystal.com
—Cut Crystal Wholesale, ☎ (574) 323-2503, ♂ www.cutcrystal.com
—📖 *Crystal Stemware Identification and Price Guide*, Bob Page and Dale Frederiksen (Collector Books, 1997)

Silverware

All things silver are fantastic buy-and-sell items, including flatware and chests, server sets, frames, and ornaments made of sterling, stainless, silver plate, and pewter. You can specialize in either new or used silverware, or combine the two. New silverware can be purchased from wholesalers, distributors, manufacturers, and liquidators, while used silverware can be purchased at garage sales, at auctions, and from private sellers advertising in the classifieds. Both new and used silverware can be sold through numerous online marketplaces (including eBay), by renting vending space at flea markets, and directly to collectors for rarer products such as a Georg Jensen Pyramid sterling silverware set valued at $6,000. Like any retail venture, the keys to success will be identifying your target market, reaching your target audience, grabbing the attention of your target market, and giving them valid reason to take action and buy. The reasons can include the best products, the best prices, special incentives, or any combination of those reasons. Also make sure that you advertise your business at online wedding sites and that you become an official wedding gift registry merchant.

Buy
Auctions, Wholesalers, Manufacturers, Garage Sales, Classified Ads

Sell
Kiosks, Collectors, Auctions, Flea Markets, Consumer Shows, eBay

Resources
—Belirams Silversmiths, ☎ 91-11-24656092 (India), ♂ www.belirams.com
—Designer Smith Inc., ☎ 91-591-2490678 (India), ♂ www.indiamart.com/designer-smith
—Silver Warehouse Wholesale, ☎ (816) 454-1990, ♂ www.silverwarehouse.com
—📖 *The Standard Encyclopedia of American Silverplate: Flatware and Hollow Ware Identification and Value Guide*, Frances M. Bones and Lee Roy Fisher (Collector Books, 1999)

Figurines

There is big money to be made buying and selling both new and collectible figurines—novelty, animals, advertising, Victorian Staffordshire, and more. All sell like crazy. Buy the most popular brand-name new figurines by Disney, Precious Moments, Cherished Teddies, and Hummel wholesale, and resell these online, and at flea markets, mall kiosks, and gift shows. Most can be purchased for 50 percent less than wholesale and off-brand figures for up to 80 percent off retail, making them very profitable. Vintage and collectible figurines by noble makers such as Royal Doulton and Wedgwood can be found at garage sales, auction sales, and estate sales, though you'll need to be a bit of a detective to uncover the best bargains. Antique figurines can be sold to collectors via antique shows, auctions, and eBay.

 BUY
Auctions, Wholesalers, Manufacturers, Garage Sales, Classified Ads

 SELL
Kiosks, Collectors, Auctions, Flea Markets, Consumer Shows, eBay

 RESOURCES
—Great Gifts Galore Wholesale, ☎ (859) 643-2082, ♂ www.giftgalore.com
—HJ Liquidators, ☎ (800) 875-7717, ♂ www.surplus.net/hj
—The Online Collector, database of figurine collectors and dealers, ♂ www.theonlinecollector.com/figurines.html
—📖 *Royal Doulton Figurines Book,* Jean Dale (Charlton Press, 2004)

Used Vehicles

Not everybody can afford to spend $30,000 on a new car. Because of this, the market for good-quality used vehicles is very strong. This is great news for entrepreneurs who decide to buy and sell used vehicles as a way to earn a living or supplement their existing income. Keep in mind, however, that mechanical repairs are very expensive, so buying and selling used vehicles is definitely best left to people who have mechanical aptitude and can thoroughly inspect vehicles to ensure they are in good working order before buying them.

Used vehicles can be purchased at auctions, from private sellers, and from car dealers who take in trades, but only resell late-model vehicles on their own lot. Dealers wholesale the older vehicles to other people to resell to the public. To maximize profits, try to buy off-season—SUVs in the spring and summer, and convertibles and sports cars in the fall and winter. Doing so can net you an additional 10 percent or more. Also go out of your way to clean up every vehicle prior to selling—polish the glass, vacuum the carpets, touch up the paint, and steam-clean the upholstery. Such little actions can increase the sales value by 10 percent or more.

Some areas of the United States and Canada have laws that prohibit nonlicensed car dealers, often referred to as curb-siders, from buying and selling cars. Make sure that you check into the legal issues in your area prior to getting started.

BUY
Auctions, Classified Ads, For-Sale Signs, Car Dealers

 SELL
Homebased Sales, Online Marketplaces, Consignment Lots

 RESOURCES
—Trader Publications, print and electronic classified advertising, ♂ www.autotrader.com
—Used Cars, buy-and-sell marketplace, ♂ www.usedcars.com
—📖 *Blackbook National Auto Research*, automotive pricing guides, ☎ (800) 554-1026, ♂ www.blackbookusa.com
—📖 *The Used Car Money Machine*, Robert Cohill (Dorrance Publishing, 2003)

Classic Cars

Many classic-car enthusiasts are prepared to pay top dollar to relive their youth or to finally reward themselves for years of hard work by buying the car of their dreams. And because demand is high, prices have exploded into the high five and in some cases, six-figure range for prized classic cars. A 1960 Porsche 356 Roadster in great shape will set you back about $40,000. A 1969 Plymouth Road Runner Hemi about $60,000, and if you are looking for a 1969 L-89 Corvette in mint condition, be prepared to write a check for more than $100,000. Perhaps these are extreme examples, and yes, great classic cars can still be purchased for under $15,000. Nonetheless, as time goes on, these former kings of the highways will only continue to increase in popularity and value.

Buying and selling classic cars is not for the faint of heart or for romantic types. You need to be educated about cars and especially about the condition, mechanical soundness, and value of collector cars. Buying sources will include estate sales, classified ads, auctions, classic-car shows, and online marketplaces. Selling will be by many of the same forums, plus direct to collectors. Also keep in mind that classic-car values in other countries can be different from those at home, which can also provide numerous additional buying and selling opportunities. For instance, Canadians buying classic cars in Canada and reselling them in the U.S. are earning an additional 30 percent on each sale because of the stronger American dollar.

BUY
Classified Ads, Auctions, For-Sale Signs

 SELL
Collectors, Homebased Sales, Online Marketplaces, Auctions, Swap Meets

 RESOURCES
—Buy Classic Cars, buy-and-sell marketplace, ♂ www.buyclassic cars.com
—Classic Car, serving the classic-car industry and enthusiasts, ♂ www.classiccar.com
—📖 *NADA Guides*, classic-car price guides, ☎ (800) 966-6232, ♂ www.nadaguides.com

Automobilia and Petroliana

Everything old is new again, and automobilia and petroliana collectibles are no exception, especially automotive and gas station antiques from the golden era of 1930 to 1960. Items such as traffic lights, highway signs, car owner manuals, books, magazines, hood ornaments, license plates, gas station uniforms, gas station signs, gas pumps, and gas station product displays are selling like crazy to people looking to add to their collections and others who are searching for nifty home and office decorations. Buy automobilia and petroliana collectibles at garage sales, flea markets, auctions, and numerous online marketplaces catering to old car and gas station buffs. In turn, sell on eBay, at auto shows and swap meets, and directly to collectors via automotive clubs and associations.

 BUY
Garage Sales, Online Marketplaces, Flea Markets, Auctions

 SELL
Collectors, eBay, Auctions, Flea Markets, Swap Meets, Homebased Sales

 RESOURCES
—The Gas Station & Auto Service Collectibles Web Site, industry information, links, and classifieds, ♂ www.oldgas.com
—📖 *Encyclopedia of Petroliana Identification and Price Guide*, Mark Anderson (Krause Publications, 2002)
—📖 *An Illustrated Guide to Gas Pumps Identification and Price Guide*, Jack Sim (Krause Publications, 2002)

Automotive Electronics

North American consumers spent more than $2 billion last year on automotive electronics such as stereos, alarms, DVD players, and onboard GPS devices, making this one of the fastest-growing segments of the automotive industry. So if you are looking to get started with buying and selling, automotive electronics may be just the right product for you. I would suggest that you stick with new electronics purchased wholesale from distributors and liquidators and avoid used merchandise. This is because in order to justify your time, you need to generate a base amount of profitable revenues, which may not be achievable dealing in used automotive electronics. Sell your goods at auto shows and swap meets, on eBay, during community events from a vendor booth, and at weekend flea markets. Also make sure when you sell live that you have functioning products on display—stereos that can be turned up loud, GPS devices that can be tested, and movies playing on automotive DVD players. The extra expense to set up these types of displays will be rewarded with increased interest in your goods and ultimately more sales. Shopping is not a spectator sport. The more excited and involved you get your prospects in the buying process, the more likely they are to buy.

Buy
Wholesalers

Sell
Auto Shows, Kiosks, Online Marketplaces, Flea Markets, Swap Meets

Resources
—Overstock B2B Wholesale, ☎ (800) 273-6063, ♂ www.overstock b2b.com
—Sylvester Electronics Wholesale, ☎ (800) 388-7344, ♂ www.sylves.com
—Vision Wholesale, ☎ (877) 379-7983, ♂ www.visionwholesale.com

Automobile Cleaning Products

The love affair with our cars does not end at the dealership. In fact, this is the beginning point; from there we spend on custom-auto appearance parts, stereos, and lots and lots of interior and exterior automobile cleaners, degreasers, polishes, and waxes. Automobile cleaning products and equipment is big business, and cashing in on the demand is very easy. Buy at rock-bottom prices from wholesalers, distributors, and manufacturers. Sell for top dollar at auto shows, on eBay and eBay Motors, at swap meets and flea markets, and through mail order advertising in automotive publications. When selling these products live, make sure you demonstrate how well they work. When people can see the benefits of a product firsthand, resistance to the sale becomes almost nonexistent.

Buy
Wholesalers

Sell
Auto Shows, Kiosks, Online Marketplaces, Flea Markets, Swap Meets

Resources
—AAA Overstock Wholesale, ☎ (800) 567-9258, ♂ www.aaaoverstock.com
—DuraGloss Manufacturing, ☎ (800) 638-7245, ♂ www.duragloss.com
—Lane's Professional Car Products, ☎ (866) 798-9011, ♂ www.car-waxes.com

Motorcycles

Motorcycles are an excellent buy-and-sell item, especially in the northern states and Canada where you can get amazing off-season deals and then wait until spring to earn as much as a 50 percent return on your initial investment, or ship them south and make a handsome profit right away. You can buy and sell street bikes, on-road/off-road motorcycles, dirt bikes, and all types of new and used motorcycle accessories such as helmets, leathers, carriers, bags, and windscreens. Concentrate on buying used motorcycles in good condition that may need a good cleaning and perhaps a few minor repairs or a tune-up. Best private-seller buying sources are for-sale signs, classified ads, auction sales, and estate sales. The best selling venues are a homebased showroom, online marketplaces like eBay Motors, and specialty publications. Motorcycle accessories can be sold at motorcycle shows and swap meets, online, and at flea markets. There are numerous selling options, giving you many ways to sell for big profits.

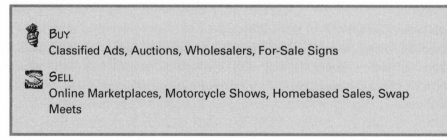

Buy
Classified Ads, Auctions, Wholesalers, For-Sale Signs

Sell
Online Marketplaces, Motorcycle Shows, Homebased Sales, Swap Meets

RESOURCES
—Hap Jones Wholesale, ☎ (209) 836-2782, ♂ www.hapjones.com
—Motorcycle Accessory Warehouse Wholesale, ☎ (800) 241-2222, ♂ www.accwhse.com
—*Trader Publications*, print and electronic classified advertising, ♂ www.cycletrader.com
— 📖 *Blackbook National Auto Research*, motorcycle pricing guides, ☎ (800) 554-1026, ♂ www.blackbookusa.com

Scooters

Soaring gasoline prices make scooters not only a wise choice for a buy-and-sell venture, but also one that can potentially make you rich. At 70, 80, and even 100 miles to the gallon, scooters may very well prove to be the only affordable transportation option for many people in the very near future. And they are also a lot of fun to ride. You can purchase new scooters wholesale and used scooters from private sellers through classified ads, for-sale signs, and auction sales; then resell both new and used from a homebased showroom if zoning permits and you have the required space. Scooters can also be marketed online and by displaying at consumer shows and swap meets. Extra revenues can be earned by selling scooter-related accessories like helmets, carriers, covers, and security devices. The truly environmentally conscious entrepreneurs might decide to specialize in electric scooters with rechargeable batteries. Green scooters are becoming very popular for urban commutes where speed and distance are secondary to efficiency, parking, and environmental friendliness.

 BUY
Classified Ads, Wholesalers

 SELL
Online Marketplaces, Homebased Sales, Consumer Shows

 RESOURCES
—MBM City Wholesale, ☎ (877) 626-2489, ♂ www.mbmcity.com
—The Scooter Company Distribution, ☎ (407) 207-1079, ♂ www.scootercompany.com
—USA Wholesale Scooter, ☎ (954) 567-1001, ♂ www.usawholesalescooter.com

Sailboats

As an avid sailor and sailboat owner, I can tell you that the main reason people buy and sell sailboats is a little disease known as two-foot-itis. You always think all your space and performance issues would be solved if your boat were just two feet longer.

I have firsthand experience in buying and selling sailboats, but one experience stands out from the others. A number of years ago I often passed a sailboat on a trailer that was for sale. In the fall, months later, the boat was still for sale. Having sold my sailboat, I decided to inquire. After some hard negotiations, I purchased the boat for about half of the $10,000 asking price. I used the boat the following season, stored it for the winter, and the following spring sold the boat through a boat broker for $8,500. I used the boat for an entire season, paid broker commissions and a few minor cosmetic changes, and still netted about $2,200.

The reason I was successful in this transaction was that I purchased the sailboat off-season and it was dirty and needed some attention. When it came time to sell the boat, I received top dollar because it was the beginning of the season, the boat was in immaculate condition, and it was in the water and could be taken for a test sail. It just goes to show you, deals are out there waiting. The best buys are desperation sales—financial problems, divorce, end of season, and boats in need of a very good cleaning.

If you are going to deal in smaller, trailer sailboats like Hobbies, Lasers, and Sunfish, you can sell directly from home and on eBay. Larger boats will require moorage, adding additional expenses to be recovered, which must be factored into the selling price. Sailboats are best sold in the water rather than in dry dock so people can take them for a test run. Out-of-water boats, which cannot be tested, always sell for less, even if they are in great shape, because of the unknown problems that might surface once in the water, especially potential mechanical problems with engine, transmission, cooling, and steering. Because the average 30-foot, late-model sailboat sells in the range of $40,000 to $120,000, it is also a good idea to invest in a professional survey before buying, to make sure you are not buying someone else's problems. In addition to boats, sell accessories such as sails, life jackets, gear, and rigging. Due to the wide variety of sailboats and construction materials, you may want to specialize—mono hull, multi-hull, cruiser, or racer.

BUY
Classified Ads, Wholesalers, Auctions

SELL
Online Marketplaces, Boat Shows, Boat Brokers

 RESOURCES
—American Boat Listing, buy-and-sell marketplace, ♂ www.ablboats.com
—Auction Sail, online buy-and-sell marketplace, ♂ www.auctionsail.com
—Used Boats, online buy-and-sell marketplace, ♂ www.usedboats.com
—📖 NADA Guides, sailboat price guides, ☎ (800) 966-6232, ♂ www.nadaguides.com

Powerboats

Like sailboats great profits can also be earned buying and selling powerboats of all sizes—skiffs, trawler fishing boats, cruisers, and speedboats—and powerboat accessories. Good deals on powerboats can be found at the end of the season in the northern climes; other good buys include boats in need of mirror repairs or a good cleaning, and boats involved in desperation sale circumstances. You might also want to strike a deal with a boat broker if your plan is to buy and sell large quantities of boats, or larger boats requiring moorage. If you choose this route, request a commission discount based on volume. Additionally, set a purchase proviso, for example, any boat costing more than $10,000 requires a full marine survey prior to buying, preferably at the seller's expense. Powerboat accessories can be purchased new from wholesalers and manufacturers, while used boating accessories are available from private sellers advertising in boating publications, local classifieds, online marketplaces, and auction sales. There are a number of ways to sell powerboats and accessories. You can utilize eBay and online power boating marketplaces, have a homebased display for smaller boats on trailers, and exhibit at boat and recreation shows.

 BUY
Classified Ads, Wholesalers, Auctions

SELL
Online Marketplaces, Boat Shows, Boat Brokers

RESOURCES
—American Boat Listing, buy-and-sell marketplace, ♂ www.ablboats.com
—Used Boats, buy-and-sell marketplace, ♂ www.usedboats.com
—📖 *American Marine Publishing*, powerboat value guides, ☎ (231) 933-0827, ♂ www.powerboatguide.com

Outboard Motors

A great opportunity exists for entrepreneurs with small-engine mechanical skills and knowledge to profit by purchasing secondhand outboard motors in need of a little TLC and reselling them for a healthy profit once tuned up. Outboard motors that do not run are for the most part valueless. In fact, they can often be purchased for a few dollars or even obtained for free from people looking to get rid of garage clutter. A tune-up, new plugs, fuel pump, or some other small repair is often all that is needed to mean the difference between a motor worth zip and one worth $500. Attend auction sales and garage sales; scan boating publication classifieds to find outboards to buy cheaply. Once cleaned up, resell the outboards with a warranty, because a guarantee that the motor will work, even if only for 30 or 60 days, will easily double the selling value. Sell from a homebased shop supported by local advertising and through online boating marketplaces. There is also a growing market for antique motors with names from the past—Neptune, Sea Kink, Buccaneer, and Seagull—which are commanding top dollar from collectors, especially if the motors are in working condition.

 BUY
Classified Ads, Auctions

 SELL
Homebased Sales, Online Marketplaces

 RESOURCES
—The Antique Outboard Motor Club, ♂ www.aomci.org
—The Mother of All Maritime Links, directory listing hundreds of marine industry links to manufacturers, clubs, collectors, and wholesalers, ♂ www.boat-links.com/boatlink.html
—📖 *Outboard Engines: Maintenance, Troubleshooting, and Repairing*, Ed Sherman (International Marine, 1997)
—📖 *NADA Guides*, outboard engine price guides, ☎ (800) 966-6232, ♂ www.nadaguides.com

Marine Electronics

Turn your knowledge and passion for boating into a profitable full- or part-time money-making venture by starting a buy-and-sell business specializing in the sale of new and previously owned marine electronics. Best-selling marine electronic items include handheld and fixed VHF radios, hailers, GPS systems, radar and autopilot systems, electronic instrument clusters, marine stereos, satellite telephone and television systems, remote spotlights, battery chargers, and fish finders. New electronics can be purchased from wholesalers, distributors, and liquidators at about 40 percent off retail, while used equipment will require a little legwork to track down through classified ads in boating publications and auction sales. New and used marine electronics can be sold through eBay and online boating marketplaces, and by exhibiting at boat and recreation shows. Additional money can be earned by installing the electronics you sell, provided you have the qualifications.

Buy
Wholesalers, Classified Ads

Sell
Boat Shows, eBay, Specialty Publications

Resources
—CWR Electronics Wholesale, ☎ (800) 527-3306, ✆ www.wholesale marineelectronics.com
—Navigator Electronics Wholesale, ☎ (877) 462-0208, ✆ www.navigator electronics.com
—Vision Wholesale, ☎ (877) 379-7983, ✆ www.visionwholesale.com

Nautical Charts

Most of the estimated 30 million boat and water-sports enthusiasts in North America have one thing in common: they need nautical charts to know where they are going, where they should be, or where they shouldn't be. Millions of nautical charts are sold every year. Cashing in on this lucrative market is easy. Start by contacting nautical-chart publishers and wholesalers, and ask questions about the most popular charts and volume pricing; even request selling tips. Charts are available in a wide range of styles and for a wide range of uses—waterproof, ocean-floor maps, general waterways maps, fishing charts, dive charts, inland lake and river charts, and electronic and PC-compatible charts and software. Sell at boat-and-recreation shows, create a Web site for online chart sales, sell through online boating and water sports Web portals, and advertise in boating magazines for mail order sales.

BUY
Wholesalers, Publishers

 SELL
Boat Shows, eBay, Specialty Publications, Mail Order, Web Site

 RESOURCES
—American Nautical Services Wholesale, ☎ (954) 522-3321, ♂ www. amnautical.com
—Map Connection Wholesale, ☎ (403) 215-4058, ♂ www.mapconnec tion.com
—National Boat Owners Association, ♂ www.nboat.com

Nautical Collectibles

The movie *Titanic* did more than smash all previous box-office records; it also ignited the marketplace for nautical collectibles, causing prices to soar. They are still strong today. The most prized nautical collectibles include cruise-liner memorabilia, model boats, brass signal lamps, sailors' sea trunks, antique sextants, glass floats, early divers' suits, ships' bells, brass cleats, portholes, wheels and propellers, barometer sets, compasses, anchors, telescopes, scrimshaw pieces, and anything and everything U.S. Navy. Buying sources include private sellers, collectible shows, auctions, and online marketplaces. Your selling options may be similar and include direct to collectors, through online specialty marketplaces, eBay, and a homebased showroom advertised locally, nationally, and internationally via your Web site and specialty publications.

 BUY
Classified Ads, Garage Sales, Online Marketplaces, Auctions

 SELL
Collectors, Auctions, Boat Shows, eBay, Homebased Sales

 RESOURCES
—The Mother of All Maritime Links, directory listing hundreds of marine industry links to manufacturers, clubs, collectors, and wholesalers, ♂ www.boat-links.com/boatlink.html
—Shipware Merchants, buy-and-sell marketplace, ☎ (800) 732-5865, ♂ www.seajunk.com
—📖 *Nautical Antiques & Collectibles*, Jan Baddeley (Philip Watson Publishing, 2003)

Recreational Vehicles

Big-ticket sales equal big profit potential, and in the case of buying and selling recreational vehicles, the prices and the profit potential don't come much bigger. The best buying source for RVs is from private sellers advertising with signs and through print and electronic classifieds. Distress sales will be a good starting point—financial troubles, divorce, death, and owner relocation can all be the basis for getting a great deal on a clean, late-model RV. Secondary buying sources include auction sales, estate sales, and bank or financier repossessions. Also look for otherwise mechanically fit RVs in need of TLC like a good cleanup, minor cosmetic repairs, and the addition of items like generators, awnings, and AC units to boost the overall value of the vehicle. Travel trailers of all sizes, from pop-up tent style to luxurious fifth-wheels, are also great buy-and-sell items, which can be purchased and sold in the same manner as motorized RVs. So can RV accessories. Your best selling options include directly from home supported by print and electronic advertising, online RV specialist Web sites, consignment RV lots, and exhibiting RV accessories at camping and RV shows.

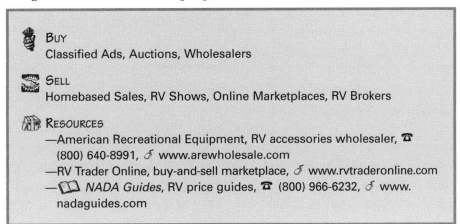

BUY
Classified Ads, Auctions, Wholesalers

SELL
Homebased Sales, RV Shows, Online Marketplaces, RV Brokers

RESOURCES
—American Recreational Equipment, RV accessories wholesaler, ☎ (800) 640-8991, ♂ www.arewholesale.com
—RV Trader Online, buy-and-sell marketplace, ♂ www.rvtraderonline.com
— *NADA Guides*, RV price guides, ☎ (800) 966-6232, ♂ www. nadaguides.com

Utility Trailers

Yard work, home renovations, and helping friends move are all reasons why owning a utility trailer has become a necessity for many people. With demand comes the opportunity to profit for entrepreneurs who decide to buy and sell utility trailers. Concentrate on both new and used utility trailer sales by purchasing new utility trailers directly from manufacturers, and used trailers from private seller classified ads and auction sales. Selling utility trailers from home should not prove difficult, provided you have the zoning permits and required space. Advertise your trailers in your local newspaper in the classified section, on bulletin boards, and with the use of attention-grabbing signage on display models. You might also want to market directly to contractors and landscape companies—any business that needs work trailers. Given that new work trucks cost about 20 times as much as a new utility trailer, many opt to purchase a utility trailer when it comes time to expand the fleet and increase productivity. Once you are set up, word will spread quickly, and it won't take long before people needing a trailer will call or stop by to inquire

BUY
Manufacturers, Classified Ads, Auctions

SELL
Homebased Sales

RESOURCES
—BNM Trailer Manufacturing & Sales, ☎ (989) 862-5252, ♂ www.bnm trailersalesinc.com
—RETCO Trailer Manufacturing, ☎ (573) 472-5165, ♂ www.retco trailers.com
—Wholesale Trailers Inc., ☎ (800) 871-7793, ♂ www.wholesaletrailers inc.com

All-Terrain Vehicles (ATVs)

Buying and selling used all-terrain vehicles, or ATVs, suits people with some mechanical aptitude and an interest in the sport. Buy from private sellers advertising online and in the classifieds, and sell from a homebased showroom and on eBay. You can also purchase new ATV accessories such as carriers, helmets, and clothing from wholesalers and sell them retail at ATV shows, sportsmen shows, online, and from home. Because the average late-model ATV retails for $2,000 to $5,000, earning just 15 percent on every sale will come to $300 to $750. Sell two a month and you will earn an additional $7,000 to $18,000 per year. Not a bad return on such a small initial investment.

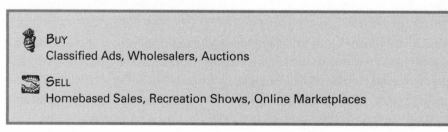

BUY
Classified Ads, Wholesalers, Auctions

SELL
Homebased Sales, Recreation Shows, Online Marketplaces

RESOURCES
—ATV Source, industry information, resources, and link, ♂ www.atv source.com
—Jiangsu Fenghua Motors, ATV and accessories manufacturer, ☎ 86-511-6531330 (China)
—📖 *Blackbook National Auto Research*, all-terrain vehicle pricing guides, ☎ (800) 554-1026, ♂ www.blackbookusa.com

Snowmobiles

Buying and selling used snowmobiles and new accessories such as clothing and helmets is an excellent choice for people with an interest in the sport, who are also looking to operate a seasonal venture. In the northern states and most of Canada, riding snowmobiles is a very popular recreational pastime enjoyed by millions of enthusiasts. Selling directly from home, it is possible to earn $50,000 a year part-time. This would only necessitate selling 50 machines with a $1,000 profit each, which is not an unrealistic goal when you consider that late-model snowmobiles sell in the range of $4,000 to $6,000. Buy from private sellers advertising in the classifieds and at auction sales. Obviously, the best time to buy is spring and summer, after the season and long before the excitement of the next season builds. New accessories can be purchased from wholesalers and resold at snowmobile and recreation shows. Also make sure you join numerous snowmobile associations and clubs so that you can network for customers and spread the word about your business.

BUY
Classified Ads, Wholesalers, Auctions

SELL
Homebased Sales, Recreation Shows, Online Marketplaces

RESOURCES
—Sled Swap, buy-and-sell marketplace, ♂ www.sledswap.com
—Snowmobile Links, industry information and resources portal, ♂ www.snowmobilelinks.com
—📖 *NADA Guides*, snowmobile price guides, ☎ (800) 966-6232, ♂ www.nadaguides.com

Designer Fashions

Almost everyone would like to dress in top designer fashions, but unfortunately, economics does not afford all the opportunity to wear $1,000 Gucci outfits. There are basically two ways you can help people buy designer fashions for a fraction of the normal cost and still make a handsome profit for yourself. First, purchase new off-brand and replica designer fashions from overseas manufacturers and wholesalers and resell these from a homebased showroom, online through eBay, and by hiring salespeople to organize and host designer-fashion sales parties in their homes. Second, purchase used, but real, designer fashions from the top houses like Prada, Fendi, Nicole Miller, Armani, and Ferrangamo by scouring garage sales, secondhand shops, flea markets, and auction sales; then resell them in much the same way you would new replica designer fashions.

BUY
Wholesalers, Manufacturers

SELL
Homebased Sales, Fashion Shows, Home Parties, eBay

RESOURCES
—1 AAA Wholesale Liquidators, ☎ (800) 661-9430, ♂ www.1aaawhole saleliquidators.com
—American Apparel and Footwear Manufacturers' Association, ☎ (800) 520-2262, ♂ www.americanapparel.org
—Jaclyn Manufacturing, ☎ (201) 868-9400, ♂ www.jaclyninc.com
—Luxury Brands Wholesale, ☎ (215) 248-3576, ♂ www.luxurybrands llc.com

Secondhand Clothing

Secondhand clothing sales definitely rank as one of the top ten buy-and-sell items for a number of reasons. First, there is an excellent supply in every community and at rock-bottom prices. Second, previously owned clothing is no longer the fashion statement for disenfranchised teens; people from every walk of life, age, and economic class view purchasing secondhand clothing as a frugal means of getting name-brand clothing at reasonable prices. Third, many people also view purchasing secondhand clothing as a way to help the planet by recycling perfectly good clothes, which ten years ago would have ended up in landfill sites.

Buy secondhand clothing at garage sales, estate sales, and by running clothing wanted ads in the classified section of your local newspaper. There are also companies wholesaling secondhand clothing that can be purchased unsorted by the pound, sorted by the pound, or sorted and pressed by the garment. Your selling options include flea markets, online marketplaces such as eBay, and hosting your own garage sales. Before merchandising any clothing, repair small tears, replace buttons and zippers as required, press or iron, and display neatly on hangers and racks. Doing so will double the sales value.

BUY
Garage Sales, Flea Markets, Wholesalers, Classified Ads

SELL
Flea Markets, Garage Sales, Online Marketplaces

RESOURCES
—Eagle Liquidators, used clothing wholesaler, ☎ (305) 634-4760, ✆ www. eagletrade.com
—Trans American Trading, used clothing wholesaler, ☎ (718) 383-3445, ✆ www.tranclo.com
—📖 *Garage Sale & Flea Market Annual* (Collector Books, 2004)

Vintage Clothing

Spending weekends scouring flea markets, garage sales, and auctions for vintage clothing and fashion accessories has the potential to make you rich! A Chanel suit from the sixties can fetch $5,000. Levi blue jeans from the turn of the last century can net you $10,000, and a vintage Emilo Pucci dress can sell for well into the five-figure range. You simply cannot go wrong buying vintage clothing and reselling it, providing you know what to buy and how much to pay. Therefore, you will need to educate yourself about vintage clothing values, and the best way to do this is to purchase vintage clothing pricing guides. The vintage clothing and accessories you purchase can be sold for a profit directly to collectors and vintage clothing retailers or through vintage clothing online marketplaces and eBay. You may also want to convert a spare room in your home into a vintage clothing boutique and advertise your products locally and through wedding and event planners.

BUY
Garage Sales, Auctions, Classified Ads, Secondhand Clothing Shops

 SELL
Collectors, B2B, eBay, Flea Markets, Web Site, Homebased Sales

 RESOURCES
—Antiques Web, vintage clothing collectors and retailers directory, ♂ www.antiqueweb.com /links/clothingandfashion.html
—Linda White Antique Clothing, vintage clothing and accessories buyer, ☎ (508) 529-4439, ♂ www.vintageclothing.com
—📖 *The Official Price Guide to Vintage Fashion and Fabric*, Pamela Smith (House of Collectibles, 2001)
—📖 *The Vintage Fashion Directory: The National Sourcebook of Vintage Fashion Retailers*, Daniela Turdich (Streamline Press, 2002), which lists every vintage clothing retailer in the United States.

Maternity Clothing

When you stop to consider that more than four million babies are born each year in the United States and Canada, you quickly realize the great opportunity that exists for clever entrepreneurs to buy wholesale maternity fashions and resell them to moms-to-be. One of the better ways to sell maternity fashions is to hire contract sales representatives to organize and host maternity fashion sales parties in their own homes. Ideal candidates, of course, are moms-to-be. Remuneration to the sales host can be by way of commission, revenue split, free product, or any combination. Establishing a homebased boutique in your own home is also a great way to sell your goods. Advertise locally and build alliances with midwives and daycare centers, which can refer their clients to your business. Also don't overlook the possibility of selling to a global audience by creating your own e-commerce Web site and posting maternity fashions on eBay and other online marketplaces. Weekend flea markets and kiosk space in malls may also prove to be a profitable way to market and sell your products, and both certainly warrant further investigation.

 BUY
Manufacturers, Wholesalers

 SELL
Flea Markets, Homebased Sales, Kiosks, eBay

RESOURCES
—American Apparel and Footwear Manufacturers' Association, ☎ (800) 520-2262, ♂ www.americanapparel.org
—Cotlon India Manufacturing, ☎ 91-11-26431288 (India), ♂ www.cotlon.com
—Liquidation Merchandise, ☎ (800) 574-5304, ♂ www.liquidationmerchandise.com
—Maximum Mama Maternity, ☎ (415) 585-3139, ♂ www.maximummama.com

Children's Clothing

There is no better time than right now to start a simple buy-and-sell enterprise that enables you to cash in on the huge demand for children's clothing. Buy the latest children's fashions directly from national and international apparel manufacturers, wholesalers, and liquidators at deeply discounted prices, especially if you purchase end-of-season and slightly blemished merchandise. Double and even triple your purchase price and resell the clothing at flea markets, from a homebased showroom, and on eBay. Boost revenues by accepting used children's clothing trade-ins on new purchases. Offer a 20 percent rebate, and then double the price of the used clothing for resale. Doing so means you will earn a 100 percent markup on the used clothing sales and be able to increase your overall revenues and profits.

 BUY
Manufacturers, Wholesalers

 SELL
Flea Markets, Homebased Sales, Kiosks, eBay

 RESOURCES
—1 AAA Wholesale Liquidators, ☎ (800) 661-9430, ♂ www.1aaawholesaleliquidators.com
—Children's Apparel Manufacturers' Association, ♂ www.cama-apparel.org
—Children's Wholesale Apparel, ☎ (727) 934-1109, ♂ www.childrenswholesale.com
—Kids Resource Wholesale, ☎ (800) 552-1610, ♂ www.kidsresource.com

Leather Fashions

Armed with only your entrepreneurial savvy and a few thousand dollars in seed capital, you can cash in on the incredible consumer demand for leather fashions by starting a leather fashions sales business. Working right from a homebased boutique, you can sell high-quality leather fashions for less than most retailers simply because you don't have to pay the big overhead costs they do in rent, advertising, staff, and utilities. Advertise your boutique in your local newspaper, by posting fliers on community bulletin boards, and by word-of-mouth referral. Buy wholesale from importers and distributors in the United States or pay even less for leather fashions by purchasing larger quantities directly from overseas leather-fashion manufacturers. The best leather fashions to sell include jackets, vests, pants, and chaps. In addition to homebased selling, also sell on eBay and exhibit at motorcycle and automotive shows.

 BUY
Wholesalers, Manufacturers

 SELL
Homebased Sales, Online Marketplaces, Consumer Shows, Flea Markets

 RESOURCES
—Leather Up Wholesale, ☎ (888) 467-0222, ♂ www.leatherup.com
—Om Impex Manufacturing, ☎ 91-11-25749187 (India), ♂ www. om-impex.com
—Royal Merchandising Wholesale, ☎ (732) 571-3100, ♂ www.royal merchandising.com

Wedding Apparel

With more than two million weddings taking place each year in the United States, the prospects for a buy-and-sell venture specializing in wedding gowns, bridal dresses, and accessories are very bright indeed. New gowns and accessories can be purchased directly from manufacturers, designers, and wholesalers, while used gowns and accessories can be purchased from classified ads and online marketplaces. Set up a boutique right at your home and advertise locally, making sure to build alliances with people in the industry, such as wedding planners, invitation printers, cake bakers, and photographers. All can refer your business to their clients. Gowns also sell extremely well on eBay and other online wedding-themed marketplaces. Count on earning in the range of 20 to 30 percent of the retail selling price of new gowns and accessories, and as much as 50 percent on secondhand gowns.

BUY
Wholesalers, Manufacturers, Classified Ads, Online Marketplaces

SELL
Homebased Sales, Bridal Shows, eBay

RESOURCES
—American Apparel and Footwear Manufacturers' Association, ☎ (800) 520-2262, ♂ www.americanapparel.org
—Cocoon Manufacturing, ☎ 852-21997184 (China), ♂ www.cocoon weddinggownfactory.com
—Discount Bridal Service, ☎ (800) 708-3363, ♂ www.workwith brides.com
—Used Wedding Dresses Online, buy-and-sell marketplace, ☎ (972) 365-7603, ♂ www.usedweddingdresses.com

Lingerie

Lingerie can be sold on numerous online marketplaces including eBay, by creating your own e-commerce Web site, via mail order, and at a homebased boutique. Another sales method is to hire contract sales consultants to organize and host lingerie sales parties in their homes. This is one of the better ways to grow your business and revenues with only a minimal initial investment. Buy lingerie at deeply discount prices from wholesalers, liquidators, and manufacturers. This is the type of product that can be marked up by 100 to 200 percent for retail sales. To earn an additional $1,500 each month, all that is needed is to achieve sales of twice that of less.

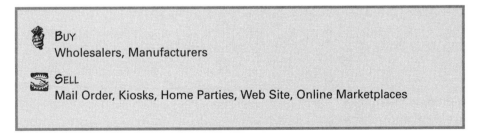

BUY
Wholesalers, Manufacturers

SELL
Mail Order, Kiosks, Home Parties, Web Site, Online Marketplaces

RESOURCES
—1 AAA Wholesale Liquidators, ☎ (800) 661-9430, ♂ www.1aaawhole saleliquidators.com
—American Apparel and Footwear Manufacturers' Association, ☎ (800) 520-2262, ♂ www.americanapparel.org
—Sheer Fashions Wholesale, ☎ (888) 241-9813, ♂ www.sheerfash ions.net
—VX Intimate Wholesale, ☎ (866) 968-4412, ♂ www.vxintimate.com

Western Apparel

Howdy, partner! Anything and everything Western is hot. Hats, boots, shirts, jackets, belts and buckles, and any other garment with a decisively Western flavor are hot sellers in Texas—and elsewhere. Buy for half of retail value or less from wholesalers, liquidators, and manufacturers of fine Western-themed apparel and accessories. Selling through online marketplaces like eBay, at flea markets, at community rodeos and events, and right from a homebased showroom will net you your highest return. Also consider buying and selling Native American-made clothing and crafts direct from southwestern Indian tribes. Though these items are great sellers in the U.S. and Canada, the absolutely huge market is Europe and Japan.

 BUY
Manufacturers, Wholesalers

 SELL
Flea Markets, Homebased Sales, Online Marketplaces, Consumer Shows

 RESOURCES
—American Apparel and Footwear Manufacturers' Association, ☎ (800) 520-2262, ♂ www.americanapparel.org
—Nitches Manufacturing, ☎ (212) 696-5660, ♂ www.nitches.com
—Western Express Wholesale, ☎ (800) 245-1380, ♂ www.western expressinc.com

Imprinted T-Shirts

As mentioned in the introduction, a 15-year-old high school girl made over $5,000 per month part-time selling vintage T-shirts online. She was doing nothing more than purchasing her stock at garage sales, flea markets, and used clothing stores, paying as little as $1 per shirt, and reselling them to collectors and consumers through various online marketplaces. In addition to vintage T-shirts, you can also sell new T-shirts emblazoned with all sorts of designs, captions, and logos. Buy from manufacturers, wholesalers, and liquidators—there are hundreds in the U.S. alone selling T-shirts, and many more hundreds worldwide. Like vintage T-shirts, you can sell new T-shirts on eBay, at flea markets, mall and beach kiosks, community events, and wherever people gather in your community.

BUY
Wholesalers, Manufacturers, Secondhand Clothing Shops, Garage Sales

SELL
Kiosks, Flea Markets, Community Events, eBay

RESOURCES
—FTH Wholesale, ☎ (888) 708-1090, ♂ www.fthwholesale.com
—T-Shirt King Wholesale, ☎ (800) 493-7887, ♂ www.wholesale.t-shirt king.com
—T-Shirt Wholesaler, ☎ (888) 245-8141, ♂ www.t-shirtwholesaler.com

Uniforms

Most people would not consider uniforms as one of the best products to buy and sell for a profit. But when you consider the vast number of people who are required to wear uniforms for work, you quickly begin to understand the opportunity and income potential. Think about all the people in uniforms—hospital staff, security personnel, auto mechanics, fire and police personnel, many school students, amateur sports teams, food and beverage workers, airline workers—the list goes on. Establish an in-home uniform showroom for sales, and go to places of work or business armed with samples to take orders. Many corporations, organizations, and government agencies that require a large number of uniforms usually put their purchases out to tender annually, or every few years. So it is important to make inquiries and be placed on the tender list. Both nationally and worldwide, there are hundreds of companies engaged in uniform-apparel manufacturing, so securing wholesale buying sources such as the ones shown below should not prove difficult.

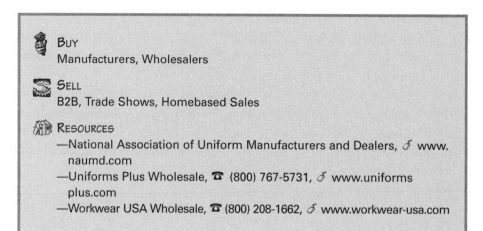

BUY
Manufacturers, Wholesalers

SELL
B2B, Trade Shows, Homebased Sales

RESOURCES
—National Association of Uniform Manufacturers and Dealers, ♂ www.naumd.com
—Uniforms Plus Wholesale, ☎ (800) 767-5731, ♂ www.uniformsplus.com
—Workwear USA Wholesale, ☎ (800) 208-1662, ♂ www.workwear-usa.com

Handbags

Whether new, used, vintage, or replica, the handbag marketplace is hot and a prime candidate for a super profitable buy-and-sell enterprise. If you decide to sell only new handbags, stick with buying off-brand names and replicas from overseas manufacturers, from liquidators for out-of-season and end-of-run handbags, or from emerging domestic handbag designers/manufacturers. Sell at flea markets, consumer shows, fashion shows, on eBay, and from mall and public market kiosks. Vintage bags from top designers like Fendi, Gucci, Prada, Versace, Valentino, and Alviero Martini will take a little bit of detective work to uncover and buy at flea markets, garage sales, estate sales, and secondhand clothing shops. These can be sold for top dollar on eBay, through collector shows and auctions, and directly to collectors via clubs and associations, especially if they are in great original condition, and rare.

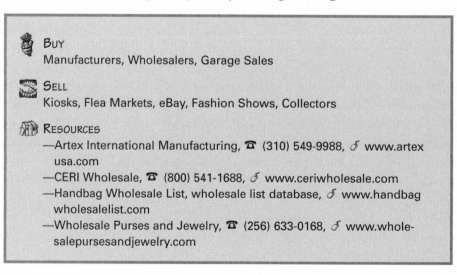

BUY
Manufacturers, Wholesalers, Garage Sales

SELL
Kiosks, Flea Markets, eBay, Fashion Shows, Collectors

RESOURCES
—Artex International Manufacturing, ☎ (310) 549-9988, ♂ www.artexusa.com
—CERI Wholesale, ☎ (800) 541-1688, ♂ www.ceriwholesale.com
—Handbag Wholesale List, wholesale list database, ♂ www.handbagwholesalelist.com
—Wholesale Purses and Jewelry, ☎ (256) 633-0168, ♂ www.wholesalepursesandjewelry.com

Shoes

Buying and selling new shoes has the potential to earn you a king's ransom. Sports, fashion, children's, and work shoes, you can sell them all or specialize in one particular type. You can also trade in vintage shoes, especially ladies' fashion shoes; prices have recently hit the stratosphere for prized, top-fashion labels from the '40s, '50s, and '60s. These can be found by scouring garage sales, flea markets, and estate sales. Resell them on eBay and directly to vintage shoe collectors via collectible shows and online marketplaces. New shoes can be purchased very cheaply if you buy direct from the manufacturer, though as a general rule you have to order larger quantities. For resellers with smaller budgets, buy from wholesalers and liquidators, who often are the source of well-below-wholesale pricing and end-of-run and out-of-season shoes. Sell at weekend flea markets, fashion shows, and directly to businesses for safety and work footwear.

BUY
Manufacturers, Wholesalers, Garage Sales

SELL
Kiosks, Flea Markets, eBay, Fashion Shows, Collectors

RESOURCES
—American Apparel and Footwear Manufacturers' Association, ☎ (800) 520-2262, ✆ www.americanapparel.org
—Kristoff Shoes Wholesale, ✆ www.kristoffshoes.com
—Shoe Balance International Wholesale, ☎ (866) 494-4094, ✆ www.shoebalance.com
—Salvage Export, ☎ (800) 506-5191, ✆ www.salvageexport.com

Hats

Become known as the King or Queen of Hats by stocking every type imaginable—fashion hats, work hats, licensed sports hats, sun hats, garden hats, Panama hats, straw hats, Western hats, novelty hats, pillbox hats, berets, visors, fedoras, trucker, and outdoorsmen hats. Buy from wholesalers, liquidators, and factory direct for the lowest pricing. Sell at flea markets, from a homebased showroom, at consumer shows, by creating your own Web site, and on eBay. Aim to generate $5,000 a month in sales, and with a 100 percent markup, you will earn $30,000 a year. It should not prove difficult given that hats are always a popular fashion statement and in demand.

BUY
Manufacturers, Wholesalers, Garage Sales

 SELL
Kiosks, Flea Markets, eBay, Fashion Shows

 RESOURCES
—The Hat Site, links to hat manufacturers and wholesalers, ♂ www.the hatsite.com
—Kraft Hat Manufacturing, ☎ (718) 620-6100, ♂ www.krafthat.com
—Village Hat Shop Wholesale, ☎ (619) 683-5533, ♂ www.villagehat shop.com

Belt Buckles

Biker, Western, automotive, animals, licensed logos, and more, belt buckles come in every imaginable design. Belt buckles are great buy-and-sell items for a number of reasons. First, they are in demand as gifts and fashion statements. Second, they can be purchased very cheaply and marked up by 300 to 400 percent for retail. Third, they are small, easy to store and ship. Fourth, they can be sold in any number of ways, including through eBay, flea markets, mall kiosks, community events, and specialty shows such as auto shows, swap meets, and motorcycle shows. So what are you waiting for? If you want to get rolling in an easy buy-and-sell enterprise that can be started for peanuts and has the potential to earn you an extra few hundred dollars a day, week, or month, depending on how much time you want to commit, then you have found it.

 BUY
Manufacturers, Wholesalers, Craftspeople

 SELL
Kiosks, Flea Markets, eBay, Consumer Shows, Community Events

 RESOURCES
—The Belt Buckle Shop Wholesale, ☎ (800) 962-5003, ♂ www.beltbuckle shop.com
—Belt House Manufacturing, ☎ 91-11-3551729 (India), ♂ www.india mart.com/fashionhouse
—Fun Buckles Manufacturing, ☎ (514) 421-6238, ♂ www.funbuckles.com

Leather Products

Leather goods and crafts such as gloves, wallets, billfolds, business card holders, leather crafts, cellular telephone cases, belts, hunting sheaths, and business organizers are fantastic items to sell for profits at weekend flea markets, on eBay, at consumer shows, and by renting kiosk space in malls and public markets. What makes leather goods and crafts such great products for a buy-and-sell venture is they are small, easy to store and ship, always in demand for personal use and gift giving, and readily available through a great number of manufacturing and wholesale sources nationally and internationally. And they can easily be sold for three to four times their wholesale costs. As always, when displaying merchandise, keep it clean and organized and your booth well-signed.

BUY
Manufacturers, Wholesalers

SELL
Kiosks, Flea Markets, eBay, Consumer Shows

RESOURCES
—Artex International Manufacturing, ☎ (310) 549-9988, ✆ www.artex usa.com
—Crazy Discounts Wholesale, ✆ www.crazydiscounts.com
—Indian Leather Portal, directory listing leather products manufacturers and wholesalers, ✆ www.indianleatherportal.com

Luggage

Luggage is one of those little-thought-about products that has the potential to be very profitable when bought and sold by entrepreneurs with innovative marketing skills. Buy luggage cheaply from wholesalers, distributors, and importers, or really decrease your discount pricing by purchasing in larger quantities directly from national and international manufacturers. Sell on eBay, from a homebased showroom, through travel and leisure shows, and at mall kiosks. Also build alliances with local travel agents who can refer their clients to your homebased showroom for their luggage needs. Maintaining a 50 percent markup and achieving monthly sales of a mere $5,000 will net you $20,000 annually.

BUY
Manufacturers, Wholesalers

 SELL
Kiosks, Flea Markets, eBay, Consumer Shows

 RESOURCES
—AAXIS Wholesale Luggage, ☎ (310) 719-1837, ♂ www.aaxiswhole
    sale luggage.com
—Al Khayam Manufacturing, ☎ 971-4-2252872 (UAE), ♂ www.buy
    luggageonline.com
—Crazy Discounts Wholesale, ♂ www.crazydiscounts.com

Fabric

Fabrics from around the world are very unique products to sell to consumers, seamstresses, and tailors. Spread the word by joining sewing and crafts clubs in your area, and online craft groups to network for business. Create your own Web site so you can sell fabrics to consumers from around the world. In the bricks-and-mortar world, you can sell your fabrics at fashion shows, home-and-garden shows, and flea markets. You can also rent temporary space in malls and public markets and host weekly or monthly fabric sales. A homebased fabric boutique could also prove to be very profitable and could be advertised locally in the classifieds, on bulletin boards, and by networking at craft and sewing club events. You can purchase fabric wholesale through a number of national and international sources. However, if you can afford it, import fabrics directly from manufacturers in India and China. You will obtain absolutely insane, rock-bottom prices, which will enable you to crush your competitors by offering customers the widest selection of fabrics at the guaranteed lowest prices.

 BUY
Manufacturers, Wholesalers, Importers

 SELL
Kiosks, Flea Markets, Online Marketplaces, Homebased Sales, B2B

 RESOURCES
—Emmaress Manufacturing, ☎ 91-22-23721232 (India), ♂ www.emma
    ress.com

—Narmada Manufacturing, ☎ 62-361-486-071 (Indonesia), ♂ www.narma datextiles.com

—Nick of Time Textiles Wholesale, ☎ (877) 447-8370, ♂ www.nickof time.net

—Textile Web, industry information and links, ♂ www.textileweb.com

—Trade India, directory listing textile exporters and manufacturers, ♂ www.tradeindia.com

Bed and Bath Linens

Towels, shower curtains, area rugs, comforters, shams, sheets, and curtain panels are just a few of the bed and bath linen products you can sell at flea markets, home-and-garden shows, mall kiosks, in-home parties, and on eBay. Buy from wholesalers, liquidators, and manufacturers at low prices, especially for end-of-run and seconds merchandise. Grow your business by hiring contract salespeople to organize and host bed and bath linen sales right in their own homes. Remuneration can be by way of a commission, profit split, or free product based on sales levels. This sales and marketing method enables you to dramatically grow your business, both geographically and in terms of gross revenues on a minimal investment.

Buy
Manufacturers, Wholesalers

Sell
Kiosks, Flea Markets, eBay, Home and Gift Shows, Home Parties

Resources
—Kimlor Innovative Home Fashion Wholesale, ☎ (800) 762-0007, ♂ www.kimlor.com

—Tinsley-Clark Wholesale Bed & Bath, ☎ (800) 255-2384, ♂ www.house oflinens.com

—Towels & Linen Wholesale, ☎ (305) 624-1331, ♂ www.towelsand linen.com

Sewing Machines and Notions

Earn a bundle buying and selling new and used sewing machines and accessories like bobbins, needles, thread, scissors and shears, pattern books, instructional videos, thread stands, and sewing lamps. Buy factory direct from manufacturers for the lowest prices, and buy smaller quantities at slightly higher prices from wholesalers. Sell from a homebased showroom supported by local advertising, on eBay, and by displaying at crafts shows, fashion shows, and home shows. Also join sewing and crafts clubs and associations offline and online to network for customers. Don't overlook buying and selling vintage sewing machines and notions as an extra source of revenue, because values have recently taken off. Find vintage items at garage sales, flea markets, and estate sales, and sell direct to collectors through organizations such as The International Sewing Machine Collectors' Society, ♂ www.ismacs.net.

Buy
Manufacturers, Wholesalers, Classified Ads, Auctions

Sell
Homebased Sales, Kiosks, Flea Markets, eBay, Fashion Shows

Resources
—Brewer Wholesale, ☎ (800) 444-3111, ♂ www.brewersewing.com
—Mico International Wholesale, ☎ (305) 599-1831, ♂ www.mico
  sew.com
—Wholesale Sewing Supplies, ♂ www.wholesalesewingsupplies.com

Fine Jewelry

You can earn lots of money buying and selling fine jewelry, especially secondhand jewelry purchased at distress prices. When money is needed in a hurry, often the first belonging people sell off at fire-sale prices is fine jewelry—rings, watches, necklaces, and diamond earrings. You see the ads all the time in the classifieds: "Diamond ring, must sell, worth $5,000. Will take $1,000 or best offer." In addition to buying from private sellers through the classified ads, you can also purchase at auctions and estates sales. Of course, you will need to educate yourself about fine jewelry and values because when you are dealing in purchases of $1,000 to $10,000 on average, the last thing you want to do is learn by trial and error. Fine jewelry can be sold to collectors, advertised in the classifieds, presented at auctions, and offered via online marketplaces.

 Buy
Manufacturers, Wholesalers, Classified Ads, Auctions

SELL
Collectors, Homebased Sales, Jewelry Shows, Auctions

 RESOURCES
—Belirams Jewelry Manufacturing, ☎ 91-11-24656092 (India), ♂ www.belirams.com
—First Class Trading, ☎ (877) 787-2346, ♂ www.fctdiamondjewelry.com
—Sell Jewelry, ☎ (800) 876-5490, ♂ www.selljewelry.com
—Treasures International Wholesale, ☎ (800) 554-4950, ♂ www.treasuresjewelry.com
—📖 *Antique Trader Jewelry Price Guide*, Kyle Husfloen (Krause Publications, 2000)

Costume Jewelry

You can also specialize in costume jewelry sales. It has the advantage of reduced financial risk because, except for antique costume jewelry, most sells for a fraction of the cost of fine jewelry. Billions of dollars' worth of costume jewelry is sold annually—earrings, rings, necklaces, and brooches. And you can make a financial killing by purchasing costume jewelry at super low prices directly from manufacturers, wholesalers, and even local craftspeople, and reselling it in some cases for ten times your cost. The best sales venues include online marketplaces such as eBay, flea market vending, kiosk sales in malls and markets, selling from a cart at community events, and by hiring a team of contract salespeople to organize and host monthly costume jewelry sales parties right in their homes. Costume jewelry is one of the best buy-and-sell products because there is huge profit potential, limited financial risk, easy storage and shipment, and incredible demand.

 BUY
Manufacturers, Wholesalers, Craftspeople

 SELL
Kiosks, Flea Markets, Community Events, eBay, Consumer Shows

 RESOURCES
—Accessory Wholesale, ☎ (800) 525-8793, ♂ www.awnol.com
—Wholesale Jewelry, ☎ (888) 563-4411, ♂ www.wholesalejewelry.net
—World End Imports, ☎ (800) 722-2309, ♂ www.trendyjewels.com
—📖 *The Official Guide to Costume Jewelry*, Harrice Simon Miller (Collector Books, 2002)

Rock and Gem Products

Calling all rock and gem hounds! It is time to start profiting from your knowledge by buying and selling rocks, gems, and related supplies. Purchase rocks, gems, equipment, and related supplies from wholesalers as well as directly from rock and gem hounds like you who spend weekends scouring the countryside for treasures hidden in the soil, riverbeds, and sides of mountains. Sell to crafters, costume jewelry makers, enthusiasts, and consumers looking for neat home and office decoration items. Your products can be sold on eBay, at industry trade shows, and by renting vendor space at weekend flea markets. If there are no rock and gem shops in your city, consider opening one in your home—a converted garage would make a fantastic rock and gem boutique.

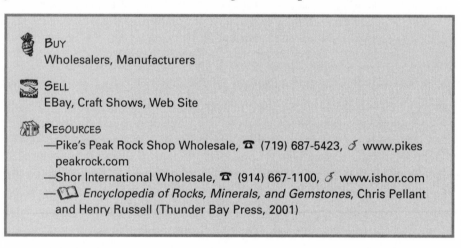

BUY
Wholesalers, Manufacturers

SELL
EBay, Craft Shows, Web Site

RESOURCES
—Pike's Peak Rock Shop Wholesale, ☎ (719) 687-5423, ✆ www.pikes
  peakrock.com
—Shor International Wholesale, ☎ (914) 667-1100, ✆ www.ishor.com
—📖 *Encyclopedia of Rocks, Minerals, and Gemstones*, Chris Pellant
  and Henry Russell (Thunder Bay Press, 2001)

Cosmetics

For the innovative entrepreneur, there are numerous ways to sell cosmetics and make a bundle. You can enlist contract salespeople to organize and host home cosmetics sales parties. You can sell cosmetics in any number of online marketplaces, including eBay. You can establish a customer base via community advertising and direct contact methods like telemarketing and mail, and offer home delivery and consultations much like Mary Kay and Avon. You can rent kiosk space in malls and sell cosmetics on weekends. You can rent vendor space at fashion, health, and beauty shows and sell cosmetics. Or you can combine any or all of these selling methods to maximize sales and profits. The first step to getting started in cosmetics sales is to source a reliable supply of decent-quality cosmetics. You can create your own cosmetics brand and have it manufactured under a private labeling agreement. Or you can strike a deal with an existing cosmetics manufacturer or distributor and market that line on an exclusive or nonexclusive basis. You may also want to specialize in organic cosmetics products and market to people with skin sensitivity or allergies.

> **BUY**
> Wholesalers, Manufacturers
>
> **SELL**
> Home Parties, Direct Delivery, eBay, Kiosks
>
> **RESOURCES**
> —Independent Cosmetic Manufacturers and Distributors, www. icmad.org
> —Liquidation Merchandise, ☎ (800) 574-5304, www.liquidationmer chandise.com
> —Top Fashion, ☎ 886-6-2507450 (Taiwan), www.wholesale-cosmetic-supply.com

Vitamins and Nutritional Supplements

The time has never been better to cash in on the health craze by selling vitamins and nutritional supplements. Sell general vitamins and supplements, or specialize in one particular area such as diet or sports supplements. Or offer customers a wide product selection, including vitamins, nutritional supplements, holistic products, aromatherapy and essential oils, and natural health products. Buy direct from manufacturers and wholesalers at deeply discount prices, and resell through any number of venues like mall kiosks, online sales, health fairs, and mail order. Also consider seminars and home parties as two viable sales options. Organize free community health seminars focused on the benefits of vitamins and nutritional supplements, and enlist the services of health experts to speak, while you sell at the back of the room. Likewise, hire salespeople to organize and host vitamin and nutritional supplements sales parties right from their homes.

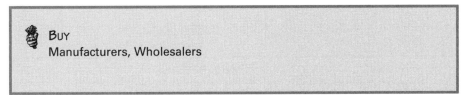

> **BUY**
> Manufacturers, Wholesalers

SELL
Mail Order, Online Marketplaces, Kiosks, Health Fairs, Seminars, Home Parties

 RESOURCES
—CA Vitamin Wholesale, ☎ (626) 336-7338, ♂ www.cavitamin.com
—TID Health Wholesale, ☎ (800) 824-2434, ♂ www.tidhealth.com
—📖 *Earl Mindell's Vitamin Bible for the 21st Century*, Earl Mindell (Warner Books, 1999)

Bath Products

Bath product gift baskets and gift sets are becoming very popular gifts at Christmas and virtually any other time of the year. For entrepreneurs looking for a simple, yet potentially very profitable, buy-and-sell option that can be started for less than $500, look no further than buying and selling bath products. Purchase from manufacturers and wholesalers at up to 60 percent off retail, and be sure to stock a wide variety of products: gels, scrubs, salts, aromatherapy oils for the bath, and creams, balms, and powders for after the bath. Hire salespeople to organize and host bath product sales parties from their homes, develop your own Web site for online sales, and display your products at health fairs and home shows. Also be sure to rent portable kiosk space in malls for days close to Christmas, Valentine's Day, and Mother's Day.

 BUY
Wholesalers, Manufacturers

 SELL
Kiosks, eBay, Flea Markets, Consumer Shows, Home Parties

 RESOURCES
—Bath and Body Wholesale, ☎ (888) 935-2639, ♂ www.wholesalebathproducts.com
—Healthy Products Plus Wholesale, ☎ (888) 909-1658, ♂ www.healthyproductsplus.com
—Simply Pampered Wholesale, ☎ (877) 624-8342, ♂ www.simplypampered.com

Home Medical Equipment

The trend toward an aging population in North America suggests that if you choose to buy and sell home medical equipment, you will be entering an explosive growth industry with incredible opportunity to profit. Convert your garage into a lavish showroom stocked with the best-quality previously owned home medical equipment. Best-selling products include power and manual wheelchairs, walkers, mechanical lifts and slings, scooters, and bath safety products. Use your negotiation skills to buy at low prices through online marketplaces and from private sellers advertising in classified ads, as well as at auctions and estate sales. You can design a Web site for online sales, display at health fairs, and sell through eBay and online used medical equipment portals. Thoroughly cleaning and tuning up all equipment, as well as providing a warranty, will greatly increase the value of your inventory. Also be sure to build alliances with doctors, physiotherapists, and chiropractors, so they can refer your business to their clients in need of home medical equipment.

 BUY
Online Marketplaces, Classified Ads, Estate Sales

 SELL
Homebased Showroom, Web Site, Health Fairs, eBay

 RESOURCES
—Intellamed, used medical equipment marketplace, ♂ www.auctionmart.com
—Med Marketplace, used medical equipment marketplace, ♂ www.medmarketplace.com
—Med Matrix, used medical equipment marketplace, ♂ www.classifieds.medmatrix.com

Hand and Power Tools

Hand and small power tools such as hammers, screwdriver sets, socket sets, cordless drills, circular saws, and wrench sets are without question some of the best and most profitable products to buy at deeply discounted prices. Simply mark up and resell to do-it-yourself enthusiasts at huge profits. Because retail sales value is not terrifically high on most small hand and power tools, especially on nonmotorized hand tools, you are well advised to stick with selling new products, not used. Purchase from wholesalers, manufacturers, distributors, and liquidators. Hand and power tools are perfect items to sell on eBay, at flea markets, at automotive and woodworking shows, and by renting vacant storefronts in malls and commercial districts for a week at a time to conduct small hand and power tool sales.

 BUY
Wholesalers, Manufacturers

 SELL
Temporary Locations, Flea Markets, Online Marketplaces, Home Shows

 RESOURCES
—Hand Tools Net, manufacturers directory, ♂ www.hand-toolsmanufac turers.com
—Mammoth Tool Wholesale, ☎ (516) 942-0905, ♂ www.mammoth tools.com
—My Crazy Tools Wholesale, ☎ (416) 944-8605, ♂ www.mycrazy tools.com
—Quality Tools 4 Less Wholesale, ☎ (808) 779-1311, ♂ www.quality tools4less.com

Shop Tools

Shop tools such as table saws, chop saws, band saws, lathes, drill presses, joiners, planners, welders, air compressors, metal breaks, metal sheers, metal presses and stamps, and pipe benders are excellent buy-and-sell items, especially used shop tools, which can often be purchased for a fraction of their true value. Where, you might wonder? Buy primarily at auctions and bankruptcy sales that are liquidating the assets of woodworking shops, metal shops, glass shops, contractors, and factories that have closed, are updating equipment, or gone bankrupt. Sell from home supported by advertising in the classifieds and by way of direct mail campaigns aimed at small-business owners in the building, woodworking, and fabrication trades. You can also sell the equipment at flea markets, on eBay, and on numerous additional online marketplaces. Elbow grease and minor repairs as may be needed will go a long way to ensure you get the most for every product. Providing a 30- or 60-day warranty on all equipment will greatly increase the value of your merchandise.

BUY
Manufacturers, Wholesalers, Auctions, Classified Ads

 SELL
B2B, Online Marketplaces, Trade Shows, Homebased Sales

 RESOURCES
—Baer Supply Wholesale, ☎ (800) 289-2237, ♂ www.baeroco.com
—Quality Tools 4 Less Wholesale, ☎ (808) 779-1311, ♂ www.quality tools4less.com
—Used Equipment Network, buy-and-sell marketplace, ☎ (800) 526-6052, ♂ www.buyused.com
—Wiha Quality Tools Wholesale, ☎ (763) 295-6591, ♂ www.wihatools.com

Reclaimed Building Products

You can make a fortune buying reclaimed building products such as bricks, lumber, kitchen cabinets, plumbing fixtures, windows, doors, hardware, ceiling tins, fireplace mantels, light fixtures, patio stones, and hardwood flooring. These materials may be purchased cheaply, and resold for a profit. The value of used building products has soared in recent years as the price of new materials has skyrocketed. Especially valuable are architectural antiques such as clear-stock casings, stained-glass windows, columns and capitals, claw-foot bathtubs, and cut-glass door-knobs. Your main buying sources will include contractors specializing in renovation, flooring installers, window replacement companies, demolition companies, plumbers, and homeowners doing their own renovations. Build alliances with these companies so that you can get first dibs on the best and most valuable reclaimed building products as they become available. Equally valuable are other reclaimed building products such as barn board, barn timbers, and split cedar-rail fencing. Go for a drive in the country and strike deals with farmers—they demolish old barns and you sell the products, splitting the proceeds on a 50-50 basis. Sell to homeowners, collectors, designers, and architects through online and offline marketplaces.

 BUY
Contractors, Homeowners, Auctions, Government Tenders

SELL
Online Marketplaces, Trade Shows, Collectors, Homebased Sales

RESOURCES
—Architectural Antiques, buy-and-sell marketplace, ✆ www.architec
turals.net
—The Used Building Materials Association, ✆ www.ubma.org
—Used Building Materials Exchange, buy-and-sell marketplace, ✆ www.
build.recycle.net

Building Project Plans

The rise in popularity of do-it-yourself home renovations and woodworking projects has made selling building project plans very profitable. You can sell building plans for a number of projects, including house blueprints, decks, garages, arbors, gazebos, furniture, woodworking, birdhouses, toys, and patio furniture. Building and project plans can be purchased wholesale individually or grouped together into book format from wholesalers, or directly from building plan publishers. Plans can be sold online, by mail order, at home-and-garden shows, and at flea markets. You may even decide to branch out and hire architects and woodworkers to design plans for you under your copyright and sell the plans wholesale through retail outlets and to consumers via the aforementioned selling venues.

 BUY
Publishers, Wholesalers

 SELL
Online Marketplaces, Flea Markets, Woodworking and Home-and-Garden Shows, Mail Order

 RESOURCES
—Garlinghouse Publishing, ☎ (800) 235-5700, ✆ www.garlinghouse.com
—Sumerset House Publishing, ☎ (800) 444-2540, ✆ www.sumerset
house.com
—U-Bild Publishing, ☎ (800) 828-2453, ✆ www.u-bild.com

Specialty Woods

A terrific opportunity to make big bucks exists for the homebased handyman with woodworking experience by buying and reselling specialty and exotic woods commonly used in cabinet making, instrument making, and fine woodcrafts industries. In addition to specialty woods like teak veneers, burls for turning, tulipwood, and bloodwood, you can also stock and offer traditional domestic hardwoods such as ash, maple, walnut, cherry, and oak. Buy in large volume wholesale, and resell by the lift, board foot, or individual piece. Extra revenues can be earned if you have the space and machinery required to offer customers milling services such as resawing, dimensioning, bending, and gluing. Sell right from home, through online woodworking portals, and by displaying products at woodworking and crafts shows. You can also sell direct to businesses that require specialty woods—cabinetmakers, boat refinishers, wood turners, furniture makers, and renovation specialists.

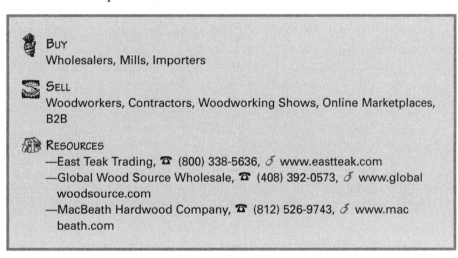

BUY
Wholesalers, Mills, Importers

SELL
Woodworkers, Contractors, Woodworking Shows, Online Marketplaces, B2B

RESOURCES
—East Teak Trading, ☎ (800) 338-5636, ♂ www.eastteak.com
—Global Wood Source Wholesale, ☎ (408) 392-0573, ♂ www.global woodsource.com
—MacBeath Hardwood Company, ☎ (812) 526-9743, ♂ www.mac beath.com

Long-Life Light Bulbs

Did you know that the oldest working light bulb in the world is over 100 years old? Since the early 1900s, a single incandescent light bulb has burned continuously at Fire Station #6 in Livermore, California. The light bulb is so popular that PBS had a documentary about it and a preservation society was formed to educate visitors about the light bulb. The latter can be found online at ♂ www.centennialbulb.org. I am not suggesting you aim to sell light bulbs that last 100 years, but you can make a bundle selling long-life light bulbs just the same. Even long-life bulbs lasting 10,000 hours are, on average, 15 times longer lived than regular bulbs. You can sell these at a retail price of about $2.50, compared to $7.50 for 15 regular light bulbs costing 50 cents each. You can save your customers $5 for each light in their building, while still earning a 100 percent markup on each bulb for yourself. Five dollars might not sound like a lot of money, but consider that a factory, school, hospital, apartment building, office building, or big-box retailer may have 1,000 bulbs burning at all times. You can save this kind of customer thousands of dollars a year in light bulb costs. Buy from wholesalers and directly from manufacturers, and sell to large-volume users by setting appointments and showing them how much money they will save by purchasing your long-life light bulbs.

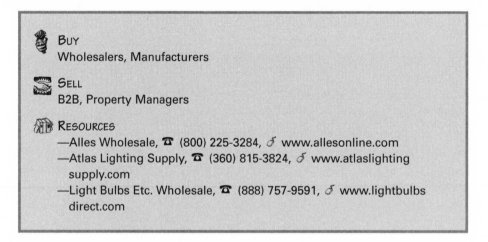

BUY
Wholesalers, Manufacturers

SELL
B2B, Property Managers

RESOURCES
—Alles Wholesale, ☎ (800) 225-3284, ♂ www.allesonline.com
—Atlas Lighting Supply, ☎ (360) 815-3824, ♂ www.atlaslighting supply.com
—Light Bulbs Etc. Wholesale, ☎ (888) 757-9591, ♂ www.lightbulbs direct.com

New Books

New books are a fantastic buy-and-sell product that has incredible upside profit potential. Buy from book distributors, wholesalers, liquidators, retailer returns, and direct from publishers at deeply discounted prices that can often reach 80 percent off cover. One of the best ways to sell is on Amazon, right alongside the new books they sell but for slightly less to entice people to buy yours. You can also hold monthly book sales by renting empty storefronts for a few days, through other online book marketplaces, at flea markets, and by renting mall kiosk vendor space, especially close to Christmas. Specialty books can be sold by mail order supported by advertising in publications related to the book titles for sale. And if there is limited competition in your area, you can even convert a room in your home and sell new books right from home. Some new booksellers even go as far as to sell their books online at cost plus listing fees or commissions and make their money on the shipping charges.

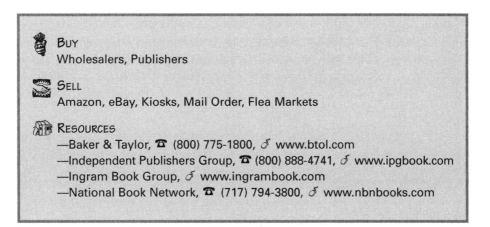

Buy
Wholesalers, Publishers

Sell
Amazon, eBay, Kiosks, Mail Order, Flea Markets

Resources
—Baker & Taylor, ☎ (800) 775-1800, ♂ www.btol.com
—Independent Publishers Group, ☎ (800) 888-4741, ♂ www.ipgbook.com
—Ingram Book Group, ♂ www.ingrambook.com
—National Book Network, ☎ (717) 794-3800, ♂ www.nbnbooks.com

Used and Rare Books

You have the potential to hit the jackpot if you specialize in rare books such as first editions, antique, and author-autographed copies. There are an infinite number of used books available at rock-bottom prices. You can buy them at garage sales, flea markets, online marketplaces, auctions, estate sales, library sales, and secondhand shops. Even better, few people take the time to find out the true value of the books they are selling, and because of this, many rare and valuable books can be purchased in the process. For instance, you might stumble upon a first-edition copy of *The Old Man and the Sea*, by Ernest Hemingway and purchase it for far less than the $600 to $1,000 it is currently worth to a collector. You will want to invest in rare-book pricing guides so you are armed with the resources needed to make wise purchasing decisions. Whether or not the books you sell are run-of-the mill used books for $10 or rare ones worth hundreds, the Internet is your best marketing tool. List books for sale on Amazon, eBay, and on any number of the used and collector book marketplaces on the Net. Also, if you plan on volume selling, be sure to invest in barcode scanning software such as Scanner Pal (www.scoutpal.com), which automatically scans all book information retrieved from the barcode for simple listing.

BUY
Garage Sales, Online Marketplaces, Flea Markets, Secondhand Shops

 SELL
EBay, Collectors, Flea Markets, Online Marketplaces, Amazon

 RESOURCES
—Abe Books, buy-and-sell marketplace, ♂ www.abebooks.com
—International Rare Book Collectors Association, ♂ www.rarebooks.org
—Swapbooks, textbook and used book buy-and-sell marketplace, ♂ www.swapbooks.com
—Used Book Central, buy-and-sell marketplace, ♂ www.usedbookcentral.com
— *Bookman's Price Index: A Guide to the Values of Rare and Other Out of Print Books*, Anne F. McGrath (Gale Group, 2004)

Movie DVDs

Because DVDs are a relatively new technology, there is an incredible opportunity to earn amazing profits buying DVDs wholesale and reselling them retail to the millions of people who are converting their VHS movie collections to DVD. Buy new DVDs from wholesalers, distributors, and liquidators, often for prices starting at $1 a disk for B-movies and up to $15 for first-run hits. These same DVDs can be sold at flea markets, through eBay, and from mall and market kiosks for as much as ten times your wholesale costs. If you choose to sell at flea markets and from kiosks, you will need to follow simple merchandising rules to ensure success. These include keeping your selling booth clean and organized, and using attention-grabbing signs that scream out your biggest customer benefit, such as, "Buy One DVD and Get a One Free!"

 BUY
Wholesalers, Classified Ads

SELL
Kiosks, eBay, Flea Markets

RESOURCES
—Buy Rite DVD Wholesale, ☎ (877) 867-3837, ♂ www.buyritedvd.com
—JM Distribution, ☎ (866) 306-2563, ♂ www.jmdistribution.net
—Treasures On Video Wholesale, ☎ (800) 630-7213, ♂ www.treasuresonvideo.com

Movie Memorabilia

Movie and celebrity fans cannot get enough of everything Hollywood—movie ticket stubs, celebrity autographs, movie scripts, posters, movie and television props, clothing, promotional items, and toys—you name it. If it has anything to do with the movies, television, or celebrities, it is valuable and will be quickly snapped up. The trading of Hollywood memorabilia is not new. It has been going on for more than 60 years, but recently values have greatly increased, mainly because of easy access to online marketplaces such as eBay, which provide new collectors the opportunity to buy like professional collectors without having to travel the world scouting for goods and attending auctions. Your buying sources for everything Hollywood will include garage sales, estate sales, Internet sites, and classified ads. Online marketplaces such as eBay will be your best choice for selling, enabling you to reach a global audience of movie buffs with money to spend. Additionally, you can sell your goods at flea markets, collectible shows, and memorabilia auctions.

 BUY
Garage Sales, Online Marketplaces, Auctions, Classified Ads

 SELL
Collectors, Auctions, Flea Markets, Memorabilia Shows, eBay

 RESOURCES
—Hollywood Memorabilia Center, buy-and-sell marketplace, ♂ www.hollywoodcollector.com
—📖 *Big Reel Magazine*, movie memorabilia collectors' information, Krause Publications, ☎ (800) 258-0929, ♂ www.collect.com
—📖 *The Official Guide to Movie Autographs and Memorabilia*, Daniel Cohen (House of Collectibles, 2004)

Music CDs

In spite of emerging digital technologies that will in the future change the way music is distributed, compact disks will remain a profitable hot seller for the foreseeable future. New CDs can be bought cheaply from wholesalers and distributors, starting at about $1 each for B-list titles, and sold for five to ten times cost to music enthusiasts by way of flea markets, eBay, and music shows. Used music CDs are in many respects a currency of their own: when fast cash is needed for whatever reason, one of the first things to be sold is often the music collection. Look to buy used CDs from people advertising entire collections for sale in the classifieds, or on bulletin boards, and run your own ads stating that you buy entire CD music collections. Hang fliers advising that you buy and sell music CDs, and include contact information, on community notice boards, especially those in close proximity to colleges and universities.

BUY
Wholesalers, Garage Sales, Classified Ads

SELL
Kiosks, eBay, Flea Markets, Consumer Shows

RESOURCES
—CD Plus Entertainment Wholesale, ☎ (727) 639-7780, ♂ www.cdplus dolphinvideo.com
—Wholesale Music CDs, ☎ (217) 344-3988, ♂ www.wholesalemusic cds.com
—Wholesale Discs, ♂ www.wholesalediscs.com, ♂ sales@whole salediscs.com
—Warner Elektra Atlantic Corporation, ♂ info@weac.com, ♂ www. wea.com

Vintage Vinyl Records

Vinyl records have one of the largest followings of people who collect for hobby and listening enjoyment. Rock 'n' roll, jazz, country, blues, and Big Band are all equally popular in 33⅓, 45, or 78 RPM format. They can sell for big bucks, especially rare first-run vinyl in mint condition. The best buying source is, without question, garage sales, so be prepared to spend some time every weekend hunting for vintage vinyl. Typically, you'll find boxes full at nearly every sale at prices of less than $1 each. Price guides will assist you in accessing value and condition. In addition to garage sales, you can also buy from online marketplaces and from private sellers who often use classifieds to advertise their entire collection. Vintage vinyl can be sold to collectors through record collecting clubs, on eBay, at flea markets, and at music and collectible shows. Fortunately, there is no shortage of vintage vinyl to buy, or people looking to buy it all that is required to succeed is finding the right vinyl at the right prices and reselling to collectors willing to pay top dollar.

BUY

Garage Sales, Online Marketplaces, Auctions, Classified Ads

 SELL

Collectors, Flea Markets, Memorabilia Shows, Online Marketplaces

 RESOURCES

—Record Collectors Guild, ♂ www.recordcollectorsguild.org

—Vinyl Web, industry information and links to dealers and collectors, ♂ www.vinylweb.com

—📖 *Goldmine Record Album Price Guide: The Ultimate Guide to Valuing Your Vinyl*, Tim Neely (Krause Publications, 2003)

Music Memorabilia

Concert ticket stubs, autographs, instruments, stage clothing, posters, sheet music, handwritten lyrics, and anything Woodstock—all music memorabilia items are in high demand and command top dollar from collectors worldwide. The best buying sources include garage sales, private seller classified ads, online marketplaces, auctions, estate sales, and collectible shows. The best selling options are similar, including eBay, auctions, flea market vending, and directly to collectors by joining music memorabilia clubs and networking with members, online and off. Additionally, get to know concert managers and promoters, as they can be an excellent buying source for incredible, one-of-a-kind music memorabilia items. Also, don't overlook the reproduction music memorabilia market either, because as the price of real collectibles continues to soar, it leaves many fans no options but to buy reproductions. These items can be purchased from wholesalers and manufacturers. You can find them by conducting Internet keyword searches on any of the popular search engines or directories.

 BUY

Garage Sales, Online Marketplaces, Auctions, Classified Ads

 SELL

Collectors, Flea Markets, Memorabilia Shows, Online Marketplaces

RESOURCES
—E-Rock, online music memorabilia auctions, ♂ www.e-rock.net
—Music Collectors, buy-and-sell marketplace, ♂ www.musiccollectors.com
— *Rock & Roll Treasures: Identification & Value Guide*, Joe Hilton and Greg Moore (Collector Books, 1999)

Karaoke Systems

If you are searching for a fun and unique product to buy and sell that has the potential to easily earn you an extra $1,000-$2,000 per month, look no further than karaoke equipment sales. Your main buying source will be from wholesalers in smaller quantities, keeping your capital investment to a minimum, or you can search for secondhand equipment. But because karaoke is relatively new, at least in North America, used equipment is scarce. Set up a homebased showroom for sales, and advertise locally in the newspaper, on bulletin boards, and by word-of-mouth. You can also sell the equipment through numerous online marketplaces such as eBay, and even at consumer shows.

 BUY
Wholesalers

 SELL
Homebased Sales, eBay, Consumer Shows

RESOURCES
—DTS Karaoke Wholesale, ☎ (800) 588-1868, ♂ www.dtskaraoke.com
—Karaoke Now Wholesale, ☎ (888) 669-7464, ♂ www.karaokenow.com
—Karaoke Wholesale, ☎ (888) 900-3472, ♂ www.karaoke-wholesale.com

Musical Instruments

The sound of music could prove to be the sound of the cash register humming if you decide to buy and sell new and used musical instruments and related accessories. Specialize in any one or all of the following types of musical instruments: drums, keyboard, piano, acoustic and electric guitar, saxophone, bass, violin, bagpipes, or harmonica. A valuable prerequisite is the ability to play, repair, and tune the instrument(s) you sell. This ability will assist in buying, especially used instruments that help maximize profit potential. It is perhaps more difficult to purchase new, recognizable brand-name musical instruments on a wholesale basis for the simple reason that most manufacturers and distributors prefer to have large, authorized retailers servicing geographical areas. In spite of this, you can find smaller manufacturers and distributors prepared to sell wholesale to a small-order reseller; it will just require a little research. Used musical instruments are no problem to buy; there is a plethora of them available in every area through classified ads, organized band sales, auctions, and garage sales. A homebased showroom is best suited for sales, as well as listing on eBay and exhibiting at music shows.

BUY
Manufacturers, Wholesalers, Auctions, Classified Ads

SELL
Homebased Sales, eBay, Flea Markets, Music Shows

RESOURCES
—Echo Trade Marketing, ☎ (888) 271-4208, ♂ www.echotrademarket ing.com
—The Shubb Company, ☎ (707) 876-3001, ♂ www.shubb.com/trade
—📖 *Blue Book of Acoustic Guitars*, S.P. Fjestad (Blue Book Publications, 2001)
—📖 *Blue Book of Electric Guitars*, Zachary Fjestad (Blue Book Publications, 2003)

Sheet Music

With millions of musicians worldwide, the prospect of a venture engaged in buying and selling sheet music appears to be very bright. All beginners, many novices, and even a few seasoned professional musicians rely on sheet music in order to play their instruments. Fill this need, and sell the sheet music they need by purchasing loose and bound sheet music from wholesalers and publishers cheaply, and then reselling it for big profits. Sell at flea markets and music shows, on eBay, and through various other online marketplaces. Also create your own e-commerce Web site listing all the sheet music you stock, so you can sell to music lovers around the globe. Because there are so many styles of music—including rock, jazz, country, opera, choir, and classical—you may want to find a niche in the market and become known as a specialist there.

BUY
Publishers, Wholesalers

 SELL
Online Marketplaces, Music Shows, Flea Markets

 RESOURCES
—Hal Leonard Corporation, ☎ (414) 774-3630, ♂ www.halleonard.com
—National Music Publishers Association, ♂ www.nmpa.org
—Southern Music Company, ☎ (800) 284-5443, ♂ www.southern
music.com

Jukeboxes

Antique, new, and reproduction jukeboxes are hot sellers that can earn you a fortune, especially when you consider that classic art deco Wurlitzers from the '40s command five figures, reproductions can sell for up to $10,000, and new Rowe CD models can also reach $10,000. Because the retail value of jukeboxes is high, it is possible to make $100,000 a year and only have to buy and sell perhaps 20 to 40 units, not to mention the extra money that can be earned selling related accessories such as new and used parts, 45 and 78 RPM records, manuals, signs, and souvenirs. To get started searching for antique jukeboxes to buy low, keep an eye on classified advertising, online marketplaces, collectible shows, and auctions. New and reproduction jukeboxes and related accessories can be purchased directly from manufacturers and distributors. New, antique, reproduction, and accessories, can all be sold from a homebased showroom supported by advertising online, locally, and in specialty publications. Also sell through online marketplaces such as eBay, antique and collectible shows, and auction sales, and through interior designers. Let's face it: who wouldn't want a classic Seeburg jukebox, made famous in "Happy Days," gracing their recreation room or office?

 BUY
Auctions, Wholesalers, Classified Ads

 SELL
Collectors, Collectible Shows, Homebased Sales, eBay

RESOURCES
—BMI Gaming Wholesale, ☎ (561) 391-7269, ♂ www.bmigaming.com
—The Complete Jukebox, industry information and resources, ♂ www.
tomszone.com
—Game Room Antiques, buy-and-sell marketplace, ♂ www.game
roomantiques.com

Arcade Games

If you want to combine fun and profit, consider buying and selling arcade games. The market is red-hot for new, used, and vintage arcade-style video and nonvideo games. It is not uncommon for vintage pinball machines to fetch a few thousand dollars, PAC MAN and Frogger games $1,500, and late-model Harley Davidson L.A. riders $5,000. New machines can be purchased through wholesalers and distributors, while used arcade games can be purchased at auctions, through classified ads, and on various online marketplaces. Sell directly to business owners, especially coin-operated machines, which can earn them money. Homeowners also love them for the recreation room, and professionals for the office as a nifty decoration, conversation piece, and the occasional quick game for an escape from work. You will want to invest in arcade-game price guides to help value machines for purchase and resale.

 BUY
Online Marketplaces, Auctions, Classified Ads, Wholesalers

 SELL
Online Marketplaces, Collectors, Homebased Sales, Collectible Shows,
B2B

 RESOURCES
—BMI Gaming Wholesale, ☎ (561) 391-7269, ♂ www.bmigaming.com
—Game Room Antiques buy-and-sell marketplace, ♂ www.gameroom
antiques.com
—📖 *The Official Price Guide to Classic Video Games: Console,
Arcade, and Handheld*, David Ellis (House of Collectibles, 2004)

Fitness Equipment

Buying and selling fitness equipment, especially used equipment, ranks as one of the best things to buy and sell. There is always great supply and great demand for all types of fitness equipment. Fitness equipment is best described as a savior purchase. The majority of people purchase fitness equipment new, hoping it will be their savior and put them on the path to better health and fitness. Unfortunately, once set up at home, reality sinks in—working out day in and day out is hard work and very time-consuming. And in no time the very expensive piece of exercise equipment becomes a very expensive clothes rack. Pick up any buy-and-sell newspaper, and you will find they are full of ads like, "Treadmill used only 10 times. Paid $2,500, sell $750 OBO." Go in with a firm cash offer of half, and there is a good chance you will be successful.

Even though excellent-quality equipment can be purchased cheaply, that does not mean you cannot resell it for huge profits; you can. Remember, much of the buy-and-sell game is timing, and in the case of fitness equipment, it does not take long before someone else will come along, also seeking a savior. As mentioned, fitness equipment can be purchased through classified ads, but also at garage sales, gym closeouts, auctions, and estate sales. New equipment can be bought from wholesalers and also directly from manufacturers. Best sellers include treadmills, steppers, elliptical trainers, rowing machines, exercise bikes, free weights, and universal multi-station machines. You can establish a homebased sales showroom and advertise locally in the paper and on community bulletin boards, and you can also list your equipment for sale on any number of online marketplaces.

BUY
Manufacturers, Wholesalers, Classified Ads, Auctions

SELL
Homebased Sales, Sports and Fitness Shows, Online Marketplaces

RESOURCES
—Fitness Equipment Trader, classifieds and auction, ♂ www.fitness equipmenttrader.com
—Hubie Equipment Manufacturing, ☎ 86-27-87454115 (China), ♂ www.hbcmec.com
—JIH KAO Equipment Manufacturing, ☎ 886-2-25373397 (Taiwan), ♂ www.jkexer.com.tw

Licensed Products

Well-branded, recognizable companies, professional sports teams, organizations, producers, publishers, and even individual people often license their likeness, logo, name, characters, or mottos to other companies and manufacturers to be featured on a wide range of consumer products. These products range from T-shirts featuring a likeness of John Lennon to hats embroidered with the famous Harley Davidson logo, to children's lunch pails covered with Disney characters, to sporting goods autographed by professional athletes, to dog collars with the familiar NHL logo printed on them—and the list goes on and on. Wholesalers will be your main buying source for licensed products for resale, though it is also possible to purchase directly from manufacturers that produce products with licensed images. Best sales venues will include eBay, flea markets, community events, and rental kiosks in mall and public markets. Pretty much all licensed products sell well, whether it is a bottle opener bearing a beer company logo or a hat with a sports team logo, mainly because people want to be associated with whatever the licensee represents. And they know the brand, thus eliminating any fear of making an unknown purchase.

BUY
Wholesalers, Manufacturers

SELL
Flea Markets, eBay, Kiosks, Consumer Shows

RESOURCES
—Big Apple Card Company, ☎ (800) 883-8090, ♂ www.bigapplecard.com
—Cavalieri Distributors, ☎ (516) 639-1532, ♂ www.cavalieridistributors.com
—Smooth International Wholesale, ☎ (800) 790-1440, ♂ www.smoothtalkinc.com

Golf Clubs

Golf ranks as one of the most popular sports and recreational pastimes in North America, and you can make a bundle by selling new and used golf clubs and equipment. If you have some mechanical aptitude, you can dramatically increase profits by purchasing golf club components (heads, shafts, and grips) wholesale, and assembling the clubs at home to meet your clients' individual needs. That is, you build custom clubs. Or if you are not the handy type, then you can purchase preassembled new clubs from wholesalers and manufacturers. Used golf clubs and accessories such as bags, electric carts, and pull-carts can be bought at flea markets, garage sales, online golf portals, auction sales, and estate sales. New and used clubs and accessories can be sold through eBay, via a homebased showroom supported by local and online advertising, and by exhibiting at golf shows.

 BUY
Wholesalers, Manufacturers, Classified Ads, Auctions

 SELL
Homebased Sales, Online Marketplaces, eBay, Golf and Recreation Shows

 RESOURCES
—Golf Equipment Shopping Guide, new and used equipment whole-salers and manufacturers links, ♂ www.golfshoppingguide.com
—Kings Sports Wholesale, ☎ (800) 344-1480, ♂ www.kingssports.com
—Wholesale Golf Equipment, ☎ (800) 752-6406, ♂ www.wholesale golfequipment.net
—📖 *Antique Golf Collectibles: A Price and Reference Guide*, Chuck Furjanic (Krause Publications, 2000)

Bicycles

One of the best buying sources for used bicycles are police auctions, because bicycles are among the most commonly stolen items, and the vast majority of those recovered by police go unclaimed by owners. Most metropolitan police forces hold auctions once or twice a year, auctioning recovered stolen items that were not claimed by their owners. Bicycles make up a large percentage of auctioned items, and it is not uncommon to purchase high-quality, late-model bikes for a fraction of their resale value. Additional buying sources include private sellers advertising in the classifieds, as well as wholesalers, manufacturers, and distributors of new bicycle accessories and parts, which can also be sold to boost revenues. Some mechanical aptitude is beneficial so you are able to make minor repairs as required, tune up each bike before selling, and give each bike a good cleaning. All of this will increase the sales value of each bike by perhaps 50 percent or more. Best-selling venues include a homebased showroom, listing bikes for sale on eBay, and exhibiting at sports and recreation shows.

BUY
Police Auctions, Wholesalers, Manufacturers, Classified Ads

SELL
Sports and Fitness Shows, Homebased Sales, Flea Markets, eBay

RESOURCES
—AMANO Cycle Manufacturing, ☎ 886-2-2531-9145 (Taiwan), ♂ www.amanocycle.com.tw
—F&R Company Manufacturing, ☎ (562) 630-3213, ♂ www.fnrco.com
—Jee Ann Bicycle Manufacturing, ☎ 880-49-2253116 (Taiwan), ♂ www.jeeann.com.tw
—📖 *Bicycle Collectibles Pricing Guide*, Dan Gindling (Van Der Plas Publications, 2000)

New Sporting Goods

More than any other hobby, activity, or pastime, sports engages more people—hockey, football, racket sports, skiing, baseball, skateboarding, base jumping, rock climbing, bowling, and the list goes on. Needless to say, an incredible opportunity exists in buying and selling new sporting goods. Due to the sheer number of sports people participate in, you may want to specialize in one, such as rock climbing, or in a small group of related sports, such as selling racket-sports equipment. Your buying sources include wholesalers, manufacturers, liquidators, importers, and distributors. The best sales venues include a homebased showroom, flea market vending, listing on eBay and online sports equipment marketplaces, and rental kiosks in malls and public markets. You will also want to join sports clubs and associations relative to the types of equipment you deal in to network for business.

BUY
Wholesalers, Manufacturers

SELL
Homebased Sales, Online Marketplaces, Sports and Recreation Shows, Kiosks

RESOURCES
—Jerry's Sports Center Wholesale, ♂ www.jerryssportscenter.com

—Regro Sports Wholesale, ☎ (877) 384-4374, ♂ www.regrosports.com
—Sporting Goods Manufacturers Association International, ♂ www.sports link.com

Used Sporting Goods

Much like dealing in new sporting goods, great profits can also be earned by buying and selling used sporting goods and equipment, especially if you specialize in high-end gear such as parasailing and skiing equipment. Buy at garage sales, sports swap meets, auctions, and through the classifieds. Sell from a homebased showroom supported by local advertising, at flea markets, and by utilizing eBay. Key to your success will be your ability to mingle with people who are engaged in the particular sport you choose to specialize in. This can be accomplished by joining online Web rings and chat forums, as well as offline sport clubs and associations, to network with members. I mention parasailing because a few years back, mixed in with some construction tools I purchased as a lot at auction, was a parasail, harness, and line, the type towed behind a speedboat. Not having a use for it, I placed a classified ad in the paper and had people lining up to buy. At the time, I remember wishing I had a hundred to sell.

 BUY
Classified Ads, Online Marketplaces, Auctions, Garage Sales

 SELL
Homebased Sales, eBay, Flea Markets, Sporting Goods Swap Meets

 RESOURCES
—Sporting Goods Guide, sporting goods marketplace, ♂ www.sporting-goods-guide.com
—U.S. Free Ads, free online sporting goods and equipment classified advertisements, ♂ www.usfreeads.com/_sports/

Trading Cards

The value of trading cards continues to rise year after year, and because of this, it is never too late to jump in with both feet and grab your share of the lucrative trading card market. In addition to traditional sports trading cards like baseball, football, hockey, and basketball, there are a great number of people who also collect nonsports trading cards such as cartoons, comics, movie celebrities, science fiction, space, automotive, wrestling, and the military cards. Having an interest and some knowledge of trading cards will help you get started. But those who are new to the business can educate themselves about the trading card industry by way of online forums, books, trading card clubs, and swap meets. New prepackaged trading cards can be purchased from wholesalers and distributors, while used cards can be bought from collectors, classified ads, auctions, flea markets, garage sales, and numerous online trading card marketplaces. You can also utilize many of the same venues for reselling the cards for a profit. Price guides will be an important tool to help you valuate both purchases and sales, so be sure to acquire up-to-date trading card price guides.

 BUY
Wholesalers, Garage Sales, Online Marketplaces, Auctions

 SELL
Collectors, Auctions, eBay, Flea Markets

 RESOURCES
—Baseline Sports Wholesale, ☎ (877) 834-6522, ♂ www.blsports.com
—Diamond Comics Distributors, ☎ (410) 560-7100, ♂ www.diamond comics.com
—Sports Card Depot, buy-and-sell marketplace, ♂ www.carddepot.com
—Sportsline Distributors, ☎ (847) 656-0300, ♂ www.sportslined.com
—📖 *The Official Price Guide to Baseball Cards*, James Beckett (House of Collectibles, 2004)
—📖 *The Official Beckett Price Guide to Football Cards*, James Beckett (House of Collectibles, 2003)
—📖 *Beckett Basketball Card Price Guide*, James Beckett and Keith Howes (Beckett Publications, 2004)
—📖 *Beckett Hockey Card Price Guide*, James Beckett, Clint Hall, and Allan Muir (Beckett Publications, 2002)

Sports Memorabilia

Calling all sports fanatics! It is time to put your knowledge of sports to good use and make a bundle of cash by buying and selling sports memorabilia. If you know what you are doing, you can buy team jerseys, autographs, photographs, sports magazines, action figures, novelties, posters, ticket stubs, and sports equipment at bargain-basement prices and resell to collectors and diehard sports fans just like you for a profit. Not only can this be an exciting way to supplement your income, you might just find you can replace your current income altogether and trade in sports memorabilia full-time. Devote time to rummaging through garage sales, flea markets, secondhand shops, online marketplaces, and auctions to find valuable sports memorabilia items that you can buy dirt cheap. Sell your valuable finds directly to collectors via online sports memorabilia Web sites and auctions, and directly from a homebased showroom advertised locally and nationally in specialty publications and online electronic publications.

 BUY
Garage Sales, Auctions, Classified Ads, Online Marketplaces

 SELL
Collectors, eBay, Sports Shows, Homebased Sales

 RESOURCES
—Leland's, buy-and-sell marketplace, ♂ www.lelands.com
—Steiner Sports Memorabilia, information and sports auction, ♂ www.steinersports.com
—Superior Sports Auctions, buy-and-sell marketplace, ♂ www.superiorsports.com
—📖 *Standard Catalog of Sports Memorabilia*, Bert Lehman (Krause Publications, 2003)

Archery Equipment

Online and from home are the two best ways to sell archery equipment and supplies, especially if you have enough outdoor space to safely (and legally) establish a test range. A converted garage, stocked with bows, arrows, cases, replacement parts, and accessories such as bow stands, targets, chest guards, finger tabs, shooting gloves, and instructional videos will work well as a showroom. Most retailers of archery equipment do not limit their potential audience and carry most types of bows such as traditional, cross, compound, and recurved. You would be well advised to do the same. Though you should concentrate on selling new equipment, you can also profit on used equipment you take in on trade. Factory direct and wholesalers will be your two primary buying sources. In addition to homebased and online sales, you can also exhibit products at sports, recreation, and hunting shows.

BUY
Wholesalers, Manufacturers, Classified Ads

 SELL
Homebased Sales, Online Marketplaces, Sports and Recreation Shows

 RESOURCES
—Jakes Archery Wholesale, ☎ (801) 225-0509, ♂ www.jakesarchery.com
—Kinsey's Archery Products Wholesale, ☎ (800) 366-4269, ♂ www.kinseys archery.com
—Lancaster Archery Supply, ☎ (800) 829-7408, ♂ www.lancaster archery.com

Windsurfers

The odds of prospering in windsurfer sales will be greatly increased if you currently participate in the sport and have a good knowledge of windsurfing equipment and accessories. Providing you meet these criteria, a great full-time or part-time income can be earned buying and selling new and used windsurfers and accessories. Buying sources for new boards and accessories are manufacturers and wholesalers, while used windsurfers and accessories can be purchased from private sellers using classified ads and by word-of-mouth. In addition to boards, increase revenues by selling replacement parts such as sails, masts, booms, foot straps, and fittings and accessories like harnesses, wet suits, roof racks, board bags, and instructional videos. Sell online, from a homebased showroom, and by exhibiting products at sports and recreation shows. Also consider buying and selling kite surfing equipment, as the popularity of the sport has recently skyrocketed and is a great sales match with windsurfers.

 BUY
Wholesalers, Manufacturers, Classified Ads

 SELL
Homebased Sales, Online Marketplaces, Sports and Recreation Shows

 RESOURCES
—American Windsurfing Industries Association, ♂ www.awia.com

—International Windsurfing Association, ♂ www.internationalwind surfing.com

—Windsurfing Classifieds, online classifieds, ♂ www.windsurfingclassi fieds.com

Trampolines

Not only do trampolines offer a fun activity for the entire family to pursue, but as a buy-and-sell product, there is a very good chance that trampolines can bring in substantial revenues, selling them right from your own backyard. There are trampolines available to suit every preference and price point—traditional for the consumer with a big backyard, floating for the cottager, mini for the space-challenged, jogger for the fitness-conscious, inflatable for portability, and tumble for gymnasts. Because used trampolines are hard to come by, other than the occasional trade-in, your supply source will probably be limited to wholesalers and manufacturers. As previously mentioned, the best place to display is right in your own backyard, and you can advertise in your local newspaper, on bulletin boards, at sports clubs, and by word-of-mouth. Recreation, fitness, and sports shows also provide good marketing venues, and don't ignore the Internet, because some consumers will know exactly the type of trampoline they want and will be more than willing to order it online, especially people living in small or remote communities without access to trampoline retailers in their area.

 BUY
Wholesalers, Manufacturers

 SELL
Homebased Sales, eBay, Sports and Recreation Shows, Community Events

 RESOURCES
—A. J. Landmark Trampoline Manufacturing, ☎ (800) 869-7335, ♂ www. ajlandmark.com
—International Trampoline Industry Association, ♂ www.itia-inc.org
—Tramp Master Manufacturing, ☎ (800) 553-1402, ♂ www.tramp master.com
—Trampolines USA Manufacturing, ☎ (800) 872-6765, ♂ www.1800 trampolines.com

Scuba Diving Equipment

Calling all scuba divers! Stop paying out your hard-earned money to other diving fanatics every time you buy a new piece of equipment. Instead, start paying yourself by using your knowledge of the sport to buy and sell new and used scuba equipment. Sell equipment such as wet suits, dry suits, tanks, weights and belts, fins, masks, dive computers, first-aid kits, underwater cameras, and every other type of scuba gear and equipment imaginable. Buy new items from wholesalers and manufacturers, and used items from private sellers advertising in scuba publications and online portals. Convert your garage into a mini dive shop and sell right from home. It's even better if you have a pool so customers can test equipment. If not, small but adequate above-ground pools are always available in the classifieds for a few hundred dollars and sometimes for free. Also sell at sports and recreation shows, through eBay, and by word-of-mouth in the tight-knit dive community.

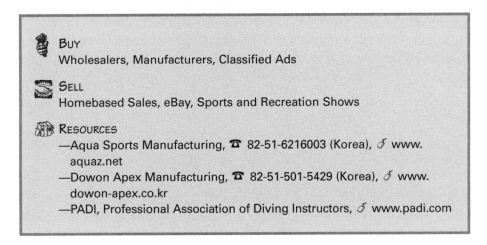

BUY
Wholesalers, Manufacturers, Classified Ads

SELL
Homebased Sales, eBay, Sports and Recreation Shows

RESOURCES
—Aqua Sports Manufacturing, ☎ 82-51-6216003 (Korea), ♂ www.aquaz.net
—Dowon Apex Manufacturing, ☎ 82-51-501-5429 (Korea), ♂ www.dowon-apex.co.kr
—PADI, Professional Association of Diving Instructors, ♂ www.padi.com

Boomerangs

If you are searching for a very unique product to sell, then it is safe to say that boomerangs will unquestionably fit the bill. In bulk, mass-produced boomerangs can be purchased for only a few dollars each and resold for five to ten times as much to consumers looking for a fun new game to play and for gifts to give to others. Boomerangs can also be sold directly to business owners as promotional specialties. Build an alliance with a local screen-printing shop; you sell the boomerangs to local businesspeople, and the printer emblazons them with the business's name, logo, and sales message. Because boomerangs make such a unique gift and fun toy, they can be sold in a number of locations online and offline, including flea markets, mall kiosks, eBay, and community events.

BUY
Wholesalers, Manufacturers

SELL
Kiosks, eBay, Flea Markets, Consumer Shows, B2B

RESOURCES
—Aussie Boomerangs, ☎ 61-2-982-45680 (Australia), ♂ www.eql.com.au/boommain.htm
—Davro Boomerangs, ☎ 44-01309-671-846 (Scotland), ♂ www.davroboomerangs.com
—W. W. Souvenirs Wholesale, ♂ www.wwsouvenirs.com

Hot Tubs

People sell hot tubs for a great number of reasons— they move, can't afford the upkeep, or simply don't use it. Regardless of the reason, used hot tubs can be purchased for a song. The reason is simple: Even though there is a huge and growing demand for new and used hot tubs, they are generally large, heavy, need equipment and a truck to move, and require a professional to install safely. Obviously, these are more than sufficient reasons to scare off many would-be buyers of secondhand hot tubs. But this is where the profitable equation begins, because you can put together all of these benefits: purchase used hot tubs cheaply, invest in transportation and equipment, and contract with professionals such as handymen for moving and electricians and plumbers for installation. Doing so will enable you to sell secondhand hot tubs as a complete package, including the tub, the transportation, professional installation, and even throw in a month's worth of chemicals. If you make it easy and convenient for people to buy the things they want, they will. In the process, you will profit handsomely.

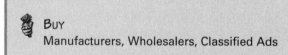

BUY
Manufacturers, Wholesalers, Classified Ads

SELL
Homebased Sales, Online Marketplaces, Home-and-Garden Shows

 RESOURCES
—National Spa & Pool Institute, ♂ www.nspi.org
—Robert's Hot Tub Manufacturing, ☎ (800) 735-5290, ♂ www.
rhtubs.com
—Spa Wholesaler, spa supplies and accessories, ♂ www.spawhole
saler.com
—📖 *The Ultimate Guide to Spas and Hot Tubs: Troubleshooting and Tricks of the Trade*, Terry Tamminen (McGraw-Hill, 2004)

Saunas

In-home saunas were a fashionable must-have item in the '70s, but as the sales of hot tubs grew in the eighties, saunas were no longer in fashion and sales greatly declined, especially in North America. But all of that has changed now. Saunas are back in vogue and a must-have for many people. There are a great number of sauna manufacturers, and many offer a do-it-yourself sauna kit requiring only basic hand tools and virtually no experience to assemble. What makes this exciting is that the saunas are in kit form, so many manufacturers can also provide drop-shipping services. This means you can sell sauna kits from home, at home-and-garden shows, recreation shows, and online marketplaces, and through specialty publications without having to worry about storage and transportation issues, as the manufacturer will ship directly to your customers. At present there is not much supply—or demand—for used saunas and equipment. However, in years to come the supply of used saunas will increase because of the recent proliferation of small sauna kits.

 BUY
Manufacturers, Wholesalers

 SELL
Homebased Sales, Online Marketplaces, Home-and-Garden Shows

 RESOURCES
—Dolphin Pacific Manufacturing, ☎ (877) 707-2862, ♂ www.amerisauna.com
—Sauna Fin Manufacturing, ☎ (800) 387-7029, ♂ www.saunafin.com
—Sauna Kits Manufacturing, ☎ (877) 663-3311, ♂ www.saunakits.com

Billiard Tables

Billiards is a recreational pastime enjoyed by millions of people. Entrepreneurs with drive can easily capitalize on this situation and turn it into money in the bank. Start a buy-and-sell enterprise specializing in the sale of new and used billiard tables and accessories such as cues, balls, chalk, replacement covers, and overhead lights. Working right from a homebased showroom, offer clients new and used equipment for less than retailers with expensive storefronts. And because you do not have the same costly overhead such as rent, commercial property taxes, and added utilities, you can pass these savings on directly to your customers in the form of lower prices, crushing the competition in the process. Buying secondhand tables will mean spending time searching classified ads and attending auction sales. New tables and accessories can be purchased directly from manufacturers and wholesalers. Keep in mind that you might want to establish a retail financing account with a bank, credit union, or leasing company so you can offer customers financing and leasing options. Doing so will greatly increase your potential market and total sales.

BUY
Manufacturers, Wholesalers, Classified Ads, Auctions

SELL
Homebased Sales, Online Marketplaces

RESOURCES
—Cuestix International Wholesale, ☎ (303) 926-2670, ♂ www.cuestix int.com
—Hi Star Manufacturing, ☎ 886-5-2217692 (Taiwan), ♂ www.hi-star. com/tw
—Yalin Billiard Goods Manufacturing, ☎ 86-531-8099666 (China), ♂ www.yalinbilliard.com
—📖 *Buying or Selling a Pool Table*, Mose Dauane (Phoenix Billiards, 2001)

Canoes

Turn your passion for paddling into a profitable pastime. Why paddle only occasionally when you can start a buy-and-sell venture trading in canoes and related equipment and doing something that you really love? Once established, in all probability you will earn enough income so you can dump your job and concentrate on canoe sales full-time. Good money can be made buying and selling both new and used canoes. Buy new directly from manufacturers. There are hundreds of them in North America, some producing thousands monthly, while others are homebased operations producing only a few each month. Specialize in fiberglass, rotomold plastic, or composites such as Kevlar, and earn additional revenues by selling paddles, dry bags and gear, rooftop carriers, and life vests. Used canoes can be purchased at auctions and garage sales, from for-sale signs, and through classified ads. New and used accessories can be sold from a homebased showroom, at sports and recreation shows, online marketplaces, and by organizing try-before-you-buy canoe sales events at local lakes and rivers.

BUY
Manufacturers, Wholesalers, Classified Ads, Auctions

SELL
Homebased Sales, Online Marketplaces, Sports and Recreation Shows

RESOURCES
—Current Designs, ☎ (250) 479-0106, ♂ www.cdkayak.com
—Mid Canada Fiberglass, ☎ (705) 647-6549, ♂ www.scottcanoe.com
—Nova Sport Equipment, ☎ (519) 455-6252, ♂ www.novacraft.com

Kayaks

Not only is kayaking fun, it is also excellent exercise, which explains why the sport has exploded in popularity over the past decade. Buying and selling ocean, river, and white-water kayaks and related accessories such as helmets, paddles, life jackets, throw bags, spray skirts, and dry bags is an excellent choice for people with an interest in the sport. Buy new or used boats and equipment for resale, or deal in both. New boats and equipment are available from numerous distributors or directly from manufacturers who are looking to establish distribution and retail accounts. Used equipment is available from private sellers through classified ads and word-of-mouth. Being an avid kayaker, who has bought and sold a few boats, I can tell you firsthand that money can be made if you are patient, buy off-season, sell in-season, and are prepared to work at marketing your products.

BUY
Manufacturers, Wholesalers, Classified Ads, Auctions

SELL
Homebased Sales, Online Marketplaces, Recreation Shows

RESOURCES
—Dagger, ☎ (800) 433-1969, ✍ www.dagger.com
—Kiwi Kayak, ☎ (800) 545-2925, ✍ www.kiwikayak.com
—Loki Kayak, ☎ (604) 908-6590, ✍ www.lokikayak.com
—Ocean Kayak, ☎ (360) 366-4003, ✍ www.oceankayak.com

Camping Equipment

Trading in camping equipment can be profitable and fun. Buy and sell new and used items like tents, stoves, water makers, sleeping bags, hiking gear, rainwear, cook sets, and more. New equipment can be purchased from wholesalers, importers, liquidators, and in some cases directly from manufacturers if you are prepared to buy in large quantities. Used equipment can be purchased from private sellers advertising in the classifieds, at auction sales, and at garage sales. Set up a showroom right at home; sell on eBay and other online recreation portals, at camping and recreation shows, and at weekend flea markets. Get the most for your products by ensuring that they are clean, in good repair and of high quality. Use attention-grabbing signs to draw people in to your sales area. Though an enormous industry, campers can be considered as belonging to a tight community, and it won't take long for word to spread about your business, providing you offer great products, fair prices, and service second to none.

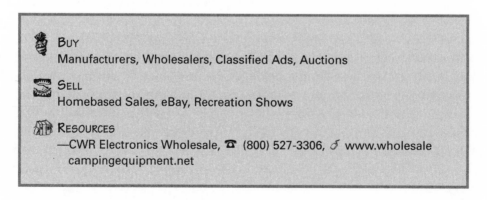

BUY
Manufacturers, Wholesalers, Classified Ads, Auctions

SELL
Homebased Sales, eBay, Recreation Shows

RESOURCES
—CWR Electronics Wholesale, ☎ (800) 527-3306, ✍ www.wholesale
campingequipment.net

—Namdhari Tents, ☎ 91-11-23543156 (India), ♂ www.indiamart.com/
namdharitents
—Outdoor Adventures Wholesale, ☎ (318) 927-5451, ♂ www.outdoor
adventuresllc.com

Fishing Tackle

For all of the entrepreneurial fishing enthusiasts out there, great profits can be earned buying low-cost fishing tackle and equipment and reselling it to fishing fanatics for huge profits. These products include rods, reels, lures, knives, fish-finder electronics, waders, clipper tools, traps, line, subject books, float tubes, vests, tackle boxes, downriggers, and electric trolling motors. The best buying sources are wholesalers and manufacturers, while the best selling sources include eBay, fishing and hunting shows, flea markets, mail order sales, and a homebased showroom. If you can afford to buy in volume, you will get the lowest prices purchasing factory direct from overseas manufacturers, especially China, which has a large fishing tackle manufacturing industry. Also do not overlook local fly tiers as a possible buying source for one-of-a-kind-ties, as these can easily be sold for two to three times cost and sell like crazy. One of the best ways to spread the word is to get out to the rivers and lakes in your area and let the fisherpeople (PC) know about your products.

BUY
Wholesalers, Manufacturers

SELL
Kiosks, eBay, Flea Markets, Recreation Shows, Mail Order

RESOURCES
—Dollar Days Wholesale, ☎ (877) 837-9569, ♂ www.dollardays.com
—Pokee Fishing Tackle Manufacturing, ☎ 8620-32234203 (China), ♂
www.pokeefishing.com
—Valor Corporation Wholesale, ☎ (800) 899-8256, ♂ www.valorcorp.com

Fishing Bait

Fishing bait is big business, and those who get into bait sales on a full-time or part-time basis can earn serious money. A prerequisite, of course, is not to have an aversion to creepy crawly-things like worms and leeches, because they will be two of your best income producers. Bait minnows, like shiners, can be caught in rivers and creeks using traps or a seine net. Or if you have the required space, you can install a minnow-breeding pond. If you catch or raise bait, a license issued by the Department of Fisheries is generally required, so be sure to check local regulations. Dew worms, a.k.a. night crawlers, are another bait. You can raise them in soil and moss boxes or purchase wholesale from worm farms and worm-picking crews, working golf courses after the sun goes down. As mentioned, leeches are another bait that can be raised or purchased in larger quantities wholesale and resold in smaller quantities for a profit. To purchase the equipment necessary to store and sell fishing bait from home will require an investment of at least a few thousand dollars. With that said, however, providing your home is in close proximity to popular fishing lakes or rivers, the investment is quickly returned and rewarded with substantial profits.

Buy
Wholesalers

Sell
Homebased Sales, B2B

Resources
—Bait Net, industry information and links, ♂ www.baitnet.com
—Forked Tree Ranch Wholesale, ☎ (208) 267-2632, ♂ www.forkedtree ranch.com
—National Bait Wholesale, ☎ (905) 278-0180 , ♂ www.nationalbait.com
—Martin's Craw Farm, ☎ (574) 965-2948, ♂ www.mcfsoftcrawfarm.com
— 📖 Shield Publications, books on raising bait for profit, ♂ www.worm books.com

Hunting Equipment

Like fishing, hunting is big business, and selling equipment and supplies directly to the millions of hunting fans in this country can make you rich. However, due to lots of red tape, regulations, and a host of storage concerns, skip selling guns and ammo. Leave that to the established shops and outfitters, and concentrate your efforts on other hunting equipment and supplies like decoys, calls, blinds and camouflage materials, scents, hearing protection, clothing, first-aid kits, survival packs, portable GPS systems, and instructional books and videos. New equipment and supplies can be purchased wholesale from manufacturers and distributors, while used equipment can be bought at auctions, through classified ads, and via online marketplaces. New and used hunting equipment can be sold at sports and recreation shows, from a homebased showroom, and on eBay.

 BUY
Manufacturers, Wholesalers, Classified Ads, Auctions

 SELL
Homebased Sales, Online Marketplaces, Recreation Shows

 RESOURCES
—Dollar Days Wholesale, ☎ (877) 837-9569, ♂ www.dollardays.com
—Hunting Fishing Gear Review, directory listing industry information and equipment wholesalers and manufacturers, ♂ www.hunting-fishing-gear.com
—Outdoor Adventures Wholesale, ☎ (318) 927-5451, ♂ www.outdooradventuresllc.com
—Valor Corporation Wholesale, ☎ (800) 899-8256, ♂ www.valorcorp.com

Table Games

Table games are an increasingly popular addition to any family recreation room, office, or employee lunchroom. For that reason they make fantastic buy-and-sell items. Purchase and resell both new and previously owned table games, including shuffleboard games, Ping-Pong tables, air hockey, chess/checker tables, poker tables, foosball games, and related equipment and accessories such as robotic Ping Pong ball servers for solo players. Set your own basement up as a showroom displaying all your products and advertise locally in the newspaper, on bulletin boards, and by word-of-mouth. You can also sell your goods through sports and recreation shows and online marketplaces like eBay. Because the average price of table games ranges from $250 to $1,000 or more, the profit potential is excellent. Used table games can be bought from private sellers by advertising locally and through auction sales. New table games can be purchased directly from manufacturers, their agents, or distributors.

BUY
Manufacturers, Wholesalers, Classified Ads, Auctions

 SELL
Homebased Sales, eBay, Home-and-Garden Shows

 RESOURCES
—Escalade Sports Manufacturing, ☎ (800) 467-1206, ♂ www.escalade sports.com
—Hi Star Manufacturing, ☎ 886-5-2217692 (Taiwan), ♂ www.hi-star. com/tw
—T. G. Enterprises, ☎ (800) 825-7664, ♂ www.americantabletennis.com

Paintball Equipment

Paintball war games have become incredibly popular over the past decade. Not a weekend goes by without thousands of people suiting up in camouflage gear and protective eyewear and hitting the woods in small groups or teams to hunt down and shoot their opponents with a paintball. You can capitalize on this craze. All it takes is securing the right wholesale source to buy from and a bit of clever marketing. Buy from wholesalers like the ones featured below, or from the many others operating in the United States, Canada, and other parts of the world. Once you have secured a reliable buying source, sell directly to paintball enthusiasts from a homebased showroom, through eBay, at flea markets, and at sports and recreation shows. Join paintball clubs and associations to spread the word about your business and network for new customers.

 BUY
Wholesalers

 SELL
EBay, Flea Markets, Recreation Shows, Homebased Sales

 RESOURCES
—Badlands Paintball Wholesale, ☎ (416) 245-3856, ♂ www.badlands paintball.com
—National Paintball Supply, ☎ (800) 346-5615, ♂ www.nationalpaint ball.com
—*Paintball Magazine*, industry information and resources, ♂ www.paint ballmagazine.com

Arts and Crafts Supplies

In North America alone, there are millions of people engaged in some sort of arts or crafts as a hobby—painting, needlepoint, costume jewelry making, folk art, and many more. All of these people have one thing in common—they need supplies in order to participate in their hobby. So where there is demand, the clever entrepreneur will make sure there is also the supply to fill it. Buy arts and crafts supplies from wholesalers and manufacturers at deeply discounted prices, up to 50 percent less than retail. Establish a homebased sales showroom to service the local market and create an e-commerce Web site to service the online global market of artists and crafters. Also sell at craft shows and flea markets, or combine all these sales and marketing methods to maximize revenue and profit potential.

BUY
Wholesalers, Manufacturers

SELL
Arts and Crafts Shows, Homebased Sales, Flea Markets, Web Site

RESOURCES
—GWI Gifts & Crafts Wholesale, ☎ (800) 666-5858, ✆ www.craftwhole saler.com
—J & R Industries Wholesale, ☎ (800) 999-9513, ✆ www.jandrind.com
—Mykonos Wholesale, ☎ (800) 695-6667, ✆ www.mykonosbeads.com
—National Craft Association, ☎ (800) 318-9410, ✆ www.craftassoc.com

Original Artwork

Oil and watercolor paintings, ink drawings, sculpture in stone, wood, and iron, and a host of other fine-art mediums can be the bases for a very profitable and personally rewarding buy-and-sell enterprise. Purchase new original works of art directly from local, national, or even world artists, as well as from companies that specialize in original artwork wholesaling. Previously owned original artwork can be purchased at auctions, online, and through classified ads. You may even stumble across the occasional rare and valuable piece at a garage sale. Establish your own Web site for promotion and sales, utilize eBay and other online marketplaces for sales, organize and host art auctions, and establish a homebased art gallery supported by local advertising and featuring weekly or monthly shows. I would opt to combine all of these selling methods to ensure maximum exposure and sales. When dealing in fine original works of art, you can never have enough knowledge. Buy price guides, study art books, join art clubs and societies, and network with artists and art dealers to learn as much as you can about the art world.

 Buy
Artists, Auctions, Wholesalers, Garage Sales

 Sell
Collectors, eBay, Auctions, Temporary Locations, Homebased Sales

 Resources
—Living Drums Company, ☎ (815) 397-9042, ♂ www.livingdrums.com
—Oil Paintings Direct, ☎ 86-592-555-9534 (China), ♂ www.oilpaintings direct.net.cn
—Oil Painting Wholesale, ☎ (626) 308-0682, ♂ www.oilpaintingwhole sale.com
—📖 Davenport's Art Reference & Price Guide, Gordon's Art Reference, ☎ (800) 892-4622 , ♂ www.gordonsart.com

Prints and Posters

Big money can be earned selling art prints and collectible posters. For art prints, you can scan classified ads and auctions to purchase secondhand from private sellers. Or buy new prints from wholesalers and directly from artists who have met with little success marketing their own prints. If you decide to deal in previously owned art prints, make sure that you acquire an art print price guide for valuation purposes. It will prove to be a very valuable tool for both buying and selling. Likewise, new posters can also be purchased directly from wholesalers, framed and mounted, or unframed and unmounted—the choice is yours. Collectible posters, including sports, advertising, theater, events, entertainment, and art, can be found by spending time at flea markets, online marketplaces, garage sales, and auctions. Market both new and used by setting up a sales kiosk at consumer shows and malls, and by listing your products for sale on eBay and other online marketplaces. Also, market your collectible prints and posters directly to collectors by joining online and offline collectible clubs and associations. You can also market art prints directly to professionals, corporations, and interior designers for home and office decorations.

BUY
Wholesalers, Auctions, Estate Sales, Garage Sales, Classified Ads, Artists

 SELL
Collectors, Kiosks, eBay, Flea Markets

 RESOURCES
—All Posters Wholesale, ☎ (510) 879-4700, ♂ www.allposters.com
—Lieberman's Print Wholesale, ☎ (800) 221-1032, ♂ www.liebermans.com
—Low Cost Prints Wholesale, ☎ (866) 422-4754, ♂ www.artlot.com
—Trade Posters Wholesale, ☎ 44-0-2392-779930 (UK), ♂ www.trade-posters.com
—📖 *Lawrence's Dealer Print Prices, Gordon's Art Reference*, ☎ (800) 892-4622, ♂ www.gordonsart.com

Specialty Soaps

With an investment of less than $500, you can be in the specialty soap business and make great money selling aromatherapy soaps, hypoallergenic soaps, dermatological soaps, novelty soaps, herbal soaps, soap-making supplies, and soap gift baskets and sets. There are just as many ways to sell soap as there are different kinds of specialty soaps. Sell from home, hire part-time salespeople to organize and host in-home soap sales parties, sell on eBay, and display at home-and-garden shows. Selling from kiosks in malls and at flea markets is another way you can earn extra money on weekends. Also consider starting a suds club. Collect customer information and send out a new bar of specialty soap every month as a free gift, but include a catalog listing all of your products along with three order forms—one for the recipient and two for friends. Buying sources for specialty and all-natural soaps include manufacturers, wholesalers, and craftspeople, or you may even decide to make your own line of specialty soaps right at home.

 BUY
Manufacturers, Wholesalers, Craftspeople

SELL
Online Marketplaces, Flea Markets, Kiosks, Consumer Shows, Home Parties, Homebased Sales

 RESOURCES
—Bath and Body Wholesale, ☎ (888) 935-2639, ♂ www.wholesalebath products.com
—Hidden Valley Farms, ☎ (866) 426-8709, ♂ www.farmsoap.com
—Vermont Soap Manufacturing, ☎ (866) 762-7482, ♂ www.vermont soap.com

Candles

Become known as the "one stop for everything candles" by selling all kinds, including aromatherapy candles, scented jar candles, floating candles, wedding candles, novelty candles, 100 percent beeswax candles, citronella candles, and decorative bowl and crock candles. Also sell candle accessories such as holders and stands, snuffers, coil incense, lamp oils, candle gift baskets, and candle making supplies. Convert space in your home for a sales showroom. Sell on eBay and create your own candle Web site. Display and sell at home-and-garden shows, and advertise in magazines for mail-order sales. You can even sell at flea markets, home parties, and from mall kiosks at holiday times. My research has led me to the conclusion that the candle-making craft has a relatively short learning curve, so you might want to consider making your own right from home. Failing that, you can buy at deeply discounted prices from manufacturers, craftspeople, and from wholesalers.

 BUY
Manufacturers, Wholesalers, Craftspeople

 SELL
Online Marketplaces, Flea Markets, Kiosks, Consumer Shows, Home Parties, Homebased Sales

 RESOURCES
—Coachlight Candle Factory, ☎ (800) 487-1180, ♂ www.coachlight candle.com
—Country Star Candles Manufacturing, ☎ (661) 269-5828, ♂ www.countrystarcandles.com

—Evolve Wholesale, ☎ (800) 869-9134, ♂ www.evolve1000.com
—National Candle Association, ♂ www.candles.org

Sun-Catchers

Sun-catchers of every shape, size, and color are fantastic buy-and-sell items. They're cheap to buy, easily marked up by 200 to 300 percent for retail sales, always in demand because they make great gifts and home decorations, and from the vendor's perspective they are easy to store, ship, and sell. Sell them on eBay, at community events, direct from a homebased boutique, at flea markets, and at gift shows. Buying cheap is also easily accomplished because there are numerous manufacturers of mass-produced sun-catchers as well as wholesalers who will be more than eager to help fulfill your needs. You may even decide to design your own custom line of sun-catchers and have local craftspeople and stained-glass workers produce them for you on a contract basis. Your buy-and-sell options are almost unlimited when it comes to sun-catchers.

BUY
Manufacturers, Wholesalers, Craftspeople

SELL
EBay, Flea Markets, Kiosks, Consumer Shows

RESOURCES
—Sun Catcher Boutique Wholesale, ☎ (800) 843-0638, ♂ www. sun-catcher.com
—Suncatcher Gallery Manufacturing, ☎ (401) 826-3070, ♂ www.sun catchergallery.com
—VNW Gift Manufacturing, ☎ 886-29531506 (Taiwan), ♂ www.vnw gift.com

Mosaic Products

People love decorative mosaic products because they are unique, colorful, great gifts, and make fantastic home, garden, or office decorations. Mosaic products are generally made of broken ceramic titles and glass, put together to form an abstract design or scene. Mosaic products can include tabletops, floor and wall titles, planters, picture and mirror frames, wind chimes, wall plaques, garden fountains, and other unique decorative items. Buying direct from overseas manufacturers who mass-produce mosaic products will secure the lowest unit price. Many importers and wholesalers right here in the United States also sell mosaic products, though the cost will be slightly higher than buying direct from manufacturers. Another buying option is to purchase mosaic products from local craftspeople, or if you have a creative flair, design your own and contract with local craftspeople to make them for you on a unit price basis or revenue split basis. Sales can be conducted on eBay, at home-and-garden shows, crafts fairs, flea markets, by renting kiosk space in malls and public markets, and at a homebased showroom.

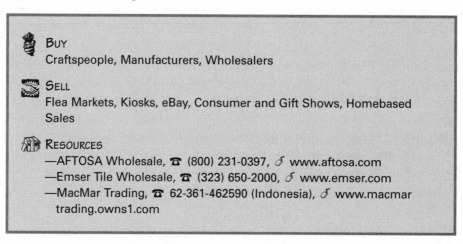

BUY
Craftspeople, Manufacturers, Wholesalers

SELL
Flea Markets, Kiosks, eBay, Consumer and Gift Shows, Homebased Sales

RESOURCES
—AFTOSA Wholesale, ☎ (800) 231-0397, ♂ www.aftosa.com
—Emser Tile Wholesale, ☎ (323) 650-2000, ♂ www.emser.com
—MacMar Trading, ☎ 62-361-462590 (Indonesia), ♂ www.macmar trading.owns1.com

Small Appliances

Small appliances such as razors, curling irons, kitchen blenders, coffee makers, clock radios, hair dryers, and air conditioners are gold mines waiting to be discovered by innovative entrepreneurs who choose to buy these products low and resell high. The best place to buy is through wholesale liquidators in pallet lots if you can afford it. Alternately, buy wholesale in smaller quantities, but expect to pay slightly more. Buying in pallet lots can get you product for as much as 50 percent less than individual wholesale pricing, money that can wisely be used for better purposes, such as buying more valuable inventory for resale. Flea markets and eBay are two of the best selling venues for small appliances. Other places to sell include consumer shows and mall-based kiosks.

BUY
Wholesalers

SELL
Kiosks, eBay, Flea Markets, Consumer Shows

 RESOURCES
—1 AAA Wholesale Liquidators, ☎ (800) 661-9430, ♂ www.1aaawhole
saleliquidators.com
—Dollar Days Wholesale, ☎ (877) 837-9569, ♂ www.dollardays.com
—Fountain Run Wholesale, ☎ (270) 434-4678, ♂ www.fountainrun
wholesale.com

Portable Electronics

There are lots of people selling portable electronic devices on eBay making a small fortune in the process, and so can you. You can sell CD players, DVD players, MP3 players, and good old-fashioned boom boxes. Get started by establishing your eBay account. Next, secure a reliable source for good-quality portable electronics that you can buy at rock-bottom prices. I have included a few wholesale sources below, but there are also hundreds more. Be sure to use the power of the Internet to find the right supplier in sync with your specific needs and budget. On that note, the more you buy, the lower your unit price goes, which may enable you to undercut the competition and sell for less. In addition to selling your portable electronic devices on eBay, you can also increase sales by selling at flea markets, mall kiosks, and consumer shows—basically, any busy location in the community where you can set up a portable tent or kiosks to sell from.

 BUY
Wholesalers

 SELL
Kiosks, eBay, Flea Markets, Consumer Shows

 RESOURCES
—1 AAA Wholesale Liquidators, ☎ (800) 661-9430, ♂ www.1aaawhole
saleliquidators.com
—Dollar Days Wholesale, ☎ (877) 837-9569, ♂ www.dollardays.com
—Open Box USA Wholesale, ☎ (877) 673-6872, ♂ www.openbox
usa.com

Cigars

Selling premium handmade and machine-made cigars has the potential to be very profitable. In fact, many people are earning six-figure incomes selling cigars online. However, there are also a few drawbacks. First, you will need to invest in cigar storage humidors and humidifying devices to protect your valuable inventory. Second, you will need to apply for and obtain a state tobacco tax and products license. These generally cost around $100 per year, though each state is different and has its owns seller's guidelines and fee schedule. For more details, visit the Bureau of Alcohol, Tobacco, and Firearms Web site located at ♂ www.atf.gov/alcohol/info/faq/tobacco.htm for information. Third, you will need to develop a sound marketing plan because this is a very competitive business. Buy directly from manufacturers and cigar wholesalers. Create your own Web site for online sales, and hire salespeople to organize and host cigar sales parties right in their own homes. You can also create a catalog listing all of your cigar brands and accessories and deliver the catalog to hotels, golf courses, businesses, restaurants, resorts, bars, and social clubs, offering free delivery on orders. To boost revenues also sell cigar accessories such as clippers, cases, humidors, gift box sets, lighters, and smokeless ashtrays.

BUY
Manufacturers, Wholesalers

SELL
Online Marketplaces, Direct Delivery, Kiosks, Homebased Sales

RESOURCES
—Cheap Cigars Wholesale, ☎ (813) 969-0523, ♂ www.cheap-cigars.com
—Cigar Family Wholesale, ☎ (800) 477-1884, ♂ www.cigarfamily.com
—Gotham Cigars Wholesale, ☎ (888) 468-0033, ♂ www.gothamcigars.com
—Neptune Cigars Wholesale, ☎ (800) 655-3385, ♂ www.neptune cigars.com

Watches

Wristwatches are among the most popular gifts for any number of special occasions—birthdays, Christmas, graduation, retirement—making them a terrific buy-and-sell product. Wristwatches can be purchased wholesale for as little as a few dollars each and retailed for five to ten times as much. There are a number of great places to sell watches—flea markets, eBay, and rental kiosks in malls and public markets. There is also enormous demand for high-quality used watches and antique collectible watches. For instance, a secondhand stainless steel Rolex Submariner watch with an oyster face still commands in the range of $3,500 to $4,000. If you decide to deal in collectible and secondhand fashion watches, educate yourself about brands and values; do this by purchasing wristwatch price guides, joining collectible-watch clubs, and subscribing to collectible watch publications. Your best buying sources for used watches will be flea markets, estate sales, auction sales, garage sales, and private sellers advertising in the classifieds.

BUY
Manufacturers, Wholesalers, Auctions

SELL
Flea Markets, eBay, Kiosks, Consumer Shows, Collectors

RESOURCES
—Anytime Watch and Clock Wholesale, ☎ (610) 380-4518, ♂ www.any timewholesale.com
—Ashford Wholesale, ☎ (866) 274-3673, ♂ www.wrist-watches.com
—MBK Wholesalers, ☎ (770) 631-8940, ♂ www.mbkwholesale.com
—National Association of Watch and Clock Collectors, ☎ (717) 684-8261, ♂ www.nawcc.org

Sunglasses

You can purchase good-quality sunglasses in bulk wholesale for as little as $2 each and resell the same sunglasses for $20 or more! Sunglasses are one of the best buy-and-sell items. They are cheap to buy, easy to store and transport, and even easier to sell because they are always in demand. Sell them on eBay, by setting up a portable kiosk at the beach, during community events, car show-and-shine events, and local weekend flea markets; or place them in retail stores on consignment and split the profits with the shop owner. However, key to success will be your merchandising skills. Keep your selling area clean and organized, invest in attention-grabbing signage, offer lots of types of sunglasses, place mirrors all around so customers can see how great they look with the sunglasses on, and simply ask people passing by to try on a pair of sunglasses. The sunglasses will do the rest.

BUY
Manufacturers, Wholesalers

 SELL
Flea Markets, eBay, Kiosks, Consumer Shows, Community Events

 RESOURCES
—Elite Image Wholesale, ☎ (800) 340-7642, ♂ www.eliteimagesun
glasses.com
—KW Sunglasses Wholesale, ☎ (212) 255-0122, ♂ www.kwsun
glasses.com
—L.E.X. Wholesale, ☎ (866) 549-6404, ♂ www.wholesalesun
glasses.com

Clocks

Grandfather clocks, wall clocks, alarm clocks, travel clocks, mantle clocks, cuckoo clocks, carriage clocks, pendulum clocks, dial clocks, novelty clocks, toy clocks, advertising clocks, ship's clocks, calendar clocks, melody clocks, digital display clocks, Braille clocks, and talking clocks. It seems there's a clock available for every occasion, use, and price point imaginable. Wholesalers, manufacturers, liquidators, and importers will be your best bet for purchasing new clocks at low discount prices. There is also money to be made in buying and selling antique clocks. For instance, stumble across a 100-year-old Swiss-made mini carriage clock and you could bring home $5,000. The best places to look for valuable used and antique clocks include garage sales, auctions, flea markets, online marketplaces, and classified ads. As always, antique clock price guides will prove to be an indispensable business tool for acquiring and selling. New, used, or antique clocks can be sold on eBay, from a homebased showroom, and at home shows, mall kiosks, collectible shows, and flea markets. Try all, and stick with the ones that prove to be the most profitable.

 BUY
Manufacturers, Wholesalers, Auctions, Garage Sales, Classified Ads, Estate Sales

 SELL
Online Marketplaces, Flea Markets, Kiosks, Consumer Shows, Collectors

RESOURCES
—Dollar Days Wholesale, ☎ (877) 837-9569, ♂ www.dollardays.com
—LungMe Manufacturing, ☎ 86-769-5386428 (China), ♂ www.
clocks-manufacturer.com
—National Association of Watch and Clock Collectors, ☎ (717) 684-
8261, ♂ www.nawcc.org
—📖 *Price Guide to Antique Clocks*, Robert Swedberg and Harriett
Swedberg (Krause Publications, 2001)

Fireworks

There are two major stumbling blocks to get past before you can sell fireworks. First, can you legally sell fireworks in your state? Second, if you can legally sell fireworks, can you meet minimum storage and transportation regulations? From a federal perspective, you can legally sell fireworks classified as "consumer fireworks." However, every state has further regulations about the sale, storage, and transportation of fireworks. Some states such as Arizona and Georgia do not allow the sale of any fireworks, while others like Iowa and Ohio allow novelty fireworks sales. Still other states such as Texas and Washington allow the sale of all consumer fireworks, including cone fountains, Roman candles, sky rockets, firecrackers, sparklers, revolving wheels, and others. To find out more about the purchase, sale, transportation, and storage of fireworks, visit the National Council of Fireworks Safety at ♂ www.fireworksafety.com or call ☎ (301) 907-7998. Providing you can meet the legal requirements, buying and selling fireworks can be extremely profitable because you can purchase at up to 50 percent off retail directly from manufacturers and obtain lesser discounts from wholesalers. The best sales locations are temporary rental storefronts in highly visible and high-traffic areas in your community, especially just before July 4th, Labor Day, and Halloween. Once again, providing you meet the legal requirements, you can also sell fireworks at flea markets, from your own Web site, and by mail order.

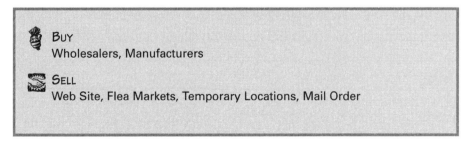

BUY
Wholesalers, Manufacturers

SELL
Web Site, Flea Markets, Temporary Locations, Mail Order

RESOURCES
—Fireworks R Us Wholesale, ☎ (888) 811-2666, ♂ www.fireworks rus.com
—HAMCO Fireworks Manufacturing, ☎ (405) 527-2688, ♂ www.hamco fireworks.com
—Patriotic Fireworks Manufacturing, ☎ (410) 287-2365, ♂ www.pat fire.com

Knives

Knives, knives, and more knives. They come in every size, and there is one for every purpose—hunting, fishing, cooking, hiking, dining, woodcarving, etc. Antique knives and swords have long been prized collectors' items. Selling any or all can be very financially rewarding. You can sell all types of knives or opt to specialize in just one or two kinds. New knives can be purchased from wholesalers and distributors and sometimes directly from manufacturers, though they require orders in larger quantities. Antique and collectible knives and swords can be purchased from private sellers advertising in the classifieds, and at auction sales, online marketplaces, and collectible shows. Selling can be accomplished in much the same manner with the addition of renting kiosks in malls, vending at flea markets, and listing on eBay.

 BUY
Wholesalers, Manufacturers, Garage Sales, Online Marketplaces

 SELL
Kiosks, Collectors, eBay, Flea Markets, Consumer Shows

 RESOURCES
—Buy N Save Wholesale, ☎ (909) 272-2227, ♂ www.buynsave direct.com
—Hot Dandy Wholesale Superstore, ☎ (800) 875-8211, ♂ www.hot dandy.com
—JD Wholesale, ☎ (866) 220-7103, ♂ www.jdwholesale.com

Cameras

New and previously owned film and digital cameras and camcorders are great buy-and-sell products, especially for people with an interest in photography. You can offer customers new cameras, digital cameras, camcorders, vintage cameras, and accessories such as lenses, cases, tripods, darkroom equipment and chemicals, film scanners, and the like. Because there are so many types of cameras and equipment you may want to focus on one particular specialty. Buy new cameras and equipment from wholesalers, and resell on eBay—on which, by the way, digital cameras are one of the hottest-selling products. Also sell at photography shows, at flea markets, and directly from a homebased showroom. Used and antique cameras and equipment can be purchased from private sellers advertising in the classifieds, from online marketplaces, at auctions, and by scouring weekend flea markets and garage sales. Not long ago a friend purchased a 1950s Super Ikonta for $40 at a garage sale, which was in great working order. He kept it for a while until a chance encounter with a collector left him without a camera but $600 wealthier.

 BUY
Wholesalers, Manufacturers, Classified Ads, Online Marketplaces

 SELL
Collectors, eBay, Flea Markets, Photography Shows, Homebased Sales

 RESOURCES
—AmeriCam Manufacturing, ☎ (800) 632-2824, ♂ www.privatelabel cameras.com
—Diversified Photo Supply, ☎ (800) 544-1609, ♂ www.diversified photo.com
—Gamla Enterprises Wholesale, ☎ (800) 442-6526, ♂ www.gamla photo.com
—📖 *McKeown's Price Guide to Antique and Classic Cameras*, Jim McKeown (Centennial Photo Service, 2001)

Telescopes

Telescopes and binoculars are great buy-and-sell items because they retail in the range of $100 to $1,000. Based on one-third gross profit margin, it does not take a lot of sales each month to really add up. Stick with retailing new telescopes and binoculars because used ones are just too hard to come by on a regular basis to be considered a viable option. Buy directly from manufacturers and through wholesale distributors such as the ones featured in Resources. Sell online, from a homebased showroom and at consumer shows. Join astronomy clubs and associations to network for business. To boost sales and revenues, also sell accessories like tripod stands, replacement parts, carrying cases, night sky map software, eyepieces, filter kits, and photographic telescopic and binocular lenses.

BUY
Manufacturers, Wholesalers

SELL
Online Marketplaces, Homebased Sales

RESOURCES
—Crazy Discounts Wholesale, ☌ www.crazydiscounts.com
—Discount Telescopes Wholesale, ☎ (877) 523-4400, ☌ www.discount-telescopes.com
—Kostek Technology Manufacturing, ☎ 886-2-22045881 (Taiwan), ☌ www.akostek.com

Military Collectibles

The Civil War, Mexican-American War, WWI, WWII, Korean War, Vietnam War, and the Gulf War. Military items such as helmets, swords, guns, uniforms, official documents, medals, knives, artillery, and photographs from these and other wars from around the world are very collectible and highly sought-after. Consider: if you wanted to purchase a M1850 Civil War infantry officer's sword, you would have to spend about $1,200. Or if you wanted a WW II M-1 infantry helmet, you would have to write a check for $300 to $400. The price of military collectibles continues to rise annually and shows no signs of slowing down. Buying military collectibles for resale requires legwork. You will have to dig through garage sales, scour flea markets, attend auctions, surf collectibles Web sites, and bid on items through estate sales to find the best and most valuable items to purchase. You will also need to know how much these items are worth when you find them. To accomplish this you will need to invest in military collectibles price guides. List on eBay and other collectibles Web sites to sell. Also exhibit at collectibles shows, and sell through auctions to ensure that you get the highest prices.

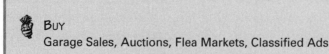

BUY
Garage Sales, Auctions, Flea Markets, Classified Ads

> SELL
> Collectors, Auctions, Collectible Shows, eBay, Homebased Sales
>
> RESOURCES
> —The Online Collector, dealers and collectors, ☎ www.theonlinecollector.com/military.html
> —📖 *Military Trader Magazine*, Krause Publications, ☎ (800) 942-0676, ☎ www.collect.com
> —📖 *The Official Price Guide to Military Collectibles*, Richard Austin (House of Collectibles, 2004)

Coins and Paper Money

There is a real possibility you can find valuable coins and paper money at garage sales, estate sales, auctions, private seller classified ads, and at flea markets. But to be able to do so, you need to educate yourself not only about the value of coins and paper money, but also about how they are graded by condition for valuation. This can be accomplished by studying price guides and by reading coin and paper money collectors' publications. Timing often comes into play as well, and deals can be had when there are no other interested parties to purchase. So when you find a 1937-D 3-legged buffalo error nickel for a buck at a garage sale, you'll have stumbled across a $150 find. Or perhaps you will find a collector liquidating his collection and you will be able to acquire a 1934 A $20 Hawaii Star note for a few thousand dollars, which is about half of its current value. Look to purchase collector coins and paper money at garage sales, flea markets, estate sales, through classified ads, and at auction. When selling, try eBay and other online marketplaces, as well as coin shows. By joining coin and paper money collecting clubs, you will have the ability to sell your finds directly to other collectors.

> BUY
> Auctions, Online Marketplaces, Stamp Shows, Classified Ads
>
> SELL
> Collectors, Online Marketplaces, Specialty Publications, Stamp Shows
>
> RESOURCES
> —Heritage Coin, online coin buy-and-sell marketplace, ☎ www.heritagecoin.com

—*Coin World,* online magazine serving coin collectors and dealers, ♂ www.coinworld.com

—📖 *The Official Blackbook Price Guide to U.S. Coins*, 42nd Edition, Marc Hudgeons and Thomas Hudgeons (House of Collectibles, 2003) Book lists coin values.

—📖 *The Official Blackbook Price Guide to U.S. Paper Money*, Thomas Hudgeons (House of Collectibles, 2004)

Stamps

Stamps have long been a highly prized collectible of people from all over the world. In fact, stamp-collecting is the number-one collectible hobby in the United States. Capitalize on your philatelic knowledge, and profit from buying stamps cheaply and reselling them for huge gains. Scan classified ads, garage sales, flea markets, online marketplaces, and stamp shows for stamps to purchase below value. Resell to collectors via auction sales, online marketplaces, stamp shows, and through specialty stamp publications. You will need to be well-versed in stamp grading and values, but there are numerous price guides available to help you in this endeavor. Who knows, you might find a US #96 10-cent stamp in mint condition at a garage sale for a few bucks, and laugh all the way to the bank when you resell it for more than $2,000. Also make sure you join online and offline stamp-collecting clubs so you will have the ability to sell your finds directly to other collectors.

 BUY
Auctions, Online Marketplaces, Stamp Shows, Classified Ads

 SELL
Collectors, Online Marketplaces, Specialty Publications, Stamp Shows

 RESOURCES
—American Philatelic Society, ♂ www.stamps.org
—Stamp Show, directory listing stamp shows worldwide, ♂ www.stamp shows.com
—📖 *Scott Catalogs*, stamp valuation guides, ☎ (800) 572-6885, ♂ www.amosadvantage.com

Religious Products

Look no further than to the success of the film *The Passion of the Christ* for proof that religion is a hot topic in North America and around the world. Books, Bible cases, religious bookmarks, crucifixes, plaques, rosary beads, religious jewelry, pins, religious games and novelties, figurines, and First Holy Communion products are all items you can buy wholesale and resell for a profit. Buy from wholesalers, distributors, liquidators, importers, and even factory direct for the best prices. Sell online, through church and Bible groups, from a homebased showroom, at flea markets, and at religious-themed consumer shows and exhibitions. Of course, follow your faith, and concentrate your marketing efforts on the religion you know best.

BUY
Manufacturers, Wholesalers

SELL
Mail Order, eBay, Flea Markets, Kiosks, Consumer Shows

RESOURCES
—Dollar Days Wholesale, ☎ (877) 837-9569, ♂ www.dollardays.com
—Knight Light Candle & Imports, ☎ (248) 745-9035, ♂ www.knight
  lightcandle.com
—Roden Surplus Imports, ☎ (256) 355-4751, ♂ www.rodenimports.com

Gift Baskets

When buying gift baskets for resale, you have two choices. First, purchase them from wholesalers and producers preassembled and ready to sell. Second, purchase the products and baskets separately, and assemble the gift baskets yourself at home, or hire someone experienced in crafts to assemble them. Your decision will depend on your needs, budget, the types of gift baskets you want to sell, and your target customers. Don't fret if you decide to assemble the baskets yourself, because gift baskets are easy to assemble and all the products and baskets are readily available from any number of wholesale sources. Simply select items such as specialty foods, flowers, or personal health products, arrange them in attractive wicker baskets or similar containers, wrap in foil or colored plastic, and the gift basket is complete. I suggest that you concentrate your marketing efforts on gaining repeat corporate clients, professionals, small-business owners, and sales professionals, such as real estate agents. Basically, focus on individuals and companies that would have reason to regularly send out gift baskets to existing and new clients. Promote your baskets using a direct-mail brochure and by networking with your target audience at business and social functions in your community; places like the chamber of commerce are excellent. Also sell the gift baskets at community events, flea markets, and public markets on weekends and holidays.

BUY
Wholesalers, Manufacturers, Craftspeople

SELL
B2B, Kiosks, Online Marketplaces

RESOURCES
—Bacon Basketware Wholesale, ☎ (905) 841-1525, ♂ www.bacon basket.com
—Country Baskets Imports, ☎ (703) 818-9173, ♂ www.baskets imports.com
—Flower Inc. Balloons Wholesale, ☎ (800) 880-9759, ♂ www.flowers incballoons.com
—📖 *Gift Basket Review Magazine Online*, ♂ www.festivities-pub.com

Greeting Cards

In spite of the popularity of electronic greeting cards, billions of dollars' worth of paper greeting cards are sold annually around the globe, thereby qualifying them as a fantastic buy-and-sell product. Service both the high-end and regular greeting card market by purchasing mass-produced greeting cards wholesale and selling them on consignment through gift shops and other retailers, a practice commonly referred to as job racking. Likewise, also sell high-end, one-of-a-kind original greeting cards by contracting with local artists to paint original watercolor scenes to fit every occasion. Use blank greeting card stock, effectively making each card a highly collectible piece of artwork. The artists' greeting cards can be sold through retailers, direct to business for promotional reasons, and to consumers via mall sales kiosks, eBay, and by establishing alliances with wedding and event planners who can refer your one-of-a-kind artist cards to their clients.

BUY
Wholesalers, Publishers, Artists

 SELL
B2B, Flea Markets, Kiosks, Online Marketplaces

 RESOURCES
—Art Galaxy Wholesale, ☎ (905) 469-9937, ♂ www.artgalaxy.com
—Dollar Days Wholesale, ☎ (877) 837-9569, ♂ www.dollardays.com
—Greeting Card Association, ♂ www.greetingcard.org
—SNAFU Card Designs, ☎ (651) 698-8581, ♂ www.snafudesigns.com

Silk Flowers

You can make a bundle selling beautiful silk flowers to consumers, crafters, event planners, and wedding planners. Your supply source will be national and international manufacturers, wholesalers, and importers of silk flowers. Or you might find craftspeople in your local area to produce them for you, based on your designs or theirs. Call and set up appointments with wedding and event planners to show them your goods and explain the benefits of purchasing from your business. You can also sell at flea markets, through online marketplaces, at craft shows, and by exhibiting at home-and-garden shows. Join crafts clubs and associations in your area to network for new business, and build alliances with other business es that can refer your products to their clients, including photographers and interior decorators.

 BUY
Manufacturers, Wholesalers, Craftspeople

 SELL
Kiosks, Consumer Shows, Flea Markets, Online Marketplaces, B2B

 RESOURCES
—Flowers By Design Wholesale, ☎ (630) 665-9333, ♂ www.flowers-by-design.com
—Kong Hing Silk Flowers, ☎ 852-2755-6738 (Hong Kong), ♂ www.silkflower.com.hk
—The Silkmaster Depot Wholesale, ☎ (877) 468-7455, ♂ www.silkmasterdepot.com

Holiday Decorations

Holiday decorations are big business, especially at Christmas, Easter, New Years Day, Thanksgiving, Halloween, Valentine's Day, and Mardi Gras. You can buy and sell decorations and accessories such as lights, ornaments, costumes, masks, nativity seems, outside yard displays, wreaths, bells, and artificial Christmas trees. One of the best aspects of buying and selling holiday decorations is that you can buy them for less than wholesale at insanely low prices by waiting to purchase out of season, hanging on to your goods until the following year, and then realizing full retail in the flurry of holiday shopping. Sell online, at flea markets, and by renting kiosks at malls and public markets. The value of antique and vintage holiday decorations has also recently taken off, especially Christmas ornaments and figurines, so keep your eyes peeled for bargains at garage sales and auctions.

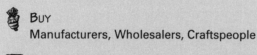

BUY
Manufacturers, Wholesalers, Craftspeople

SELL
Flea Markets, Kiosks, eBay, Consumer Shows, Homebased Sales

RESOURCES
—Four Season General Merchandise, ☎ (323) 582-4444, ♂ www.4sgm.com
—KIP International Wholesale, ☎ (215) 289-2447, ♂ www.kipintl.com
—Scottish Christmas Wholesale, ☎ (800) 259-6785, ♂ www.scottish-christmas.com

Lighters

In spite of the decline in the numbers of people who smoke, cigarette lighters continue to be popular collectibles, gifts, and handy items to have around the house. Zippo, Camel, Ronson, and Scripto are all highly sought after lighter brands, both new and collectible. You can buy new lighters wholesale for peanuts, as little as a couple dollars each for great quality products and only a dollar a dozen for disposables. Mark up the lighters by 300 to 400 percent for resale on eBay, and at flea markets, auto shows, and community events. Also boost revenues and profits by investing in a simple engraving machine, enabling you to personalize your customer's lighter purchases right on location. Collectible lighters can be found by rummaging through flea markets, garage sales, and online marketplaces and sold on eBay and to collectors via clubs and associations.

BUY
Wholesalers, Manufacturers

 SELL
Kiosks, Flea Markets, eBay, Collectors, Consumer Shows

 RESOURCES
—Crazy Discounts Wholesale, ☌ www.crazydiscounts.com
—Dollar Days Wholesale, ☎ (877) 837-9569, ☌ www.dollardays.com
—Indy Wholesaler, ☌ www.indywholesaler.com

Umbrellas

I am sure that when you think about great products to buy low and sell high, umbrellas probably don't quickly come to mind. But they should because they are a fantastic buy-and-sell product for two reasons: They can be resold for two to three times wholesale cost, and they are always in demand. There are numerous types of umbrellas—standard rain umbrellas we keep in the closet, mini carry-along umbrellas, beach umbrellas, patio umbrellas, market umbrellas, and promotional umbrellas emblazoned with logos for businesses. Umbrellas can be purchased from wholesalers, manufacturers, importers, and distributors, from both U.S. and overseas companies. Flea markets, consumer shows, community events, eBay, and mall kiosks are all excellent locations to sell. And don't overlook the possibility of forming a partnership with a silkscreen printing company so you can sell umbrellas to corporations, organizations, and small businesses as a promotional item bearing their name, logo, and promotional message.

 BUY
Manufacturers, Wholesalers

 SELL
Kiosks, B2B, Home-and-Garden Shows, eBay

 RESOURCES
—Seagull International Manufacturing, ☎ (800) 666-9300, ☌ www.seagullintl.com
—Umbrella Mart Manufacturing, ☎ 91-20-244-56944 (India), ☌ www.anchorumbrella.com
—The Umbrella Shop Wholesale, ☌ www.umbrellashop.com

Wicker Products

Interior and exterior wicker furniture and decorative items are wonderful buy-and-sell products. Whether new or used, wicker is always in demand. New wicker products purchased by the container load from foreign manufacturers at incredibly cheap prices is the best way to fly if your budget permits. If not, U.S. and Canadian wholesalers and importers are a good alternative for buying in smaller quantities, but you will pay higher prices, though not so high that the venture cannot be profitable. Used wicker products can be purchased from private sellers advertising in the classifieds, by digging through garage sales, and by attending auctions. Both new and used wicker merchandise can be sold via eBay, flea market vending, a homebased showroom supported by advertising, and exhibiting at home-and-garden shows. Once again, wicker furniture and decorative items are popular and always in demand. Finer pieces and vintage wicker sell for incredibly big bucks; not uncommon is $1,000 for a wicker rocking chair, $2,000 for a complete patio set, and thousands for antique wicker baskets.

BUY
Manufacturers, Wholesalers, Auctions

SELL
Homebased Sales, Kiosks, Flea Markets, eBay, Home-and-Garden Shows

RESOURCES
—Bali Bintang, ☎ 62-361-7429745 (Indonesia), ♂ www.bali-bintang-art-gallery.com
—Baskets Galore Wholesale, ☎ (800) 749-1155, ♂ www.basketsgalore inc.net
—Cindy Rattan Manufacturing, ☎ 62-231-342576 (Indonesia, ♂ www.cindyfinishing.com

Dollar-Store Items

Dollar-store items are the ultimate buy-low, sell-high flea market items—hand soap, bags of marbles, paintbrushes, picture frames, fly swatters, decks of cards, shampoo, and a ton more products move out of the booth at lightning speed. If it's cheap and useful, as almost all dollar-store items are, it will sell fast and furiously. Buy in bulk from wholesalers and especially from liquidators handling out-of-season and damaged merchandise, because you can often purchase for as much as 50 percent below even wholesale pricing. These products can generally be marked up 300 percent or more. While because of their low retail value you have to sell lots of merchandise to realize substantial profits, about three-quarters of all your revenues will be pure profit. Dollar-store products are notoriously easy to store and transport, so working from home with even a hatchback car to move from vending location to vending location will be more than sufficient. Because you pay next to nothing for your goods, offer flea market shoppers lots of great deals and reasons to buy: two-for-one specials, fill a bag for $20, and other promotional gimmicks get the cash register ringing. Aim to sell $1,500 worth of products at a busy weekend flea market, and you will take home $1,000 for yourself.

BUY
Wholesalers

SELL
Flea Markets, Kiosks, Consumer Shows

RESOURCES
—1 AAA Wholesale Liquidators, ☎ (800) 661-9430, ♂ www.1aaawhole saleliquidators.com
—Buck Wholesale, ☎ (770) 939-9334, ♂ www.buckwholesale.com
—Liquidation Merchandise, ☎ (800) 574-5304, ♂ www.liquidation merchandise.com

Metaphysical Products

Metaphysical products, also known as New Age products, cover a wide range of items, including tarot cards, magnets, zodiac pendants, astrology products, crystals, healing wands, fountains, meditation supplies, yoga mats and books, pagan products, crystal balls, pyramids, hypnosis tapes, and hemp products. And that only scratches the metaphysical products' surface. Therefore you might want to specialize or at least start with a few items and expand your offerings as your buy-and-sell venture grows. Though there are certainly no personal prerequisites to sell metaphysical products, an interest and belief in New Age ideology will help. Metaphysical products can be purchased directly from manufacturers and wholesalers, and you may even find local craftspeople in your area who can also supply or make what you would like to sell. The nature of these products means that online marketing will be your best bet. Join New Age chat rooms and user groups so that you can network for customers and spread the word about the benefits of your products. Also sell your goods at flea markets, consumer shows, and rental kiosk space in malls on busy weekends.

 BUY
Wholesalers, Manufacturers, Craftspeople

 SELL
Consumer Shows, Online Marketplaces, Kiosks, Flea Markets

 RESOURCES
—Azure Green Wholesale, ☎ (413) 623-2155, ♂ www.azuregreen.com
—Just Winging It Wholesale, ☎ (888) 430-4594, ♂ www.jwi.com
—*The New Age Wholesale Directory*, over 1,200 distributors, wholesalers, manufacturers, and publishers of New Age and metaphysical products, ♂ www.newagereseller.com

Vintage Advertising

Vintage advertising products from the late 1800s to the 1970s are super hot collectibles commanding top dollars from eager-to-buy collectors worldwide. They want it all—posters, advertising specialties, clocks, signs, packaging, tins, calendars, boxes, glassware, pins, soda industry advertising, distillery advertising, business cards, Christmas ornaments, matchbooks, work uniforms, clothing, and just about any other type of product featuring an advertising logo, image, or message. Be prepared to comb through garage sales, auctions, and estate sales because these are the places where you are likely to make your best purchases for the lowest prices. Sell to collectors through online marketplaces and shows, as well as eBay and right from home.

 BUY
Auctions, Flea Markets, Garage Sales, Estate Sales, Classified Ads

 SELL
Homebased Sales, eBay, Collectors

 RESOURCES
—Antique and Collectibles Dealers Association, ♂ www.antiqueand collectible.com/acda.shtml

—The National Association of Antique Malls, ✆ www.antiqueand
collectible.com/naam.shtml

—📖 *Warman's Advertising: A Value and Identification Guide*, Don
Johnson and Elizabeth Johnson (Krause Publications, 2000)

Reproduction Tin Signs

Reproduction tin signs are the latest craze in the reproductions collectibles market, and with good reason. They look and feel exactly like real antique tin signs, but are available for a fraction of the cost. The heyday of tin and ceramic advertising signs was from the 1920s until the sixties, at which point tin and ceramics were replaced by cardboard and plastic. However, a few years ago reproductions become available because the supply of originals was limited and the price of authentic antique advertising signs soared beyond the reach of most hobby collectors. The great majority of these reproduction signs feature advertising, everything from Coke to cars to clothes. Current retail prices for tin signs range from $10 to $50, depending on size and subject. Wholesale, these same signs can be purchased for as little as $2 each, which makes retailing them very financially attractive. Sell reproduction tin signs online, at flea markets, consumer shows, and directly to businesses for use as nifty store and office decorations.

BUY
Wholesalers, Manufacturers

SELL
Consumer Shows, eBay, Flea Markets, Kiosks, B2B

RESOURCES
—Collector Images Reproduction Tin Signs, ☎ (765) 557-0487, ✆ www.
collectorimages.com
—Cornhusker Reproduction Signs, ☎ (402) 332-5050, ✆ www.corn
huskersign.com
—Desperate Tin Sign Reproductions, ☎ (800) 732-4859, ✆ www.
desperate.com

Balloons

If you are searching for a low-investment, yet potentially very high-profit buy-and-sell venture to start, then look no further than balloon vending. There are three ways to buy balloons wholesale. First, you can presell advertising balloons to local businesses and salespeople to promote a sale or special event. The balloons are silkscreened with your customer's business name, logo, and sales message. Potential customers include car dealers, restaurateurs, retailers, schoolteachers, politicians, and home sellers. The main benefit of this type of sale is that you find your customer first, get a deposit for the order, and order from the wholesaler after you are assured the sale. Many balloon wholesalers offer this type of service, and B&C Balloons listed below is one. Second, you can purchase latex or foil balloons with preprinted messages such as Happy Birthday, Happy Fourth of July, Happy New Year, and Get Well Soon, and resell them from kiosks, at community events and at flea markets. Third, you can purchase balloons and related products like ribbon and confetti and offer a balloon decoration service for weddings, parties, and special events. If you choose this route, you will need to invest in a helium tank and a few other pieces of equipment. To market this venture, build alliances with wedding, event, and party planners, as well as with banquet-hall owners and restaurateurs.

BUY
Wholesalers

SELL
Community Events, B2B, Kiosks, Flea Markets

RESOURCES
—Balloons Wholesale, ☎ (800) 239-2000, ✂ www.balloons.com
—B&C Balloons Wholesale, ☎ (888) 629-8545, ✂ www.bcballoons.net
—Wholesale Balloons, ☎ (919) 676-5998, ✂ www.wholesale balloons.com

Novelties

Novelty and gag products such as key chains, lasers, light-up pens, gag gifts, adult-themed items, fake money, and pencil sharpeners in the shape of a train are some of the hottest and most profitable items to sell at flea markets. You can easily double or triple your money on every single sale. In addition to flea markets, you can also sell novelty items right from a rented kiosk at malls, at the public market, or during community events like fairs and parades. Some novelty products, especially adult-themed, may also be offered via suitable online marketplaces and through print and electronic mail-order catalogs. There are a great number of wholesale sources for novelty products, such as the ones featured below. To locate more, conduct *Wholesale Novelty Products* keyword searches on any of the popular search engines or directories.

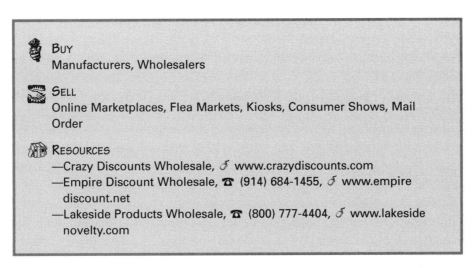

Buy
Manufacturers, Wholesalers

Sell
Online Marketplaces, Flea Markets, Kiosks, Consumer Shows, Mail Order

Resources
—Crazy Discounts Wholesale, ♂ www.crazydiscounts.com
—Empire Discount Wholesale, ☎ (914) 684-1455, ♂ www.empire discount.net
—Lakeside Products Wholesale, ☎ (800) 777-4404, ♂ www.lakeside novelty.com

Temporary Tattoos

Today's peel-and-stick tattoos are nothing like the kind you used to get out of penny gumball machines 30 years ago. The ones now available rival the best authentic tattoos in terms of color and design, and can last for a week. Of course, there are two major differences between temporary tattoos and their real counterparts: they are not permanent, and they cost a mere fraction of the real McCoy. In fact, temporary tattoos can be purchased in bulk for as little as five cents apiece. Granted, at a retail price of one to five dollars each, you will have to sell a great number to realize large revenues, but almost all of the money you do earn will be pure profit. You will want to concentrate your marketing efforts on the main target market for temporary tattoos—kids and teens. Go to where the kids are and set up a portable kiosk. Excellent locations include the beach, and community events like fairs, flea markets, parades, and music concerts.

BUY
Manufacturers, Wholesalers

 SELL
Community Events, Flea Markets, Kiosks

 RESOURCES
—Dune Temporary Tattoos Wholesale, ☎ (877) 444-0615, ♂ www.temp tats.com
—Tattoo Manufacturing, ☎ (800) 747-8016, ♂ www.tattoosales.com
—Wholesale Jewelry and Accessories, ☎ (888) 653-4411, ♂ www. efashioncatalog.com

New Toys

Billions of dollars' worth of toys are sold every year in the United States; the numbers are absolutely staggering. You will get rock-bottom wholesale prices on toys by purchasing factory-direct out of China. In fact, prices are so low it is possible to buy items for less than $1 that retail for ten times as much here. The toy retailing industry is super competitive, one of the most competitive segments of the retail industry. Therefore, look for unusual toys new to the marketplace, and try to get exclusive marketing rights for North America, if possible. This may seem like a tall order, but with a little hard work it is possible because there are literally thousands of overseas companies manufacturing toys, many of which would love representation in the United States, Canada, and Europe. Buying sources will be factory direct in large quantities, and domestic wholesalers and liquidators for smaller quantities. Stick to dealing only in new toys because the value of used toys is too low, except for collector toys. The best selling options include online sales and any place a crowd gathers—flea markets, consumer shows, community events, and mall kiosks close to Christmastime.

 BUY
Manufacturers, Wholesalers

 SELL
Flea Markets, Consumer Shows, Kiosks, Online Marketplaces

RESOURCES
—Big Lots Wholesale, ☎ (614) 278-3700, ✆ www.biglotswholesale.com
—ESCO Imports, ☎ (210) 271-7794, ✆ www.escoimport.com
—Toy Depot Inc. Wholesale, ☎ (213) 621-2893, ✆ www.storetoydepot inc.com
—Toy Directory, database listing toy manufacturers, ✆ www.toydirec tory.com

Collectible Toys

Just think, throughout America, Canada, and much of the world, stuffed away in dusty attics or forgotten in dark basements, are literally thousands of antique and vintage toys, worth millions to toy collectors worldwide. Perhaps you would even be fortunate enough to find a 1929 American National Fire Tower Truck pedal car for a few hundred at an estate sale and later sell it to a collector for about $5,000. Don't laugh. These treasures are found every day in every part of the country by savvy buyers scouring garage sales, flea markets, estate sales, junk shops, and auction sales. But unlike many buy-and-sell items, when you come across collectible toys, or any collectible in need of repairs, don't hesitate. Collectors want toys in original condition even if it means scratches, dents, missing parts, or in other words, wear. And values climb even higher if the toy still has the original packaging, advertisement, or receipt. Animals, cap pistols, construction sets, rocking horses, banks, and wagons are only a few of the best-selling and most highly prized collectible toys. Sell at collectible auctions, to collectors via shows, through clubs, eBay, and online collectible toy marketplaces, and right from home on weekends.

 BUY
Garage Sales, Flea Markets, Auctions, Online Marketplaces

 SELL
Collectors, eBay, Auctions, Homebased Sales

 RESOURCES
—The Online Collector, database listing toy collectible dealers and collectors, ✆ www.theonlinecollector.com/military.html

—📖 *2004 Toys and Prices*, Karen O'Brien (Krause Publications, 2004)
—📖 *Antique Trader Toy Price Guide*, Kyle Husfloen (Krause Publications, 2003)
—📖 *Toy Shop Magazine*, Krause Publications, ☎ (800) 942-0676, ♂ www.collect.com

Model Trains

The trains may be small, but the industry is not. Neither is the profit potential. Scale railroading is huge, a hobby enjoyed by millions of people worldwide. Right from home, you can sell all or any one of the most popular scale model trains and accessories: N, HO, O, G, and S, though O and HO are by far the most popular scale sizes. Best-selling accessories include scaled scenery, trees, buildings, bridges, tunnels, people, cars, track, assembly tools and paint, power and audio equipment, and model railroading books. Buy new trains and accessories from wholesalers and used from garage sales and flea markets. In addition to home-based sales, sell on eBay, through model railroading clubs, and directly to collectors for any vintage finds you stumble across.

 BUY
Wholesalers, Online Marketplaces, Garage Sales, Flea Markets

 SELL
Flea Markets, eBay, Collectors, Consumer Shows, Homebased Sales

 RESOURCES
—Lionel Trains Inc. Manufacturing, ☎ (810) 949-4100, ♂ www.lionel.com
—Micro Trains Wholesale, ☎ (541) 535-1755, ♂ www.micro-trains.com
—Pasco Group Wholesale, ☎ (800) 667-6121, ♂ www.pascotoys.com
—📖 *O'Brien's Collecting Toy Trains: Identification and Value Guide*, Elizabeth A. Stephen (Krause Publications, 1999)

Die-Cast Toys

Not long ago I purchased a half dozen old die-cast cars at a secondhand shop. Not because I am a collector, but because I thought they were cool. While writing this book, I wondered if they were worth anything, and if so, how much? As it turns out, the $10 I spent to buy all six, is one-tenth of what I would get if I were to sell. A bit of time spent scouring garage sales, flea markets, and secondhand shops looking for die-cast cars and toys at rock-bottom prices to resell could be financially rewarding. Brand names such as Dinky, Corgi, Matchbox, and Maisto are common in the world of die-cast toys. Though most people think of scale cars when they hear die-cast, in reality die-cast toys represent many things, including figurines, action figures, farm tractors, boats, animals, trains, planes, military equipment, and soldiers, all of which can be valuable. Consider that a die-cast Vindex piggy bank from the 1930s in good condition is worth $100 to $150. In addition to collectible die-cast toys, the market for new die-cast toys is enormous. Products can be purchased from wholesalers, manufacturers, and liquidators. Your main marketing forums will be eBay and other online marketplaces, direct to collectors via auctions and shows, and vending at flea markets and community events.

 BUY
Wholesalers, Online Marketplaces, Garage Sales, Flea Markets

 SELL
Collectors, eBay, Flea Markets, Kiosks, Consumer Shows

 RESOURCES
—Empire Discount Wholesale, ☎ (914) 684-1455, ♂ www.empire
discount.net
—Jada Toy Manufacturing, ☎ (626) 810-8382, ♂ www.jadatoys.com
—Maistro International Manufacturing, ☎ (909) 357-2020, ♂ www.
maistro.com
—📖 *Toy Car Collectors' Guide: Identification and Price Guide*, Dana
Johnson (Collector Books, 2002)

Baby Items

So what are the best new and used baby items to sell? The list is long and includes cribs, strollers, car seats, swings and rockers, changing tables, highchairs, audio and video monitoring systems, bumper jumpers, bath and crib mobiles, hampers, bedding, and bassinets, just to get started. Absent from the list is sit-in walkers, as the sales of these, new or used, have recently been banned in Canada because of safety issues, and many other countries are planning to follow suit. New items can be purchased at deeply discounted prices direct from manufacturers and wholesalers, while used equipment can generally be found in good condition at garage sales and via private seller advertisements. New or used, establish a home-based showroom for sales, and sell online and through eBay, at flea markets, and by spreading the word through local day-care centers, parent-to-be groups, and birthing classes.

 BUY
Manufacturers, Wholesalers, Garage Sales, Classified Ads

 SELL
EBay, Kiosks, Flea Markets, Homebased Sales

 RESOURCES
—1 AAA Wholesale Liquidators, ☎ (800) 661-9430, ♂ www.1aaawhole saleliquidators.com
—Dollar Days Wholesale, ☎ (877) 837-9569, ♂ www.dollardays.com
—Empire Discount Wholesale, ☎ (914) 684-1455, ♂ www.empire discount.net

Kites

You can get started buying and selling kites for peanuts; only a few hundred dollars is needed to establish a starting inventory and cover the cost of basic marketing materials, such as fliers, signs, and business cards. A great promotional idea is to host the occasional try-before-you-buy kite-flying event. Set up at a local park or beach, and let potential customers try out a kite before they commit to the purchase. One thing is for sure: It will not take long before a crowd assembles to see what is going on. These kinds of events really build excitement and clearly demonstrate the end-user benefit to customers—in this case, fun. Buying sources are plentiful. There are literally thousands of companies engaged in manufacturing, wholesaling, and importing kites of every size, shape, and price point. In addition to try-before-you-buy sales events, you can also sell your kites online, at sports and recreation shows, during community events, and at flea markets and public markets.

 BUY
Manufacturers, Wholesalers

SELL
Community Events, eBay, Kiosks, Homebased Sales

RESOURCES
—American Kite Fliers Association, ♂ www.aka.kite.org
—Avia Sports Composites Manufacturing, ☎ (828) 345-6070, ♂ www. aviasport.net
—Catch The Wind Manufacturing, ☎ (541) 994-9500, ♂ www.spin sock.com
—New Tech Kites Manufacturing, ☎ (512) 250-0485, ♂ www.newtech kites.com

Comic Books

Buying and selling new comic books is a snap—buy top-name publisher brands like DC, Marvel, Disney, and Gold Key from comic-book distributors and publishers, and resell online and through flea markets. The same, however, cannot be said for buying and selling used and vintage comic books. The industry is competitive, and you need a strong knowledge of comic books to succeed. Used comics values are mainly based on rarity and condition. But they are only worth what someone is willing to pay for them, so it is critical that you get them in front of the right people if you hope to get top dollar. *Comics Buyer's Guide* is the longest-running magazine about comic books, available by monthly subscription from Krause Publications, ☎ (800) 258-0929. Monthly issues feature new comic reviews, a monthly price guide, and comic convention news. *The Overstreet Guides to Comic Book Pricing and Condition*, from Gemstone Publishing, ♂ www.gem stonepub.com ☎ (888) 375-9800 is considered the industry standard for rating comic-book prices and conditions. Both are invaluable tools. Buy at garage sales, flea markets, online marketplaces, and comic-book shows, and resell in many of the same ways to collectors, through eBay, and comic-book shows.

 BUY
Wholesalers, Online Marketplaces, Garage Sales, Flea Markets, Auctions

 SELL
Collectors, Flea Markets, Comic-Book Shows, eBay, Kiosks

RESOURCES
—Cold Cut Comic Distributors, ☎ (831) 751-7300, ♂ www.coldcut.com
—Comic Link, buy-and-sell marketplace, ♂ www.comiclink.com
—Diamond Comics Distributors, ☎ (410) 560-7100, ♂ www.diamond comics.com
—FM International Wholesale, ☎ (608) 271-7922, ♂ www.fminternet.com
—Vault Auctions, comic book auctions, ♂ www.vaultauctions.com

Model Kits

Model craft is a hobby enjoyed by millions of people in North America—boats, cars, trucks, buildings, planes, motorcycles, tanks, and trains, models come in many designs and price points to meet each individual's wants and budget. Wholesalers and manufacturers will be your best purchasing sources. Though you will pay a bit more for each model when you buy from wholesalers as opposed to manufacturers, the advantage is you will not be required to buy case or container lots. This keeps your start-up investment to a minimum, enabling you to grow your venture as revenues and profits are earned. Flea market vending, exhibiting at craft shows and hobby shows, posting on eBay, renting mall kiosks, and selling from a homebased showroom are all suitable retailing methods for selling model kits. Also be sure to join hobby clubs and associations to spread the word about your venture and network for customers.

 BUY
Wholesalers, Manufacturers

 SELL
Kiosks, Flea Markets, eBay, Consumer Shows, Homebased Sales

 RESOURCES
—Empire Discount Wholesale, ☎ (914) 684-1455, ♂ www.empire discount.net
—Spacecraft International Manufacturing, ☎ (626) 398-4800, ♂ www. spacecraftkits.com
—Toy Directory, database listing toy manufacturers, ♂ www.toy directory.com

Piñatas

Piñatas aren't just for kids' birthday parties anymore. There are piñatas for just about any special occasion and function imaginable—anniversary parties, weddings, bachelor and bachelorette parties, baby showers, and more. The big difference between these, of course, is what is hidden inside the piñata. You definitely won't find the same prize in a birthday piñata as you will in a bachelor party piñata. Therefore, if you are going to buy and sell piñatas for profit, keep your inventory divided so the right piñata goes to the right occasion. You can buy piñatas directly from manufacturers or wholesalers. However, if you want to be unique, you can also enlist the services of local craftspeople to make piñatas per your designs, filled with the items your customers select. Sell your products online, at flea markets, and in malls, utilizing kiosk space. Also be sure to build alliances with wedding planners, day-care centers, event planners, and restaurants that host birthdays and other special occasions.

 BUY
Manufacturers, Wholesalers, Craftspeople

 SELL
Event Planners, Kiosks, Consumer Shows, Homebased Sales

 RESOURCES
—Lisa's Mexican Imports, ☎ (956) 726-9470, ♂ www.lisasmexican imports.com
—Piñatas Wholesale, ☎ (888) 764-2827, ♂ www.pinatas.com
—Talking Piñatas Manufacturing, ☎ (915) 591-7868, ♂ www.talking pinatas.com

Remote-Controlled Models

When I was a kid, remote-controlled toys were nothing more than a handheld controller attached to the toy by a wire; in effect, they were not really remote-controlled. All of that has changed. Gone are connected wires. Some of today's remote-controlled toys can reach speeds of 100 miles per hour and have a range of a mile. Best of all, from a financial aspect, remote-controlled models can sell for as much as a few thousand dollars, which means they are definitely not just for kids. These toys are available as race cars, classic cars, planes, helicopters, boats, motorcycles, and all-terrain vehicles. They are also available at just about every price point: $20 retail to a few thousand dollars. Remote-controlled models can be purchased from wholesalers, distributors, and in some instances directly from the manufacturers or their authorized agents. Sell through online marketplaces including eBay, from a homebased showroom, consumer shows, and flea markets. It does not take long for a crowd to assemble when these models start whizzing about, and even less time for the wallets to come out when people see how much fun they are.

BUY
Manufacturers, Wholesalers

SELL
Kiosks, Flea Markets, eBay, Consumer Shows

RESOURCES
—Interactive Toy Concepts Manufacturing, ☎ (866) 214-2220, ♂ www. interactivetoy.com
—Megatech Manufacturing, ☎ (847) 564-9945, ♂ www.megatech.com
—Toy Yard Manufacturing, ☎ 86-769-7791967 (China), ♂ www.toy yard.com

Dolls

Next to stamp collecting, doll collecting is the biggest collectible hobby in the United States. Needless to say, sales of new and used dolls and accessories are best described as gigantic. Depending on your knowledge and objectives, you can concentrate your buy-and-sell efforts on either new or collectible dolls. New dolls can be purchased from manufacturers, wholesalers, and craftspeople, while collectible dolls will require you to spend time scouring garage sales, doll shows, flea markets, and online doll portals to unearth valuable hidden treasures. Who knows, you might be lucky enough to stumble upon a 1960 Ponytail Barbie at a garage sale for a few bucks and resell it to a collector for about $350, and twice that if it is still in the original packaging. Collectible dolls are best sold directly to collectors via eBay and doll shows, while new dolls can be sold via flea markets, kiosks, eBay, and community events. You will also want to give some thought to the type(s) of dolls you want to sell, because there are lots, and every doll consumer has his or her own preference—porcelain, rag, Barbie, wooden, cloth, toy, and artists, to name a few. Additional revenues and profits can be earned by selling doll accessories such as clothing, houses, and doll-making supplies.

BUY
Manufacturers, Wholesalers, Garage Sales, Auctions

 SELL
Collectors, Online Marketplaces, Kiosks, Flea Markets, Community Events

 RESOURCES
—Corolle Dolls Manufacturing, ☎ (800) 628-3655, ♂ www.corolle dolls.com
—The Doll Net, database listing doll manufacturers and wholesalers, ♂ www.thedollnet.com
—Roden Surplus Imports, ☎ (256) 355-4751, ♂ www.rodenimports.com
—📖 *Blue Book Dolls and Values*, Jan Foulke (Hobby House Press, 2001)

Stuffed Animals

There are two ways to profit from buying and selling stuffed animals. First, buy new stuffed animals on a wholesale basis, and resell them for a profit. Second, purchase antique stuffed animals at auctions and estate sales, and resell them to collectors for a profit. You can combine both, but because the buying processes are very different, that may prove difficult to sustain because of time commitment. If you elect to buy new stuffed animals direct from manufacturers, distributors, importers, and wholesalers, they can be marked up and resold at community events, on eBay, and at flea markets. If you decide to specialize in collector stuffed animals and teddy bears, you need to devote time to hunting them down at garage sales, flea markets, secondhand shops, and auction sales. Make sure you obtain collectible stuffed animal and teddy bear pricing guides so you will know how much to pay and what your purchases can be resold for. Antique stuffed animals can be sold to collectors through online clubs and marketplaces, on eBay, at flea markets, through exhibiting at collectible shows, and by selling at auctions.

 BUY
Manufacturers, Wholesalers, Garage Sales

SELL
Collectors, eBay, Kiosks, Flea Markets, Community Events

 RESOURCES
—Dollar Days Wholesale, ☎ (877) 837-9569, ♂ www.dollardays.com
—Mascot Factory Inc. Wholesale, ☎ (877) 250-2244, ♂ www.mascot factoryinc.com
—Plush in a Rush Wholesale, ☎ (800) 886-8602, ♂ www.plushina rush.com
—Toy Directory, database listing toy manufacturers, ♂ www.toydirec tory.com
—📖 *Buying and Selling Teddy Bears Price Guide*, Doris Michaud and Terry Michaud (Portfolio Press, 2000)

Video Games

Console and computer video gaming is the fastest-growing segment of the entertainment industry in North America. Oddly enough, a recent survey pegged women between the ages of 18–34 as the largest emerging audience of participants. You can buy and sell used video games and accessories, and it can be a very profitable undertaking. But because the retail value of games is not large, I suggest you stick with new games and accessories and concentrate on volume sales to ensure sufficient profits. Buying from wholesalers is really your only option for obtaining new games. Used games and equipment can be purchased through online marketplaces, and at garage sales and flea markets. New or used, the best selling venues for video games and accessories are eBay, mall kiosks, gaming shows, and flea markets. Likewise, you are best to stick with the major brand names such as Nintendo, Saga, Play Station, and XBox, and the most popular games for each.

 BUY
Wholesalers

 SELL
Kiosks, eBay, Flea Markets, Consumer Shows

 RESOURCES
—D&H Wholesale, ☎ (800) 340-1001, ♂ www.dandh.com

—Pacific Games Wholesale, ☎ (213) 627-7259, ✇ www.pacific
games.com
—Regal Games Wholesale, ☎ (954) 455-8445, ✇ www.regalgames.com

Cardboard Playhouses

Become a fun broker by selling cardboard playhouses, but don't be fooled into thinking these structures are flimsy because of the construction material. Though made entirely of cardboard, these playhouses are sturdy, durable, and can last for years. Parents love them because they are portable, can be used indoors and out, and they can be packed up and taken to the beach, a local park, to Grandma's house, or brought inside in mere minutes. The best way to buy is directly from the manufacturer, thus cutting out wholesalers' markups. Selling the cardboard playhouses is very easy, especially if you can get them in front of the intended target audience, which is parents and grandparents. All kids have to do is see the gems, and their faces light up. Once that happens, the game is over for Mom, Dad, Grandpa, or Grandma, because they know it is time to start writing the check.

 BUY
Wholesalers, Manufacturers

 SELL
Homebased Sales, Kiosks, Flea Markets, Consumer Shows, Web Site

 RESOURCES
—Box Town Manufacturing, ✇ www.boxtown.com, ✇ boxtown@com
cast.net
—Pharmtec Manufacturing, ☎ (877) 833-2221, ✇ www.pharmtec
corp.com
—Playscapes Manufacturing, ☎ (608) 222-9600, ✇ www.playscapes.com

Liquidated Inventory

Retailers and manufacturers liquidate inventory for any number of reasons—slow moving, out-of-season, damaged, relocating, merging, or going out of business. Billions of dollars' worth of inventory become available every year at incredibly cheap liquidation prices or, as I like to say, fire-sale prices. Savvy entrepreneurs can earn a bundle by buying this inventory low and reselling it in the right places and to the right people at staggering markups. Traditionally, the best types of inventory to purchase are power and hand tools, music and movie disks, toys, kitchen and bath accessories, and electronics. Stay clear of products that have a limited shelf life or have special warehousing and transportation requirements. Hold monthly or quarterly sales in temporary rental locations to sell your merchandise. Or you can harness the power of the World Wide Web to buy and sell liquidated inventory and merchandise online. It's fast, easy, safe, and secure, and the only technical skill required is to be able to click a mouse. You can also sell your merchandise to retailers, flea market vendors, and eBay sellers. The choices are almost unlimited. In recent years, many merchandise liquidation services have gone live on the Web to provide retailers and manufacturers forums to list and sell inventory they wish to liquidate. A few of these liquidation Web sites are featured below.

 BUY
Online Marketplaces, Auction Sales, Trustees, Retailers, Manufacturers

 SELL
Temporary Locations, eBay, B2B, Flea Markets, Online Marketplaces, Resellers

 RESOURCES
—Liquidation Online, inventory liquidation service, ♂ www.liquidation.com
—Merchandise USA, inventory liquidation service, ♂ www.merchandise usa.com
—Quitting Business, inventory liquidation portal, ♂ www.quitting business.com

---

Government Surplus

Purchasing government surplus and seized merchandise for pennies on the dollar of the original value and reselling to consumers at marked-up prices can make you very rich. Government agencies and organizations of every sort sell off used and surplus equipment, as well as items seized for nonpayment or from criminal activity every day, through auction sales and sealed-bid tenders. A few of these agencies are the Internal Revenue Service (IRS), U.S. Postal Service, U.S. Small Business Administration (SBA), U.S. Marshals Service, and the U.S. Treasury Department. There are many more government agencies at the federal, state, county, and city level that also routinely hold auction sales to dispose of surplus, foreclosed, and seized property. Though most of these sales are conducted like traditional auction sales, sometimes the sale can be by sealed-bid tender, which means you complete a tender form and submit the amount you are willing to pay for a specific item. Tender forms are available directly from the government agency holding the sale or the auctioneer conducting the sale. Items that are routinely auctioned by government agencies include computers, real estate, automobiles, machinery and tools, jewelry, furniture, electronics, and boats. Sell the larger items you buy from home and through eBay and the smaller items at weekend flea markets.

 BUY
Auctions, Sealed-Bid Tenders

 SELL
Homebased Sales, eBay, Flea Markets, Web Site

 RESOURCES
—Public Works and Government Services Canada—Crown Assets Distribution, sales of government surplus and seized property by auctions, tenders, and public sales, including real estate, equipment, automobiles, furniture, boats, jewelry, clothing, furniture, and electronics, ☎ (905) 615-2025 ♂ http://crownassets.pwgsc.gc.ca/text/index-e.cfm
—U.S. Department of the Treasury, seized-property auctions, including automobiles, boats, jewelry, electronics, and furniture, ☎ (202) 622-2000, ♂ www.ustreas.gov/auctions/customs
—U.S. General Services Administration, government-owned asset sales, ☎ (800) 473-7836, ♂ www.propertydisposal.gsa.gov.Property/About/
—U.S. Postal Service, damaged and unclaimed items auctions, ♂ www.usps.com/auctions

Restaurant Equipment

Did you know that only 10 percent of new restaurants remain in business more than five years? So there is a fantastic opportunity to buy secondhand restaurant equipment and fixtures, such as grills, fryers, coffee machines, tables and chairs, and coolers, for a song to resell for a gain. The concept is very straightforward. When one restaurant goes out of business, simply purchase the equipment and fixtures for a fraction of their original retail value. When a new restaurant opens, sell the same equipment to them for a handsome profit. To buy restaurant equipment, establish working relationships with auctioneers and bankruptcy trustees who can keep you informed about restaurant closings in your area. Once you have accumulated some equipment, it is time to advertise it for sale in online marketplaces, in specialty restaurant publications, by developing your own Web site linked with other restaurant information Web sites, and by speaking directly to restaurateurs. Inquire about equipment needs they may have, and speak with people intending to open restaurants. You will need showroom and storage space at home for the equipment, and suitable transportation to move it. If these are not available, all can be rented on an as-needed basis.

 BUY
Auctions, Bankruptcies, Classified Ads

 SELL
Homebased Sales, B2B, Online Marketplaces, Specialty Publications

 RESOURCES
—National Restaurant Association, ☎ www.restaurant.org
—Restaurant Operator Online, information and resources, ☎ www.restaurantoperator.com
—📖 *The Official Used Restaurant Equipment Guide*, David Marketing Group, PO Box 2757, Duluth, GA 30096, Fax (770) 497-1827

Store Fixtures

The buy-and-sell concept at work here is the same as with restaurant equipment: when a retail store closes, purchase their chattels, items such as display cases, wall rack systems, light fixtures, warehouse equipment and shipping supplies, mannequins, counters, displays, and signage, and resell these items to retailers opening new stores or expanding existing ones. You can operate right from home and advertise locally. Develop a Web site to promote and sell online, list items on eBay and other online marketplaces, sell through auctions, and join business associations to network for new business, both for purchasing and selling reasons. The venture can be very lucrative because, though unfortunate for the merchants who are facing financial ruin, you will be able to purchase store fixtures at absolutely rock-bottom prices.

BUY
Auctions, Classified Ads, Bankruptcies

 SELL
B2B, Homebased Showroom, Online Marketplaces

 RESOURCES
—Recycler's World, directory listing used store fixture and display dealers nationwide, ♂ www.recycle.net/Commercial/store
—Retail Source, information and resources portal and online marketplace for retail store owners and fixture dealers, ♂ www.retail
source.com

Office Furniture and Equipment

Office furniture and equipment such as desks, chairs, photocopiers, dividers, and
file cabinets can often be bought for pennies on the dollar at bankruptcy auctions,
through the classifieds, and at surplus sales. Establish a homebased showroom for
sales; a converted garage or basement works well. Design your own Web site listing furniture and equipment available, and join business associations such as the
chamber of commerce to network for customers. This opportunity relies heavily
on patience, and good timing. I have many times attended office closeout auctions
and always been astounded by the available bargains. This part of the equation is
timing. I have also purchased lots of secondhand office furniture and equipment
from dealers, and though I paid less than retail value, I did pay substantially more
than auction and closeout prices. Patience is the key.

 BUY
Auctions, Classified Ads, Bankruptcies

 SELL
B2B, Homebased Showroom, Online Marketplaces

 RESOURCES
—Recycler's World, directory listing used office equipment and furniture
dealers nationwide, ♂ www.recycle.net/Commercial/furniture
—📖 *Office Machines and Business Equipment Used Price Guide*,
Asay Publishing Company, ☎ (800) 825-9637, ♂ www.asaypub.com

Security Mirrors

The market for security mirrors is nearly unlimited, as there are millions of potential customers right now and thousands more as new retail businesses open. In spite of the popularity of security video cameras, security mirrors will always be a popular choice for merchants. Security mirrors enable shopkeepers to keep an eye on their valuable inventory, while assisting other customers. Security and safety mirrors come in many styles and price points, ranging from inexpensive 18-inch convex mirrors, which retailers can purchase for about $75, to four-foot ceiling dome mirrors for large-surface viewing that can cost upwards of $400, which is still substantially less costly than video surveillance cameras and arguably more of a deterrent to would-be shoplifters. Even though the retail prices are reasonable, you can easily generate 30 to 50 percent gross profit on each sale.

The best way to market the security mirrors is to design a simple brochure highlighting all the benefits and features, and call on businesses directly. Go in and talk to shopkeepers. Let them know right upfront that you are there to save them money. Security mirrors are not a hard sale: if they deter just one person from shoplifting, there is a good chance they have already paid for themselves, and if they deter ten shoplifters a month, the shopkeeper will be ahead thousands every year, which is a pretty persuasive sales pitch. Additional locations where safety and security mirrors are needed include warehouses, parking lots and garages, construction sites, and factories.

BUY
Wholesalers, Manufacturers

SELL
B2B, Trade Shows

RESOURCES
—Brossard Mirror Manufacturing, ☎ (800) 222-7825, ♂ www.brossard mirrors.com
—Newport Glass Manufacturing, ☎ (800) 782-2100, ♂ www.newport glass.com
—See All Mirror Manufacturing, ☎ (800) 873-1313, ♂ www.seeall.com

How-To Information

How-to books, tapes, and software can retail for as much as $100 each and cost as little as a few dollars to buy wholesale or to produce, making this a fantastic buy-and-sell opportunity. Many publishers, authors, and media companies sell master copies or reproduction rights to their works cheaply, which means that you can purchase and reproduce the work in various print and electronic mediums and formats to resell for a profit. There are two kinds of rights: reprint rights and master rights. Reprint rights means the owner of the copyrighted material authorizes a buyer to reproduce the materials in print or electronic format for resale. Master rights means the copyright owner has also authorized the buyer to sell the reprint rights to anyone they wish. Popular how-to and self-help information has always included subjects relating to business, sales, marketing, relationships, childrearing, home renovation, health, crafts, and diet and fitness. The best selling methods include online sales, back-of-room seminar sales, trade shows, and mail order.

BUY
Publishers, Copyright Holders

SELL
Web Site, Online Marketplaces, Mail Order, Seminars

RESOURCES
—The eBook Directory, ✎ www.theebookdirectory.com
—Reprint Rights, ☎ (888) 550-8855, ✎ www.reprint-rights.com
—Total Resale, ✎ www.totalresale.com

Computers

Big profits can be earned by buying and selling new and used computers, and getting started is easier than you think. New desktop and notebook computer systems can be purchased from wholesalers, liquidators, and distributors, then marked up by as much as 50 percent and sold to businesses and consumers through online marketplaces such as eBay, direct contact with business owners, and by establishing a homebased showroom. The potential to profit is even greater buying and selling used computers, especially notebook computers, which hold their value much better than desktop computers. There are companies that even wholesale notebook computers for resale purposes. That's how big the demand and market are for used notebook computers. Though the selling methods are the same as for new computers, the buying sources are not. To buy used computer systems, scan classified ads for bargains and attend auction sales, the preferred method. Many corporations, government agencies, schools, and organizations replace their still-otherwise-good computer equipment on a scheduled basis. These computers can often be purchased for pennies on the dollar of the original cost at auctions or tender sales.

 BUY
Wholesalers, Auctions, Classified Ads

 SELL
B2B, Flea Markets, Consumer Shows, Homebased Sales

 RESOURCES
—Buy 4 Less Electronics Wholesale, ☎ (822) 251-1391, ♂ www.buy4lessinc.com
—D&H Wholesale, ☎ (800) 340-1001, ♂ www.dandh.com
—S&K Computers Wholesale, ☎ (303) 430-7500, ♂ www.skwholesale.com
—USA Notebooks Used Computer Wholesale, ☎ (888) 728-9902, ♂ www.usanotebook.com

Computer Peripherals

The best computer accessories to sell online and offline include inkjet printers, laser printers, scanners, DVD and CD writers, flat-screen and flat-panel monitors, and wireless keyboards and mouse sets. Purchase new computer peripherals at deeply discounted prices from wholesalers, especially liquidators offering these products by the pallet, but on a first-come, first-served basis. Occasionally you will find high-end used equipment to buy with good resale values, especially flat-panel LED monitors. However, unless you are prepared to spend time scanning classified ads, attending auctions, and submitting tenders, stick with buying and selling new computer peripherals. The best selling methods include direct to businesses, flea market vending, exhibiting at computer and consumer shows, selling from a homebased showroom supported by local advertising, and especially listing on eBay as computer peripherals are some of the best-sellers.

Buy
Wholesalers, Auctions, Classified Ads

 Sell
B2B, Flea Markets, eBay, Consumer and Computer Shows, Homebased Sales

 Resources
—Overstock B2B Wholesale, ☎ (800) 273-6063, ♂ www.overstock b2b.com
—S&K Computers Wholesale, ☎ (303) 430-7500, ♂ www.skwhole sale.com
—Vision Wholesale, ☎ (877) 379-7983, ♂ www.visionwholesale.com

Computer Parts

A great full-time or part-time income can be earned buying and selling new computer parts such as CDRW and DVD drives, hard drives, memory, audio and video cards, processing chips, and motherboards. Buy from wholesalers and sell directly to businesses for upgrade purposes, from a homebased showroom/repair shop, and through various online marketplaces. Additional revenues and profits can be earned if you have the skills and knowledge to install the parts you sell, because you can easily charge in the range of $30 to $50 per hour for this service. Because prices for replacement PC parts have fallen dramatically in the last few years, skip buying and selling used parts because there is not enough profit in it, unless you can get late-model computers for next to nothing and sell them for parts.

 Buy
Manufacturers, Wholesalers

 Sell
B2B, Homebased Sales, Online Marketplaces

 Resources
—Overstock B2B Wholesale, ☎ (800) 273-6063, ♂ www.overstockb2b.com
—S&K Computers Wholesale, ☎ (303) 430-7500, ♂ www.skwholesale.com
—Star Tech Wholesale, ☎ (800) 265-1844, ♂ www.startech.com

Software

There are more than 250,000 software applications currently available—diagnostics, accounting, productivity tools, database management, content, customer-relationship management (CRM), publishing, inventory, graphics, training, educational, communications, games, security, and anti-virus software, to name a few. It is safe to say that finding one or a few to buy and sell should not prove difficult. Start your search on software directory Web sites like the ones featured here in Resources. Buy right from developers or from wholesalers, and sell online, direct to businesses, and through computer-related trade and consumer shows. There is also a very healthy market for used software, especially business applications. However, when buying used, you have to make sure it is not pirated software. The best way to do that is to buy only used software that is complete with the original packaging and documentation. Buy used software at auction sales, online marketplaces, and from classified ads. There are a number of companies online offering to purchase used software, such as Soft Buyers (www.softbuyers.com), but you can make more by selling it directly to consumer and business users yourself.

 BUY
Programmers, Wholesalers, Distributors, License Agents

 SELL
B2B, Online Marketplaces, Consumer Shows

 RESOURCES
—D&H Wholesale, ☎ (800) 340-1001, ♂ www.dandh.com
—Soft Database, directory listing more than 29,000 software distributors and developers, ♂ www.softdatabase.com
—Sunnyland Software Wholesale, ☎ (888) 471-6655, ♂ www.sunny landsoftware.com
—The Software Network, business software directory, ♂ www.thesoft warenetwork.com

Automated-Teller Machines (ATMs)

The deregulation of ATMs (automated-teller machines) allows any entrepreneur to purchase one or more ATMs, place them on location, and operate them as a going business concern. Since deregulation, thousands of ATMs have been sold, and a secondary market is now emerging for the sale of secondhand ATMs. While a lucrative income can be earned by purchasing secondhand ATMs low and reselling them at a profit, the truly gigantic money lies in purchasing secondhand ATMs, locating them in a busy place where they can earn revenues, and then selling the secondhand ATMs on location and with bankable revenues as going business concerns. Doing so easily increases the value of the machine by three to four times as much as would be worth without a secure operating location. Good placement locations include taverns, nightclubs, convenience stores, grocery markets, and other buildings with high foot-traffic counts. Typically, the owner of the building or operator of the business where the ATM is located will split the revenues the machine earns with the ATM owner/operator. The revenue split can range from 50-50 to 90-10 in the favor of the ATM owner, depending on the agreement and how much revenue the machine generates.

BUY
Classified Ads, Auctions, Wholesalers

SELL
B2B, Business Opportunity Shows, Online Marketplaces

RESOURCES
—ATM Marketplace, industry information and links, ♂ www.atmmarket place.com
—ATM Wholesale, ☎ (866) 285-0208, ♂ www.atmwholesale.com

Personal Security Products

The time has never been better to buy personal security products such as mace, sirens, whistles, and stun guns at rock-bottom wholesale costs and sell them to security-minded consumers at full retail. Who can blame people for being concerned about security? Muggings, personal attacks, road rage, and home invasions have people scared to death. While many people refuse to have a gun, these same people are more than willing to use personal security products that do not have such permanent results. Of course, online marketplaces such as eBay are perfect selling venues for these products. But you can also set up displays at consumer shows, in malls, and even organize and host safety seminars by bringing in experts to talk about personal safety issues. You can also sell personal safety devices during and after the seminar. There are numerous wholesale sources for personal safety and security products. In addition to the ones featured below, you can also go online to find many more.

Buy
Wholesalers, Manufacturers

 Sell
Online Marketplaces, Flea Markets, Kiosks, Consumer Shows, Seminars

 Resources
—Cutting Edge Products Wholesale, ☎ (800) 497-0539, ♂ www.cepi.biz
—Safety Technology Wholesale, ☎ (904) 720-2188, ♂ www.safetytech
nology.com
—TBO Tech Self Defense Products Wholesale, ☎ (910) 426-5722,
♂ www.tbotech.com

Home Security Products

Like personal security products, home security products are also hot sellers that can earn you a bundle in cold hard cash in no time. These products include window security bars and roll shutters, home alarm systems, surveillance equipment, security lighting, motion-detector dog barkers, and many other devices. Also, like personal security products, home security products sell themselves. We live in a violent society. People want to protect their families, homes, and belongings, and the best way to do it is to be proactive and get the security devices that get the job done. Because there are numerous manufacturers and wholesalers of home security devices, supply at reasonable terms and prices will not be difficult to secure. Selling your products can be accomplished in a number of ways, including marketing through eBay and other online marketplaces, direct from your home supported by localized advertising, exhibiting at home-and-garden shows, and direct to business owners intent on protecting their shops, employees, customers, and livelihoods.

 Buy
Wholesalers, Manufacturers

 Sell
Homebased Sales, Consumer Shows, Kiosks, Online Marketplaces

 Resources
—Delectronix Wholesale, ☎ (888) 742-4263, ♂ www.delectronix.com

—Maziuk Wholesale Distribution, ☎ (800) 777-5945, ♂ www.maziuk.com
—Safety Technology Wholesale, ☎ (904) 720-2188, ♂ www.safetytech nology.com

Cleaning Products and Equipment

Consumers, businesses, government, and organizations spend billions annually on sanitation supplies and equipment: cleaners, paper products, mops, brooms, and disposal bags. Cashing in on this demand is probably easier than you think. Get started by securing a reliable wholesale source to buy cleaning products and equipment for rock-bottom prices. These wholesalers are easy to locate in the Yellow Pages or on the Internet, and I have included a few below. The next step is to determine how you want to sell your product line: direct to businesses or direct to consumers. If you decide to sell direct to businesses, all that is required is to start knocking on doors and making inquiries about who their current supplier is and if they would be willing to give your business a try. Offering incentives such as a special discount, free samples, and guaranteed free and quick delivery will help. If you decide to concentrate your marketing efforts on consumers, you can sell through flea markets as well as trade and consumer shows. The busiest vendors at these shows are always the people who sell miracle cleaning products, chamois, dust mops, and super powerful vacuum cleaners. This marketing method works great because you can demonstrate the products live. No need to tell customers how great your cleaners are when you can show them, and let them witness the fantastic results and benefits.

BUY
Manufacturers, Wholesalers

SELL
Flea Markets, Consumer Shows, B2B

RESOURCES
—Alles Wholesale, ☎ (800) 225-3284, ♂ www.allesonline.com
—Dollar Days Wholesale, ☎ (877) 837-9569, ♂ www.dollardays.com
—International Sanitary Supply Association, ♂ www.issa.com

First-Aid Kits

Purchasing first-aid kits wholesale and reselling them for great profits is definitely one buy-and-sell idea that could easily be overlooked because of its simplicity, but it should not be, especially if you think in terms of specialization. Who potentially needs access to first-aid kits and supplies? Millions of people every single day, including hikers, campers, sports enthusiasts, families, boaters, motorists, workers, and pet owners, and this list only scratches the surface. You have a couple of choices of how to buy the kits. First, purchase first-aid products and hard or soft cases appropriately labeled separately to suit the desired end user, and assemble the kits yourself. Second, purchase preassembled first-aid kits in bulk from wholesalers, and sell them as is, with no modifications. Some wholesale suppliers I contacted will even assemble the kits to suit their customers' needs; this is worth keeping in mind because it can save you assembly time. Sell the first-aid kits directly to business owners or consumers online, at flea markets, and at industry-specific events such as auto shows, home-and-garden shows, and sports and recreation shows.

 BUY
Manufacturers, Wholesalers

 SELL
B2B, Kiosks, Consumer Shows, Online Marketplaces

 RESOURCES
—Custom Kit Company Wholesale, ☎ (508) 943-8501, ♂ www.custom-kits.com
—First-Aid Supplies Online Wholesale, ☎ (800) 874-8767, ♂ www.firstaidsuppliesonline.com
—MP First-Aid Wholesale, ☎ (888) 332-4863, ♂ www.mpfirstaid.com

Patio Furniture

When it comes to buying and selling lawn and garden products, patio furniture has the potential to be among the most profitable. Good-quality patio furniture is available at insanely low prices from overseas suppliers, especially if you purchase by the container. You can also buy from importers and wholesalers, though prices will be higher per unit. Because patio furniture can be constructed from numerous materials—wood, plastic, iron, precast cement, marble, and fiberglass—you might decide to design your own line unique to your business and enlist local crafts-people to construct it for you on a contract basis. Regardless of the type of patio furniture you decide to sell, great sales methods include homebased displays, direct to businesses such as restaurants, exhibiting at home and garden shows, listing in online marketplaces, and vending at flea markets. Personally, I would concentrate on the high-end market, supplying only the best custom patio furniture and catering to those with substantial enough budgets to make this type of purchase.

Buy
Manufacturers, Craftspeople, Wholesalers

Sell
Homebased Sales, Home-and-Garden Shows, Online Marketplaces

Resources
—Best Adirondack Chair Company, ☎ (800) 418-1433, ♂ www.thebest adirondackchair.com
—Hansen Wholesale, ☎ (800) 365-3267, ♂ www.hansenwholesale.com
—Teak Patio Wholesale, ☎ (866) 535-6558, ♂ www.teakpatiowhole sale.com

Trees and Shrubs

Selling trees and shrubs right from home is a fantastic way to earn an extra few thousand dollars every year or even every month if you are ambitious. When you consider that Americans spend more than $5 billion annually on outdoor plants, the opportunity becomes abundantly clear. There are two main purchase options. First, purchase trees and shrubs from wholesale commercial nurseries, mark them up, and resell them. Second, if space is available, grow your own trees and shrubs right at home. Surprisingly, not much space is required. Consider that you can purchase Japanese maple seedlings for about 75 cents each, pot or plant in burlaps, wait a season or two while they grow, and resell them right from home for $25 to $50 each. A 20-foot-square garden area is large enough to support 300 of these seedlings, thus producing approximately 100 saleable trees annually when planting is alternated. That's as much as $5,000 every year in revenues from just a small patch of ground in your backyard. Of course, to maximize profit potential you might combine both methods, buying some wholesale and growing some of your own.

BUY
Wholesalers, Growers

 SELL
Homebased Sales, Online Marketplaces, Gardener Clubs

 RESOURCES
—J. Frank Schmidt & Son, ☎ (503) 663-4128, ♂ www.jfschmidt.com
—Lawyer Nursery, ☎ (406) 826-3881, ♂ www.lawyernursery.com
—Tennessee Wholesale Nursery, ☎ (866) 526-4527, ♂ www.tennessee
    wholesalenursery.com

Landscape Supplies

Much like the recent explosion in do-it-yourself home renovation, homeowners have also taken to do-it-yourself landscaping as a way to save money, improve their property, and stretch their creative wings. People take pride in their homes and want them to look as good on the outside as they do inside. The best way to accomplish this is with landscaping. This buy-and-sell enterprise necessitates that you have lots of outside storage space with proper zoning and a truck capable of carrying and dumping heavy loads. Providing you can meet the criteria, you can purchase sand, gravel, topsoil, and bark mulch by the dump-truck load wholesale and sell it to homeowners in smaller quantities for full retail. They pick up, or you deliver for an added fee. You can also stock and supply natural landscape products such as driftwood and river rock, which can be acquired for free from the beach or by striking a deal with farmers and landowners. In addition to consumer sales, you can also market your products to construction-related businesses may have a need for these products, such as paving-stone installers, foundation installers, and playground equipment installers. Contact the sources listed below to find wholesale supplies in your area.

 BUY
Wholesalers, Manufacturers, Free Sources, Farmers

 SELL
Homebased Sales, Direct Delivery, B2B

RESOURCES
—Mulch and Soil Council, the trade association representing processors of horticultural mulches and consumer potting soils, ☎ (703) 257-0111, ♂ www.mulchandsoilcouncil.org
—National Stone, Sand, & Gravel Association, ♂ www.nssga.org

Solar-Powered Products

When it comes to how we power our lives, the wave of the future is without question alternative energy sources. Therefore, if you decide to start a buy-and-sell enterprise focused on the retail sales of solar-powered products, you will be definitely engaging in a growing industry that will prove extremely profitable for years to come. Sell solar and alternative-energy products such as solar-powered interior and exterior lights, solar-cell battery systems and chargers, wind-powered generators, rooftop solar panels, and any number of other solar-cell power and storage systems for big profits. Your buying source will be new products directly from manufacturers and wholesalers, mainly because it is rare to find used solar-powered and alternative-energy products for sale. Customers will include everybody who is currently or who wants to be *off the grid*, including remote property owners, boat owners, RV owners, campers, hikers, and basically anybody else who has a need for energy to power equipment, lights, and utilities where none is available. Sell your products directly from home, supported by local and online advertising, as well as through consumer shows and online marketplaces catering to alternative-energy enthusiasts.

BUY
Manufacturers, Wholesalers

SELL
Online Marketplaces, Consumer Shows, Homebased Sales

RESOURCES
—Alternative Solar Products Wholesale, ☎ (909) 308-2366, ♂ www.alternativesolar.com
—Solar Energy Industries Association, ♂ www.seia.org
—Solar Sellers Wholesale, ☎ (562) 423-4879, ♂ www.solarsellers.com

Flags

Choices are almost unlimited in the variety of flags that can be sold, including country flags, state flags, provincial flags, sports flags, marine flags, safety flags, historical reproduction flags, royal flags, military flags, organization flags, windsocks, auto racing flags, and handheld flags. And don't forget flagpoles! Buy flags direct from manufacturers and wholesalers, such as the ones featured below, or conduct a *Wholesale Flag* keyword search on any popular search engine or directory to find more. There are also numerous places to resell flags for big profits. These include homebased sales, online marketplaces like eBay, by creating your own e-commerce Web site, and by renting booth space in malls, flea markets, consumer shows, and community events such as Fourth of July celebrations and Flag Day events. Additional revenues can be earned by offering a flagpole installation service, which can be subcontracted out to a local handyman on a revenue-split basis.

 BUY
Manufacturers, Wholesalers

 SELL
Homebased Sales, Kiosks, Online Marketplaces, Flea Markets

 RESOURCES
—American Flags Wholesale, ☎ (888) 719-9516, ♂ www.american-flags-wholesale.com
—National Independent Flag Dealers Association, ♂ www.flaginfo.com
—Patriotic Flags Wholesale, ☎ (866) 798-2803, ♂ www.patriotic-flags.com
—Sav-On Wholesale, ☎ (888) 662-1097, ♂ www.sav-on-wholesale.com

Garden Fountains

Garden fountains are a welcome addition to any garden, lawn, patio space, or interior sunroom. Nothing quite matches the soothing sounds of tinkling water for relieving the day's stresses. Garden fountains and related accessories can be purchased from wholesalers, manufacturers, and sometimes even local craftspeople who are currently or who can be contracted to build garden fountains based on your design or theirs. Sell from home, displaying your fountains in the front and backyard with appropriate signage. Or exhibit and sell at home-and-garden shows, sell through online marketplaces including eBay, and join gardening clubs to network for new business. Additionally, sell related equipment such as replacement pump motors, underwater lights, water plants, and stones.

BUY
Manufacturers, Wholesalers

SELL
Homebased Sales, Home-and-Garden Shows, eBay, Kiosks, Flea Markets

RESOURCES
—Amarc Heritage Manufacturing, ☎ 91-120-3090098 (India), ✆ www. marble-craft.com
—Art Flow Designs Manufacturing, ☎ (888) 927-8356, ✆ www.artflow designs.com
—Garden Fountains Manufacturing, ☎ (866) 207-1674, ✆ www.garden-fountains.com

Garden Ornaments

Garden statues, wall plaques, and lawn ornaments are all hot sellers, and you can get in on the moneymaking action by starting a venture buying garden ornaments wholesale and reselling them to homeowners for big profits. Garden ornaments can be constructed from ceramics, wood, stone, fiberglass, plastic, and a number of other materials. Display and sell right from your own front yard as well as on eBay, at flea markets, and at home-and-garden shows. Garden statues and ornaments can be purchased in North America and overseas from any number of manufacturers, wholesalers, and importers such as the ones featured below. To find more buying sources, simply log on to any search engine or directory and conduct a *Wholesale Garden Ornaments* keyword search.

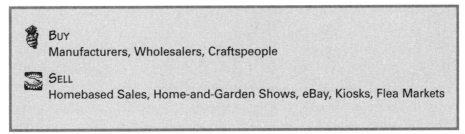

BUY
Manufacturers, Wholesalers, Craftspeople

SELL
Homebased Sales, Home-and-Garden Shows, eBay, Kiosks, Flea Markets

RESOURCES
—Double D Statuary Manufacturing, ☎ (361) 364-2115, ✆ www.
doubledstatuary.com
—Ideal Lawn Ornaments, ☎ (631) 669-0600, ✆ www.idealornaments.
com/ wholesale.html
—Kevin's Custom Crafts Manufacturing, ☎ (570) 523-0813, ✆ www.light
houseman.com

Weathervanes

Weathervanes adorn millions of homes worldwide. Though best suited to Victorian architecture or East Coast Capes and Saltboxes, these functional and attractive features add charm to any home and hark back to the days of old. You have three main options for buying weathervanes, which are manufacturers, wholesalers, and local craftspeople. If you decide to sell high-end weathervanes crafted of copper and finely detailed, then specialty manufacturers and local craftspeople will be your best buying sources. If you choose to sell in quantity at lower retail prices, then wholesalers or overseas manufacturers specializing in mass-produced vanes of cast and extruded metals will be the right choice. Once you have determined your prices and the target audience that you will cater to, your next step is to determine the best methods of marketing. Your marketing options will include homebased sales supported by local advertising, signage drive-bys, and word-of-mouth referrals. Online sales utilizing forums such as eBay, Yahoo auctions, and specialty marketplaces relating to home renovation and decoration, and offline marketplaces such as consumer shows focused on home and garden products, flea markets, and mall rental kiosks are all viable marketing and sales venues.

 BUY
Wholesalers, Manufacturers, Craftspeople

 SELL
Consumer Shows, Kiosks, Homebased Sales, eBay, Flea Markets

 RESOURCES
—Mammoth Manufacturing, ☎ 886-4-7387062 (Taiwan), ✆ www.
garden-sprinkler.com.tw

—Weather Vanes Outlet Wholesale, ☎ (801) 720-5695, ♂ www.weather-vanesoutlet.com

—Weathervanes of Maine, ☎ (207) 548-0050, ♂ www.weathervanesof-maine.com

Wind Chimes

Bamboo, anodized aluminum, cast iron, glass, seashells, and ceramic tiles are only a few of the materials used to construct eloquent and beautiful-sounding wind chimes. They are available in every size, style, and price point imaginable to suit every individual's tastes and budget. Buy direct from foreign manufacturers of mass-produced wind chimes for the lowest unit pricing, or start small by enlisting the services of a local craftsperson to make the wind chimes based on your creative designs. Regardless of the route you choose, sell the chimes on eBay, at home-and-garden shows, at weekend flea markets, and by renting kiosk space at malls and public markets. Also, don't overlook salespeople and corporations as potential clients. You may be surprised by how many would be willing to buy wind chimes to give to their best customers as appreciation gifts. And of course, if you have a few hundred displayed in your yard with For Sale signs posted, there is no doubt you will attract lots of attention and people stopping in to make a purchase.

 BUY
Manufacturers, Craftspeople, Wholesalers

 SELL
Flea Markets, Kiosks, eBay, Homebased Sales, Community Events

 RESOURCES
—Esco Imports, ☎ (800) 445-3836, ♂ www.escoimports.com
—P. T. Indonesia Export, ☎ 62-361-721-575 (Indonesia), ♂ www.source-indonesia.com
—Troop Manufacturing, ☎ 886-2-25795768 (Taiwan), ♂ www.troopcorp.com/ international

Hammocks

Next to great profit potential, the best aspect of selling hammocks is that they sell themselves. Who can resist the thought of spending a lazy summer afternoon napping in a hammock under a shady tree in the backyard? Purchase hammocks directly from importers, manufacturers, wholesalers, and craftspeople in your community who are currently making, or who can be persuaded to make hammocks for your venture. The profit potential is great because good-quality hammocks can be purchased in bulk for as little as $15 each and resold for $75. You can get as much as $300 for elaborate, finely crafted models. While the hammocks can certainly be sold through any number of online marketplaces such as eBay, do not overlook the power of demonstration. Setting up a hammock that people can try out is a very persuasive marketing tool, one that can be effectively used at flea markets, rented kiosk space in malls and public markets, at community events, and at home-and-garden shows. When people get to try out a product and realize the benefits of ownership firsthand, the resistance to the sale often disappears.

 BUY
Manufacturers, Wholesalers, Craftspeople, Importers

 SELL
Online Marketplaces, Consumer Shows, Flea Markets, Kiosks

 RESOURCES
—The Hammock Source Wholesale, ☎ (800) 334-1078, ♂ www.the hammocksource.com
—Second May Inc., ☎ 91-120-2576746 (India), ♂ www.secondmay.net/hammocks.html
—Sitting Pretty Manufacturing, ☎ (613) 267-5716, ♂ www.deluxe-hammocks.com

Hobby Greenhouses

Hobby greenhouses have become a very popular addition to any backyard or patio space, especially for the baby boomer generation as they slip into retirement and look for ways to keep active and enjoy life. Even though hobby greenhouses are a pint-sized version, they still provide many of the same features and growing capabilities as full-size models, which make them ideal for any yard or patio, including those in condominiums. Retail prices range from a few hundred dollars for basic models to $5,000 for models with all the bells and whistles. Purchasing wholesale or direct from the manufacturer, you can expect to retain 20 to 25 percent of the retail-selling price. Hobby greenhouses are generally sold in a kit, making them easy to ship. Many manufacturers even provide drop-shipping options direct to your customers, so you do not have to worry about storage and transportation issues. The best way to sell hobby greenhouses is to erect a display model right at your own home and advertise locally in the classifieds, at gardening clubs, by referral, by exhibiting at home-and-garden shows, and via online marketplaces such as gardening Web sites and eBay.

Buy
Manufacturers, Wholesalers

Sell
Homebased Sales, Home-and-Garden Shows, Online Marketplaces

Resources
—BC Greenhouse Manufacturing, ☎ (888) 391-4433, ♂ www.bcgreen houses.com
—Farm Wholesale Greenhouses, ☎ (800) 825-1925, ♂ www.farmwhole sale.com
—Pharmtec Manufacturing, ☎ (877) 833-2221, ♂ www.pharmtec corp.com
—National Greenhouse Manufacturers Association, ♂ www.ngma.com
—Hobby Greenhouse Association, ♂ www.hobbygreenhouse.org

Arbors and Gazebos

Garden arbors and gazebos made of wood, vinyl, or composite plastics are hot sellers in any area of the country. Buy from manufacturers who offer these products in kit form and who also offer direct drop-shipping options to your customers, so you need not worry about storage and transportation issues. Set up arbor and gazebo displays right in your own front and backyard, and advertise locally and through garden clubs to spread the word about your products. Additionally, display your products at home-and-garden shows and even list and sell on eBay. Signage will be an important marketing tool, especially for homebased sales. Your signs should be basic, but bold, and attention-grabbing. State your biggest competitive advantage right on your sign, whether it is best selection, made to order, free delivery and setup, best quality, or lowest prices.

BUY
Manufacturers, Wholesalers, Craftspeople

SELL
Homebased Sales, Online Marketplaces, Home-and-Garden Shows

RESOURCES
—Gazebo Depot, ☎ (561) 243-2410, ♂ www.gazebodepot.com
—Interstate Wood & Vinyl Products Manufacturing, ♂ www.interstate
woodproducts.com
—Lifetime Vinyl Fence Manufacturing, ☎ (800) 213-2539, ♂ www.avinyl
fence.com

Retractable Awnings

Retractable shade and rain awnings are a welcome addition to any patio space. They come in two basic mechanical designs: hand-crank models or motorized models operating on a switch or handheld remote control. Retail prices vary greatly depending on size, model, and fabric selection. They can range from a couple hundred dollars for mass-produced 8- by 10-foot awnings to $5,000 for large motorized awnings. Homeowners seeking protection from the sun and rain will be your number-one target audience. But don't discount recreational-vehicle owners and business owners with outdoor patio space, especially restaurants and cafés. Buying directly from manufacturers will secure your best pricing, and there are many awning manufacturers. You can also buy from wholesalers, distributors, and agents, though you will have to pay slightly higher unit prices. Sell direct from home by setting up awning displays and inviting potential customers to check them out. You can also create your own Web site so you can take online orders from around the globe. Awnings can also be sold through eBay, at home-and-garden shows, and at recreational-vehicle expositions.

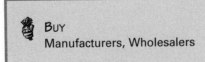

BUY
Manufacturers, Wholesalers

SELL
Homebased Shows, Home-and-Garden Shows, eBay

RESOURCES
—Ace Canopy Manufacturing, ☎ (888) 702-6082, ✂ www.ace
canopy.com
—Shade System Technology Manufacturing, ☎ (714) 630-3466,
✂ www.sstinc.com
—TCT&A Manufacturing, ☎ (800) 252-1355, ✂ www.awning-tent.com

Hydroponics Equipment

Hydroponics gardening is becoming increasingly popular, especially in urban centers where green space and living space are at a premium. When you consider the benefits of hydroponics gardening, it is not difficult to understand the rise in its popularity—no heavy soil needed, less space required, less mess, and equal or greater plant production. In combination with nutrient-rich liquids, hydroponics equipment can be used to start and grow virtually every type of indoor and outdoor plant, which can later be transplanted directly to the garden or potting container. For the entrepreneur who wants to operate a small, yet potentially profitable buy-and-sell enterprise, hydroponics equipment and supplies fit the bill perfectly. In addition to selling the equipment and supplies from a homebased showroom, be sure to market your products through online marketplaces and through home-and-garden consumer shows. Likewise, joining local gardening clubs to network for new customers will also help to spread the word, generate sales, and build a solid referral base.

 BUY
Manufacturers, Wholesalers

 SELL
Homebased Sales, Home-and-Garden Shows, eBay

 RESOURCES
—Bloomington Wholesale Garden Supply, ☎ (800) 316-1306, ✂ www.
bwgs.com
—LMC Wholesale, ☎ (866) 584-3634, ✂ www.wholesale-garden.com
—Micro Hydroponics Wholesale, ☎ (650) 968-4070, ✂ www.microhydro
ponics.com

Seeds and Bulbs

Good profits can be earned by purchasing seeds and bulbs wholesale and reselling them retail. You can buy seeds and bulbs in bulk and repackage into smaller containers, or purchase seeds and bulbs already prepackaged for retail sales. The first option has the potential to be more profitable, but the second is far more convenient. You can specialize in rare and unusual plant varieties, or in run-of-the-mill vegetable, flower, herb, fruit, and wildflower seeds and bulbs. Also, because gardening is such a broad topic appealing to millions of people, be sure to sell accessories, mainly how-to books and videos. Buying sources will be wholesalers, while your selling options include mail order, garden shows, and online marketplaces. Many seed wholesalers offer their resellers catalogs for marketing purposes. These are invaluable tools, which I recommend that you invest in for your business.

Buy
Wholesalers

Sell
Mail Order, Home-and-Garden Shows, Online Marketplaces, Kiosks

Resources
—Carter Seeds Wholesale, ☎ (800) 872-7711, ♂ www.carterseeds.com
—Hummert International Wholesale, ☎ (800) 325-3055, ♂ www.hummert.com
—Park Seed Wholesale, ☎ (800) 845-3366, ♂ www.parkwholesale.com

Outdoor Power Equipment

Put your small-engine mechanical skills and knowledge to work for you by starting an outdoor power equipment buy-and-sell venture. Purchase outdoor power equipment such as lawn mowers, trimmers, riding mowers, chain saws, garden tillers, yard trailers, snow blowers, and leaf blowers at garage sales, auction sales, and through classified ads, and resell for big profits. To get the lowest prices, buy equipment out of season or that needs minor repairs and a good cleaning. Sell from home supported by local advertising, signage, and by posting fliers listing your equipment for sale on community notice boards. Close more sales and for more money by offering customers a 30- or 60-day warranty on all equipment sold. Doing so will easily increase the value of each piece of equipment by 10 to 20 percent.

BUY
Classified Ads, Auctions, Garage Sales

 SELL
Homebased Sales, eBay, Flea Markets

 RESOURCES
—The Outdoor Power Equipment Aftermarket Association, industry information and resources, ☎ (202) 775-8605, ♂ www.opeaa.org
—The Outdoor Power Equipment Institute, industry information and resources, ♂ www.opei.org
—📖 *Repairing Your Outdoor Power Equipment*, Jay Webster (Delmar Learning, 2001)

Birdhouses

Millions of birdhouses are sold annually. So why not start a part-time enterprise buying and selling birdhouses and cash in on this existing market as so many others have? Buy birdhouses from manufacturers who mass-produce them or from local craftspeople who build a more unique model or one-of-a-kind birdhouses. Displaying the birdhouses at your home with bold attention-grabbing signage ensures that people and motorists passing by will stop in and browse through your selection. In addition to selling from home, you can also sell birdhouses on eBay, and at flea markets, home-and-garden shows, and crafts shows. You should have no problems maintaining a healthy 100 percent markup on all sales. Overall, selling birdhouses is a great way to have some fun and subsidize your income at the same time.

 BUY
Craftspeople, Manufacturers, Wholesalers

 SELL
Flea Markets, Kiosks, Online Marketplaces, Homebased Sales

 RESOURCES
—Little Log Company Manufacturing, ☎ (800) 219-3285, ♂ www.little log.com
—Mulberry Designs Manufacturing, ☎ (919) 736-0801, ♂ www.mulberry designs.com
—Woodside Gardens Manufacturing, ☎ (845) 355-8412, ♂ www.abirds home.com

Mailboxes

Like birdhouses, mailboxes are a great buy-and-sell item. Direct from the manufacturer, local craftspeople, or from wholesalers—mailboxes can be purchased in many ways at low discount prices. Sell from home, through online marketplaces, at flea markets, and by displaying your products at home-and-garden shows. Don't underestimate this somewhat simple enterprise. Elaborate mailboxes made from specialty materials such as copper, iron, and cultured stone can sell for $1,000 and more. Based on this retail sales value, you can easily pocket $250 to $350 on each sale. Sell just one of these a week, and you'll earn upwards of $15,000 per year, with only a part-time effort.

 BUY
Craftspeople, Manufacturers, Wholesalers

 SELL
Flea Markets, Kiosks, Online Marketplaces, Homebased Sales

 RESOURCES
—Brandon Industries, ☎ (972) 542-3000, ⌀ www.brandonindustries.com
—Designer Mailboxes Manufacturing, ☎ (877) 502-3548, ⌀ www.designer-mailboxes.com
—Gaines Manufacturing, ☎ (858) 486-7100, ⌀ www.gainesmfg.com

Sheds and Shelters

Sheds and portable shelters can be used for any number of needs around the home, including an affordable way to add storage or workshop space, an art studio, guest accommodation, automobile protection, garden tool and patio furniture security, or as a backyard playhouse for the kids. Recently, portable carports constructed of a basic metal frame covered by rain-resistant fabric have become a trendy alternative to building an expensive permanent garage to protect boats, automobiles, RVs, and trailers. In North America there are hundreds of companies engaged in manufacturing portable sheds and shelters made from a wide variety of materials: plastic, wood, metal, and fabric. Therefore, securing a reliable wholesale source should not be difficult. The majority of portable sheds and shelters are sold as a do-it-yourself kit. Many manufacturers also provide drop-shipping services directly to your customers, cutting out the need for you to store and transport product. You can sell the sheds and shelters online and at home-and-garden shows, but perhaps the best way to market them is by displaying them right at your home.

BUY
Manufacturers, Wholesalers

SELL
Homebased Sales, Consumer Shows, Online Marketplaces

RESOURCES
—Ace Canopy Manufacturing, ☎ (888) 702-6082, ✆ www.ace canopy.com
—Handy Home Products Manufacturing, ☎ (800) 221-1849, ✆ www. handyhome.com
—Jamaica Cottage Shop Manufacturing, ☎ (877) 397-7433, ✆ www. jamaicacottageshop.com

Seashells

Unquestionably, there is a certain allure to seashells, which makes them irresistible to most people, especially crafters who like to use them to create wind chimes, mosaics, costume jewelry, planters, and a whole host of products. I mention crafters because if you decide to buy and sell seashells, crafters will be your main target market. Though other people will also buy them for home and office decoration, the main audience is crafters. Therefore, you have to go to where the crafters are, and this includes craft shows, craft clubs, and online craft groups and chat forums. Once again, because seashells also appeal to consumers searching for nifty home and office decorations, you can also sell the shells at flea markets, public markets, and community events. If you live in an area renowned for seashells, you can collect them for free, but because (other than the grandest conch shell) they do not sell for great sums, spending your time collecting them will probably prove ineffective and unprofitable. Therefore, purchasing seashells in bulk from established wholesale sources will be the better option for most people.

BUY
Wholesalers

SELL
Craftspeople, Craft Shows, Flea Markets, Kiosks, eBay

 RESOURCES
—APN Shell Craft Wholesale, ☎ 91-4652-246368 (India), ♂ www.apn shells.com
—Shell Horizons Wholesale, ☎ (727) 536-3333, ♂ www.shell horizons.com
—U.S. Shell Wholesale, ☎ (956) 554-4500, ♂ www.usshell.com

Christmas Trees

For a great many people, there is no replacement for a real Christmas tree. They want the look and smell that only a real tree can provide, regardless of messy needles, cost, and disposal issues. And where there is demand, supply will certainly follow. In the case of real Christmas trees, North American consumers spend more than $1 billion annually to make sure that they have the real McCoy decorated and ready for Christmas cheer. Short of your having your own tree lot, you will have to rely on tree farms and wholesalers for product. But, be forewarned: Christmas trees sell fast; most are spoken for six months in advance. On a wholesale basis directly from tree farmers, bound trees ready to be shipped cost in the range of $10 to $40, depending on size and type of tree—fir, balsam, or jack pine. Retail prices also vary greatly, depending on the type and size of tree and the area where the trees are being sold. New Yorkers typically pay the most, on average $100. You can sell Christmas trees right from your own home providing your neighbors don't mind and you are located in a high-traffic location. For most, however, a better option is to rent empty lot space starting around December 1st and counting until Christmas Eve. Good locations include grocery store parking lots, busy intersections, gas station lots, and basically any other piece of empty ground that is exposed to lots of passing motorists. You will need to negotiate some sort of financial arrangement with the landlord, either a flat rental rate or perhaps a percentage of your total sales. I would opt for the second choice if you can arrange it. To increase sales and help your community, align yourself with a local charity and give a small portion of each sale, perhaps 5 percent, to the charity. Doing so enables you and your customers to help others less fortunate, which, of course, is the true meaning of Christmas.

BUY
Growers, Wholesalers

SELL
Temporary Rental Lot, Homebased Sales

RESOURCES
—All Season Trees, ☎ (570) 943-3339, ✆ www.allseasontrees.com
—Alpine Farms, ☎ (360) 674-2549, ✆ info@alpinefarms.com
—Christmas Trees Worldwide, ☎ (866) 287-2483, ✆ www.christmas treeww.com

Snack Vending

The snack-vending business is a multibillion-dollar industry in North America and continues to grow year after year. Fortunately, claiming your piece of the very lucrative snack-vending pie is easy to do. Get started by finding the right location(s) before buying equipment and inventory. Do this by starting with friends and family members: Where do they work? Is there a vending machine present? If not, would the location support a vending machine? Failing this approach, strike out into the community and look for places that are busy with foot traffic or have a large number of employees—that is, in the 25-plus person range. These locations can include car dealerships, factories, office buildings, fitness clubs, and laundromats. Once you have found the perfect location and reached an agreement with the landlord or business operator to install the vending equipment, you will be in the right position to know which type of machine(s) to purchase and the kinds of snacks to stock. Typically, you can expect to mark up your product by 300 percent for vending.

BUY
Wholesalers, Manufacturers

SELL
Vending Machines

RESOURCES
—123 Vending Supplies, ☎ (800) 303-7882, ✆ www.123vending.com

—National Automatic Merchandising Association, ⚲ www.vending.org
—Universal Vending Supplies, ☎ (877) 643-8363, ⚲ www.universal vending.com

Vegetable Stand

Whether it's a roadside stand, a rented booth at a farmers' market, or a portable kiosk set up at a local flea market, selling fresh, in-season fruits and vegetables such as corn, carrots, apples, oranges, and asparagus can be very profitable. Like any type of retail venture, the key to success is location, location, and, you guessed it, location. With that goal in mind, excellent locations include gas stations, industrial parks, busy intersections, and along roadways leading to popular attractions like the beach, garden centers, and public parks. The stand you work from needs to be nothing more than a basic framework covered by a tarp to keep the sun and heat off the veggies. Of greater importance, however, are the signs needed to advertise your products and presence. Signs should be large, colorful, and compel passing motorists to stop by screaming out statements such as, "Stop 100 yards ahead for the best deals on fresh vegetables!" Be sure to place your signs well ahead of your stand to give motorists ample warning so they have time to slow down and stop. Buy vegetables directly from farmers, or farmers' co-operatives in your area, or from produce wholesalers. Regardless of your buying sources, sell only the highest quality and freshest products available.

 BUY
Wholesalers, Farmers, Growers Co-op

 SELL
Vegetable Stand, Flea Market, Farmers' Market

 RESOURCES
—Eden Valley Growers, ☎ (716) 992-9721, ⚲ www.edenvalley growers.com
—Seminole Produce Distributing, ☎ (800) 745-1102, ⚲ www.fresh veggie.com
—Today's Market Prices, ⚲ www.todaymarket.com

Organic Food Products

Kiss chemicals and preservatives goodbye by offering your customers only the highest-quality fresh organic foods available. The potential to make a small fortune selling organic meats, vegetables, fruits, dairy products, and baked goods is well within reach, especially when you consider how many entrepreneurs are already doing it. People in general are starting to make a shift to a more healthy diet, and organic foods are leading the way. All states and provinces have numerous farmers, producers, and manufacturers engaged in growing and producing organic foods, so finding a reliable local source should not prove difficult. You can buy direct from growers, producers, manufacturers, and wholesalers and sell at venues such as farmers' markets, public markets, and online marketplaces. Also establish a solid customer base in your locale by using advertising and direct marketing to promote your organic products. Offer your customers free direct delivery of staple food items on a regularly scheduled basis.

 BUY
Wholesalers, Manufacturers, Growers, Producers

 SELL
Direct Delivery, Web Site, Kiosks, Farmers' Markets

 RESOURCES
—Access Organic Sales, wholesaler, ☎ (406) 862-0696, ♂ www.access organics.com
—B.I.N Sales, ☎ (203) 852-0827, ♂ www.binsales.com
—Garden Spot Distributors, ☎ (800) 829-5100, ♂ www.gardenspot dist.com
—Organic Trade Association, ♂ www.ota.org

Gourmet Foods

Only the finest gourmet foods from around the globe will do for your customers if you decide to start a gourmet food buy-and-sell business. Specialize in one particular type of gourmet food such as Canadian maple syrup or Italian olives, or in food categories like desserts, beverages, candy and chocolates, seafood, and baked goods. Buy from importers, wholesalers, producers, and manufacturers nationally and internationally. Establish a Web site so people from every corner of the globe can order online. Also sell at farmers' markets, public markets, and mall kiosks.

You will have to sort out storage, shipping, and possibly even licensing issues depending on the types of foods you intend to sell. However, with that said, the work is worth the effort because selling gourmet foods can be extremely profitable.

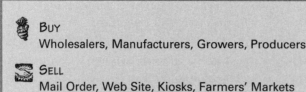

BUY
Wholesalers, Manufacturers, Growers, Producers

SELL
Mail Order, Web Site, Kiosks, Farmers' Markets

RESOURCES
—1-800-Gourmet Wholesale, ☎ (800) 468-7638, ♂ www.1800 gourmet.com
—Caviar Etc. Wholesale, ☎ (800) 819-4330, ♂ www.caviaretc.com
—The Gourmet Food & Accessory Trade Mart, database listing gourmet food producers and wholesalers, ♂ www.gftm.com

Candy

Everybody loves candy, which is why it is a great product to buy wholesale and resell for big profits. You have two options. First, buy candy prepackaged and resell. Second, buy candy in bulk and repackage it into small quantities and resell. The first option is more convenient, but the second option has the potential for greater profits because in bulk your wholesale costs are much lower than buying prepackaged. Candies can be sold directly from vending carts and kiosks in malls, and at community events, public markets, trade and consumer shows, large auction sales, sporting events, and flea markets. Buying can be from confectioner wholesalers or directly from any one of the numerous candy manufacturers in this country and abroad. One of the best candy-selling ideas that I have recently come across from a person who was purchasing wrapped candies in bulk, repackaging them into five-pound bags, and selling them to businesses so they could put them out on counters and in reception areas for their customers. The candy vendor returns each week leaving a new bag of candy and sends the bill in the mail. A very easy, low-cost way to sell candy and build a successful business with repeat customers.

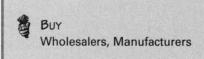

BUY
Wholesalers, Manufacturers

SELL
Kiosks, Flea Markets, Community Events, Farmers' Markets, B2B

RESOURCES
—Elite Distribution, ☎ (505) 797-1702, ♂ www.elite-distributing.com
—Family Sweets Distribution, ☎ (800) 334-1607, ♂ www.family
  sweets.com
—National Confectioners Association, ♂ www.candyusa.org

Herbs and Spices

Herbs and spices not only make food taste great, but they can also be used to treat medical conditions and physiological disorders, and as an agent to help promote weight loss. You have a couple of options for buying and selling herbs and spices. First, you can purchase them directly from wholesalers, manufacturers, or even local producers whose products are prepackaged and ready for resale. Second, you can purchase herbs and spices in bulk quantities and repackage them into small containers for resale. The first option is far more convenient, but the second option offers the most profit potential. Once you have determined your buying source and packaging method, the herbs and spices can be sold directly to restaurants and at flea markets, farmers' markets, and public markets. Also consider online marketplaces or establishing your own Web site for an online store with mail delivery.

BUY
Wholesalers, Manufacturers, Growers

SELL
Mail Order, Kiosks, Flea Market, Web Site, B2B, Farmers' Markets

RESOURCES
—Atlantic Spice Company, ☎ (800) 316-7965, ♂ www.atlanticspice.com
—The Great American Spice Company, ☎ (888) 502-8058, ♂ www.
  americanspice.com
—Herb Depot, industry information and resources, ♂ www.herbs-depot.
  com

Pet Food

It is estimated that people in the United States and Canada spend more than $5 billion annually on food to feed their cats, dogs, rabbits, birds, reptiles, fish, and other domestic pets. If hearing this made your ears perk up to the sweet sounds of profit potential, now is your chance to cash in by buying pet foods from wholesalers or directly from manufacturers and reselling it at a profit to the pet-loving public. One of the best sales methods is to establish a solid customer base through advertising and direct marketing and offer free home delivery of pet foods on a regular schedule. It will take lots of hard work and an investment of time and money to convince people to switch from their current pet food brand to yours. But your advantage is free home delivery and lower prices because you do not have the same high overhead as bricks-and-mortar retailers. You can also sell at pet shows and through online marketplaces. Don't forget about gourmet pet foods and treats, because this is the fastest-growing segment of the industry.

 BUY
Manufacturers, Wholesalers

 SELL
Direct Delivery, Pet Shows, Online Marketplaces

 RESOURCES
—American Pet Products Manufacturers Association, ✆ www.appma.org
—Metro Traders Wholesale, ☎ (877) 321-5050, ✆ www.wholesaleforpets.com
—Show Coat Manufacturing, ☎ (866) 290-7387, ✆ www.showcoat.com

Aquariums and Tropical Fish

You can make a small fortune selling aquariums, accessories, and tropical fish right from home. Turn your garage or basement into an *everything aquarium and fish showroom* stocked with inventory for sale. Sell glass and acrylic tanks, freshwater and saltwater tropical fish, and tank and fish accessories such as stands, canopies, filters, foods, lights, aquatic plants, skimmers, ornaments, and cleaning supplies. All of these items can be purchased at deeply discounted prices from manufacturers, wholesalers, and tropical fish farms. Beware that there are laws and regulations that you must comply with for importing and exporting tropical fish, so research will be required if you are planning these activities. Additional sales venues include online sales, pet shows, and even direct to businesses and offices for great conversation pieces.

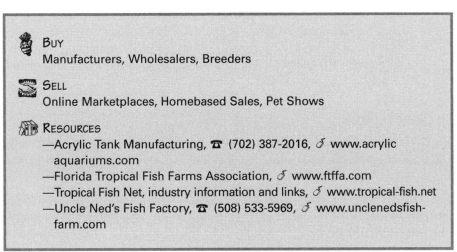

BUY
Manufacturers, Wholesalers, Breeders

SELL
Online Marketplaces, Homebased Sales, Pet Shows

RESOURCES
—Acrylic Tank Manufacturing, ☎ (702) 387-2016, ♂ www.acrylic
 aquariums.com
—Florida Tropical Fish Farms Association, ♂ www.ftffa.com
—Tropical Fish Net, industry information and links, ♂ www.tropical-fish.net
—Uncle Ned's Fish Factory, ☎ (508) 533-5969, ♂ www.unclenedsfish-
 farm.com

Pet Toys

North Americans love their pets. In fact, there are an estimated 30 million dogs and 50 million cats living in U.S. and Canadian households. Combined, that is 80 million potential customers for a buy-and-sell enterprise that specializes in toys, such as chew ropes, buddy balls, Frisbees, and bells. Our pets must have them all, and are often more spoiled than our children. To cash in on the pet toys craze, you will first need a reliable wholesale supplier. I have included a couple below, along with the Web address for the American Pet Products Manufacturers Association, which can help you locate manufacturers and distributors of many different types of toys for pets. Marketing pet toys for profit can be accomplished in many ways—online sales, flea markets, pet shows, and vending at community events. One unique way to get selling is simply to visit parks frequented by dogs and owners. On any given day, and especially on weekends, you are bound to run into 20, 30, or more pets every hour, and you can start selling and handing out information about your business and how people and their friends can buy. I have purchased a few glow-in-the-dark balls for my dog in this manner, so I can tell you firsthand that it works.

BUY
Manufacturers, Wholesalers

 SELL
Pet Shows, kiosks, Flea Markets

 RESOURCES
—American Pet Products Manufacturers Association, ♂ www.appma.org
—King Wholesale Pet Supplies, ☎ (800) 825-4647, ♂ www.kingwhole sale.com
—Purrfect Paws Wholesale, ☎ (702) 878-7297, ♂ www.purrfectpaws.com

Furniture for Pets

North Americans love to spoil their pets. Admittedly, I am one of these people. We get our pets groomed. We buy gourmet foods for them and send them to day care and dog spas. And, of course, no truly cherished pet can be without his own custom-manufactured furniture, which, surprisingly enough, could easily pass for finely crafted household furniture, if not for the small scale. So what kind of furniture is available for pets? Couches, chairs, beds, ottomans, baskets, and lots more. Furniture for pets comes in every imaginable size, design, and fabric selection. That's right, you can show your customers numerous fabric swatches and let them choose. The two main buying sources are direct from manufacturers like the ones I have included below. Or you can be creative and design your own pet furniture line, enlisting local craftspeople to produce it on a contract or perhaps even profit share basis. Develop your own Web site for sales and marketing purposes; sell on eBay, display at pet shows, and establish a pet furniture boutique right at home. To expand sales and revenues, you can also offer a line of fabric covers to protect household furniture and car seats from Fido and Kitty as well.

 BUY
Manufacturers, Craftspeople

 SELL
Web Site, Kiosks, Pet Shows, Homebased Sales, eBay

 RESOURCES
—American Pet Products Manufacturers Association, ♂ www.appma.org
—Posh Pet Furniture Manufacturing, ☎ (866) 976-7387, ♂ www.posh petfurniture.com
—Seventh Heaven Cat Furniture Manufacturing, ♂ www.7thheavencat furniture.com

INDEX